ENDURING
LIVES

ENDURING
LIVES

Living Portraits of Women and Faith in Action

CAROL LEE FLINDERS

ORBIS BOOKS
Maryknoll, New York 10545

Copyright © 2006, 2013 by Carol Lee Flinders.

Originally published in 2006 by Jeremy P. Tarcher/Penguin.

Slightly revised paperback edition published by Orbis Books, Box 302, Maryknoll, NY 10545–0302.

Manufactured in the United States of America
Manuscript editing and typesetting by Joan Weber Laflamme.

Library of Congress Cataloging-in-Publication Data

Flinders, Carol.
    Enduring lives : living portraits of women and faith in action / Carol Lee Flinders.
      pages cm
    Includes bibliographical references and index.
    ISBN 978–1–62698–034–1 (pbk.)
    1. Hillesum, Etty, 1914-1943. 2. Goodall, Jane, 1934– . 3. Tenzin Palmo, 1943– . 4. Prejean, Helen. 5. Religious biography. 6. Women—Biography. I. Title.
BL72.F56 2013
200.92'52—dc23
[B]

2013000454

*To the women everywhere
who are turning things around,
and to the men who aid and abet.*

Contents

Acknowledgments

Enduring Grace, the book to which *Enduring Lives* is a kind of sequel, was published in April 1993, and I did a reading soon after that in Denver at Tattered Cover, one of the country's largest and most vibrant independent bookstores. My host was the director of the store's religious books department, Joel Fotinos, and I realized by the end of the evening that most of the people who had come were there because they were friends of Joel: if he was keen on a particular book or author, they figured it would probably be worth their time to show up.

How thoroughly satisfying, then, that *Enduring Lives* was first published under Joel Fotino's inspired leadership at Jeremy P. Tarcher/Penguin, where he is now publisher.

To my editor at Tarcher/Penguin, Sara Carder, and her assistant, Kat Kimball, I'm deeply grateful; their reading of the manuscript and subsequent suggestions were both sensitive and astute. My copy editor, Toni Rachiele, certainly earned her keep and probably quite a bit more: thank you!

My agent, Candice Fuhrman, has been working on my behalf for more than fifteen years now, and I count myself truly fortunate that this is so.

To Will Keepin and Dena Merriam, my special appreciation for making possible my interview with the Venerable Tenzin Palmo. Thanks to Dale Peterson for answering queries regarding Jane Goodall, and to the reference librarians at Sonoma State University for initiating me into LexisNexis.

For nearly forty years I have been affiliated with the Blue Mountain Center of Meditation. It is my spiritual home and my extended family. The Center's present director, Christine Easwaran, is a model of unassuming leadership and one of my favorite answers to the question with which this book begins. She is our treasure, hidden in plain sight.

Finally, closest at hand, my husband, Tim, and our son, Mesh, have been spectacularly patient and supportive, and not just because we're family. They are both writers, too—they understand the process.

I am pleased beyond words that *Enduring Lives* is entering its own second life under the wing of Orbis Books. To Robert Ellsberg, Maria Angelini, Joan Laflamme, and the entire diligent staff at Orbis, my gratitude.

Introduction

If Saint Teresa of Avila were heading off to college today, would she study anthropology? Comparative literature? Psycho-neuro-immunology? Would Julian of Norwich drive a hybrid, ride a bicycle, or just move to a town with good public transit? Would Saint Clare of Assisi run a non-profit? Take inner-city kids on white-water-rafting trips? Would Saint Catherine of Siena be an investigative journalist, or an attorney general? Would any of these women, if they were around today, choose a cloistered life?

Playful and dead serious at once, questions like these have crossed my mind regularly over the twenty years since I wrote *Enduring Grace*. They are part of the reason I've wanted to write a companion volume that would come into the present and identify some of the contemporary great-grand-goddaughters of Saint Teresa, Dame Julian, and Saint Clare.

I researched and wrote *Enduring Grace* with a strong sense of mission; it felt sometimes as if I were staging a hostage rescue operation. I had studied primary sources closely enough to know that Clare, Catherine, and the others weren't just the chaste and obedient daughters of the church that traditional hagiography had made them out to be. Vivid, resourceful, courageous, and charismatic, they had stepped out of obscurity fully voiced and authoritative long before there was anything even faintly like a women's movement, and in cultures that were unequivocally male centered. Remarkably, they found the resources they needed in the very religious tradition that had demeaned them so as women.

I constructed those "living portraits" in the hope of stripping away the pious miasma of traditional biographies so that Teresa and her sisters in spirit could come to life in the reader's imagination—the reader's, but the writer's no less.

Tibetan Buddhists practice a visualization technique called *yidam* that instructs the meditator first to commit to memory all the features of a particular deity—how she is dressed, what her ornaments are, who the other figures are that tradition places nearby—and then use them to construct a detailed mental picture. When the image is sharply visible to the mind's eye, the practitioner holds it there and dwells lovingly on each of its aspects and the inner qualities they symbolize. In the last and most difficult stage, she moves toward the figure and unites herself with it.

Having become one with Green Tara, or the Compassionate Buddha, the meditator can expect to find herself empowered by the experience. Something of Green Tara's compassion, or Buddha's resoluteness, will flow into her thoughts and actions: a considerable something, or maybe just a faint, faint resonance, depending on the quality of attention the meditator is able to bring to the exercise.

Variations on *yidam* practice are a popular feature of women's retreats today, and for good reason. A few years ago I was leading a workshop in Southern California, and we were talking about how difficult it can be to find voice, and a young woman stood up who described her bleak upbringing in a home where it was understood that women and girls would keep quiet. The habit of silence had stayed with her until she was in her mid-twenties and joined a book club—where she was startled to discover that the other members really did want to know what she thought about the books they were reading. Before long, the burden of silence fell away, and not just within the safety of the book club. "Now," she told us, "if there's something I want to say in my workplace, or at a school board meeting, or even to my husband, I just stand up and say it. *Because I can feel my friends lined up behind me.*" As she spoke, she made a quarter-turn and seemed to gesture toward the seats just behind hers, and for a second you could almost see them—a formidable queue, short and tall, old and young, all holding copies of *The Red Tent* and *The Secret Life of Bees.*

She had expressed so winningly something many women feel today: that if we're going to work for positive change in the world, and take the often unpopular positions that kind of work requires, we need to be able to reach back and connect with "friends lined up behind us." If some of those friends are contemporary and others aren't—like Green Tara, or Shakti, or Mary Magdalene—all the better. There are families in South India that trace their ancestry back through the maternal line, and a friend who grew up in one of these clans used to swear that right along with the DNA, spiritual awareness flows down the mother-line. "*Like a river,*" he insisted, and I remember feeling a stab of envy. What a perfect simile for the sense of continuity women like me did *not* have with sustaining spiritual mother-lines.

Enduring Grace was my first attempt to fill that absence. *Enduring Lives* was undertaken with the same intention, but it's been a very different kind of project.

The *Enduring Grace* subjects lived within a kind of mono-culture in which every meaningful question was construed as a theological question, including those we'd now define as scientific, or political, or economic, or artistic. However magnificent their visionary experiences were, and however deeply they had come to understand that all of life is one interconnected whole, they could only express what they knew in the vocabulary of their inherited religious tradition. No matter how diverse the women themselves actually were, they were all palpably religious, and labels like *saint* and *mystic* seem appropriate.

Today, we move about in a world of myriad discourses of which religion is only one; Christianity is a subset, and Roman Catholicism a subset of the subset. When we see a woman now who has the radiant self-possession, courage, wisdom, tenderness, and resourcefulness we associate with the *Enduring Grace* subjects, she probably doesn't live in a convent, and the word *religious* may not be the first one we choose when describing her. The steady, stepped expansion of empathy and influence that we've seen in a Catherine of Siena or a Teresa of Avila, extending so far, at last, that it embraces the whole of life, might be just as visible in her story as theirs, but the word *saint* doesn't feel like a good fit anymore either. Maybe that's because a lot of us these days feel the way Sister Helen Prejean has said she does about sainthood: that it's a way of discounting the complexity of a human being, of putting her into a box and rendering her harmless.

Returning readers will notice, too, that while the subtitle of *Enduring Grace* called the subjects of the book *mystics*, the word doesn't come up in either title or subtitle of the present book. That isn't an accident.

It's funny how easy it is to declare someone a mystic who's been dead for five hundred years, and about whom we know almost nothing except what she wrote about her relationship with God. From what we can gather, though, Saint Catherine of Genoa probably did speak for all of the *Enduring Grace* subjects when she said she had discovered, in the depths of prayer, that "my *me* is God!" They all give every appearance of having lived, as Saint Teresa said she did, "in the light without a night."

I don't believe that the subjects of the present book would ever make such a claim, and I don't believe even their most devoted admirers would say it about them either. Each has spoken of flashes of deep insight into the unity of life—"realizations," in Tenzin Palmo's language—but none has even hinted that she is permanently established in unitive consciousness.

This is fine for my present purposes, because I decided early on that I didn't want to write this time about religiously iconic figures like Mother Teresa of Calcutta, or Ammachi, of whom it could be said unequivocally that they are mystics, but rather, individuals—call them mystics-in-the-making, or maybe mystics-under-heavy-cover—whose stories let us watch a profound transformative process even as it is still taking place. Women, these, who are more like women I know.

They include:

- A Dutch Jew, Etty Hillesum, who translated Dostoevsky and engaged in a hybrid practice of psychotherapy, palm reading, and grief counseling until her death at Auschwitz just before what would have been her thirtieth birthday.
- A world-renowned environmentalist, Jane Goodall, who spent her happiest years clambering around a Tanzanian forest stalking chimpanzees.
- The daughter of a London fishmonger, Tenzin Palmo, who went to India, became a Tibetan Buddhist nun, and travels the world today raising money for a nunnery she has established in the Himalayas.
- Another nun, this one a lawyer's daughter from Baton Rouge, Louisiana, Sister Helen Prejean, who intends to see the death penalty abolished within her lifetime—and who summers among the Northern Cheyenne Indians in Montana.

I'd planned on a larger gathering. My original list was dozens of names long. But once these particular women had taken their places around my imaginary table and started talking—first one, then two, then three, and four—the room was full: full of voices, full of ideas, full of strong opinions and compelling visions for a world that could be. And Etty Hillesum set the agenda—not just because she happened to speak first, but because the circumstances of her death place us squarely in front of what may be the defining truth of our times. The violent, state-sanctioned destruction of more than seventy million human beings between 1914 and 1945—in Europe and Russia alone—is impossible to take in. The mind just stops. Our best efforts falter, attention drifts away. But Etty Hillesum's diary is one of the rare documents of that period that arrests our attention in mid-drift. In her company, strengthened I think by her calm, her lucidity, her immense warmth, we come back and look again at what we must.

With her, we begin to ask, as we know we absolutely must: How do hearts turn to stone? And what do we do about it?

These questions haunted all three of my other subjects. Both Jane Goodall and Tenzin Palmo have actually visited Auschwitz, which might not seem extraordinary until you think about how many trips people take to Europe every year that don't include a stop at the death camps. Goodall undertook the visit as a pilgrimage. (For Sister Helen Prejean, one gathers that the executions she has attended in the United States are as close a facsimile to Auschwitz as her imagination requires. She has experienced her work on Death Row as an ongoing pilgrimage.)

Where does it come from, they've all asked—the capacity to decide that another group of human beings is fundamentally *not us*, and therefore expendable? Each of these women would confront directly some form of "othering" in her own life—as fascism, racism, misogyny, religious and ethnic hatred, and environmental destruction—and resist it with her whole being.

Etty's reply echoes the teachings of the Compassionate Buddha as well as Mahatma Gandhi: there is only one useful or effective response to hatred, and that is not hatred or even indifference, but love.

Jane Goodall would agree, but she approaches the phenomenon from a different direction. She is a scientist who believes that we must look at ourselves in context, as one life form among millions. She believes that we carry our complicated pre-human history along with us and act it out in all kinds of unconscious ways we'd be better off knowing about, and that we can't hope to establish peace among ourselves until we've learned to be loving custodians of the natural world *of which we are part.*

Tenzin Palmo would also concur with Etty where love is concerned, though she'd probably use the Pali term *metta* (compassion) instead. That there is a relationship between compassion and trained attention both Etty and Jane recognize and find interesting, but for this Tibetan Buddhist nun, that connection is everything. Because daily, deep, systematic meditation enables us to still the mind and get hold of the mechanism in consciousness that "others" our fellow beings, it is for her the highest form of activism.

Sister Helen Prejean began to struggle in earnest with Etty's question when she began visiting prisoners on Louisiana's Death Row and came to understand the death penalty as a form of torture. With Sister Helen we come, in a sense, full circle, back to the Christ-centered spirituality of the *Enduring Grace* subjects and their continuous, willed *relinquishment* of any attitude, or attachment, or reservation that might prevent full loving encounter with Christ disguised as "the Other."

Each of these women speaks for herself and in her own idiom, but like Catholic saints with a particular charism and following, each also speaks for a certain broader constituency as well: Etty for everyone who has met hatred with love; Tenzin Palmo for those who make meditation the basis of their lives; Jane Goodall for everyone who has sprung to the defense of animals, trees, and river systems; Sister Helen for those who are convinced that no one in the world is beyond redemption.

I want to offer a closer look at some of the ways in which these four women seem almost to reincarnate the *Enduring Grace* mystics, and to do that we need to pause for a moment, revisit the "golden age" for female mysticism, and determine why it was so. I suggest that the tried-and-true formula invoked in police procedurals may not be a bad way to operate: motive, means, and opportunity. Find the individual who has all three, and you have your . . . mystic. Maybe, in fact, a *great many* mystics.

Motive—the desire to know God—an "inward tug" Mechthild of Magdeburg called it—isn't the rarest thing in the world. Nineteenth-century novelist George Eliot observed as much when she began *Middlemarch* with a cameo portrait of Saint Teresa, whose spirit, she wrote, "soared after some illimitable satisfaction, some object which would never justify weariness." Eliot's heroine, Dorothea Brooke, was just such a young woman, the reader is to understand, but she had had the bad luck to have been born in a backwater village in early nineteenth-century England, where "here and there is born a Saint Theresa, foundress of nothing, whose loving heart-beats and sobs after an unattained goodness tremble off and are dispersed among hindrances."

Nobody knew better than Eliot that women are far likelier to possess a soaring spirit than the privacy and the leisure to act on it—the assurance that basic needs will be met if you give yourself over to the interior life: the *means*, in short. Necessity did not drive the life choices of any of the *Enduring Grace* subjects. Born into the aristocracy or the newly affluent middle class, they all grew up in relatively comfortable circumstances. By one means or another, each was able to secure the room of her own—and the door she could close—that allowed her to turn inward, safe from interruption. Most of them recall having been a loved and even favored child, and their stories include gestures of generous parental support. Clare's mother joined her at San Damiano, and when Julian had her visions, her mother was there in the room with her.

Motive and means, well and good. But medieval Europe provided its most intensely religious young women as well with a breadth of *opportunity* that was, perhaps, unprecedented. A tremendous spiritual awakening spread through Europe beginning in the thirteenth century. Mysticism, claiming that it is possible to know God in this life, was implicit in the sermons of Francis of Assisi and Bernard of Clairvaux. Within every human being, teachers like Meister Eckhart proclaimed, there is a core of likeness to God. Just as pear seeds grow into pear trees, he maintained, the "god-seed" within us can grow, under the right circumstances, into a god tree, in which everything that is merely personal has been annihilated.

The images of gestation and fruition that Eckhart and others invoked were of a piece with an important shift in the way people thought about their relationship with God. Metaphors for spiritual development were increasingly feminine now, and spiritual aspirants were less inclined to think of themselves as "warriors of God" than as pilgrims and lovers, filled with longing for a deity who reciprocates their warmth of feeling. Men as well as women were encouraged to think of themselves as handmaidens of God, and devotion to the Virgin Mary escalated steadily. If a woman could convince family and others that she was called to be Christ's bride, she could remain unmarried and, even more important, childless. A new emphasis on contemplative prayer as the route by which one drew closer to "the bridegroom" gave real substance to the motif.

A room of one's own is one thing—but a *life* of one's own?

Barely to be imagined.

Convents filled to overflowing, and the enclosure of so many women turned out to have unexpected consequences. Life in entirely female communities proved to be a powerful catalyst for rising feminine consciousness. So, for that matter, did the fact that women were excluded from the professional roles that were open to devout men. Unlike their male counterparts, nuns had considerable time for prayer and meditation—and to the initial surprise of their male confessors, many of them turned out to have a genius for the interior life.

They discovered Christ as indwelling, and they met him subsequently in the person of every suffering individual they encountered. All of human anguish came to be distilled, for them, into the crucifixion, and it didn't seem at all blasphemous to them to suggest that the suffering ordinary people undergo in the course of their lifetimes mysteriously unites them to Christ crucified, whose maternal aspect was plain. Nor did it seem presumptuous to think that we are meant to become *like* Christ. The Beguines were particularly adamant on this score. As members of the "order that was not an order," they determined that they could follow Christ in every meaningful way without taking permanent vows or placing themselves under male religious authority. In effect, by acting on this determination, they initiated the first women's movement. In the autumn of 2012, as American women religious await the outcome of the Vatican's "doctrinal assessment," this chapter in church history would seem to have particular resonance.

Applying the "motive, means, and opportunity" formula to contemporary women, it seems plain enough that hunger for an "illimitable satisfaction" is as strong a force in consciousness now as it was in Julian's day, or Clare's. It is powerfully visible in the lives of Etty, Jane, Tenzin Palmo, and Sister Helen, and in at least the last three cases made itself known when they were still children. The privacy, moreover, and freedom from constraint, available only to relatively well-to-do women in the Middle Ages, is within the reach of a far greater number of women today. Because contemporary Western women can be educated and hold jobs, they are under far, far less pressure to marry and/or have children, and even if they do have families they are sometimes financially comfortable enough to get away for the odd weekend retreat. They aren't unlikely to have a door they can close and a *zafu* (cushion) they can sit upon.

The question of opportunity is somewhat more complicated. For all the talk about religion that dominates news cycles today, we do not walk about in a culture that anyone would call god-intoxicated. Imagine what it must have been like to have Saint Francis standing on your corner calling you to Jesus!

Yet, thanks in part to the god-intoxicated 1960s (Eastern teachers actually began stirring Western waters more than a hundred years ago), contemporary seekers have their own diverse portals onto direct religious experience, and those portals are evident in all four of the lives examined here. Traditional religious orders still exist. Teresa could be a Carmelite all over again. But she could also be a Zen Buddhist, a Sufi, a follower of Kabbalah, or a shaman. She could explore the mysterious interconnectedness of things, moreover, outside a religious context altogether, as a cultural anthropologist, a filmmaker, a marine biologist, or a physician, and she could practice interior prayer or meditation morning and evening. She could even, with relative ease, find someone to direct her . . . could find her, for that matter, or him, by means of the Internet.

Though Etty Hillesum spoke of her morning meditations as "Buddhist moments," her direct exposure to things Eastern was limited.

Through her mentor, though, a student of Carl Jung, she absorbed a view of religiousness itself that was immensely liberating for her and that directly reflects Jung's interest in Eastern religions. It had to do with recognizing the thirst for what-we-call-God as innately human and universal, independent of any particular religion or revelation.

Jane Goodall had a brush at an impressionable age with a Theosophist who taught her about "circling thoughts" and the need to direct them. Tenzin Palmo knew even as a little girl that she wasn't at home in the West, and when she got older and found out about Buddhism, she was like an adopted child receiving a letter out of the blue from her birth mother. Sister Helen remains as Catholic as the day she was born, yet her fascination with the *flow* of things keeps striking me as pure Taoism. All three of these women maintain close connection with indigenous peoples and their earth-centered spirituality.

So yes, the convergence of motive, means, and opportunity goes a long way toward explaining why women mystics were such a visible and audible presence in medieval Europe and why this last hundred years or so may have been an especially propitious time for women like them.

I've pointed to some of the threads that join the lives and teachings of my four subjects with the lives and teachings of the *Enduring Grace* mystics, and I'd like to get still more specific. If there really is a mother-line, and something flows through it "like a river," and we're tempted to call it spiritual awareness, what do we mean?

To sharpen our sense of the relationship between Julian of Norwich and Etty of Amsterdam, or Catherine of Siena and Jane of Gombe, I suggest we take still another look at the times that allowed Julian, Catherine, and Clare to challenge so effectively conventional scripts for women. History has to be rewritten all the time because fresh insights into human experience keep putting the past in a new light. In a small way I learned that firsthand a few years ago when a string of events unfolding in "real time" made me rethink what I thought I'd understood about women mystics in the late Middle Ages.

Sometime in the year 2000, to begin with, two scientists, both of them women, were talking to one another in a laboratory at UCLA. It was what some might call a Mars and Venus moment: Why was it, they wondered, that when work at the lab was going badly, the men tended to hole up by themselves and brood, while the women came in even earlier than usual—to straighten up the lab, make coffee, and just check in with one another?

The men's behavior wasn't mystifying at all: it was a classic instance of the "fight or flight" response modern human beings are supposed to have inherited from our prehistoric and even pre-human ancestors. Under severe stress, scientists have been telling us for more than fifty years, our nervous systems react as if we were facing down a saber-toothed tiger: we stand our ground and prepare to take it on, or we run for cover. Even before we've decided, stress hormones like cortisol and adrenalin are kicking in and putting us into red-alert mode.

But what was going on with the women?

The question had barely formed when Dr. Laura Cousino Klein remembered, and told fellow researcher Dr. Shelley Taylor, that almost 90 percent of the stress research that supports the "fight or flight" paradigm had been conducted on men. Klein, whose field is bio-behavioral health, and Taylor, a psychologist, were so intrigued that they embarked on a landmark study on stress in women, and sure enough, an entirely new paradigm has emerged that they call "tend and befriend." They see this as an adaptive behavior just as firmly rooted in our evolutionary past as "fight or flight." Because whether a woman is pregnant when she is threatened, or nursing, or surrounded with children, neither fight nor flight will be of much use. She certainly isn't going to leave the kids. She gathers them in close, rather, and feeds them and soothes them so that they don't arouse antagonism. She forms alliances with other females that are protective as well as comforting. She grows curiously calmer and, in the process, still more resourceful and resilient.

Prompting these two very different responses are two markedly contrasting hormonal reactions. Testosterone drives one, oxytocin the other. Oxytocin is a hormone that is released during childbirth and breastfeeding, and it regulates moods as well, decreasing anxiety and depression and promoting affiliation. When women bond with others still more oxytocin is produced, and so are endorphins, the "juices" that make people feel so good after a swim or a run. Men have oxytocin, too, but in highly stressed situations it tends to be swamped by testosterone. Indeed, estrogen, the female sex hormone, amplifies the calming effect of oxytocin, while androgens, the male sex hormones, tend to lessen its effects.

The implications of this research are considerable. A number of other studies had already found that social ties lower blood pressure, heart rate, and cholesterol. The fact that women under stress tend to strengthen their connections with both family and other women may help explain, then, why women outlive men as consistently as they do. What I find just as striking, though, is the fact that this information only emerged because two highly trained scientists who were also women were able to fraternize (sororize?) and compare their impressions of their workplace and male colleagues, both as women and as scientists. Their *affiliation*, that is, which would never have occurred had the women's movement not made the strides it has, gave rise to good science as well as good mental health. Just so, we will see, empathy for her subjects hasn't just delighted Jane Goodall; it's given her access to information that would otherwise have been hidden from her. Not long after the "tend and befriend" paradigm was identified, three more women, each of them a highly trained professional, had their own "lightbulb" moments. Each had become aware of glaring malfeasance within the institution where she worked, and each had issued alarms to her colleagues and superiors. Their concerns were ignored and/or silenced, and all three of them felt compelled, eventually, to turn to outside authorities. These were the so-called whistle blowers that *Time* magazine declared "Persons of the Year" for 2002: Colleen Rowley of the FBI, Sherron Watkins of Enron, and Cynthia Cooper of WorldCom. (They were, in fact, not the only whistle blowers to make headlines that year. Just as visible were the individuals, men as well as women, who challenged the code of secrecy that had been protecting dozens of Catholic priests from prosecution for the sexual abuse of children. It wasn't a good year for what my generation used to call the establishment.)

Anita Hill drew on her own experience as a whistle blower when she wrote of these three women that they had all risen through the ranks of male-dominated institutions to become insiders.[1] They had access to information, for example, and authority over others. But their institutional homes had been exclusively masculine so recently—and remained so in a thousand unspoken ways—that these women were nonetheless outsiders simply *because* they were women. They had become what Hill calls "outsider-insiders"—a variant on the terms "outsider within" or "conditional insider" that black feminist sociologist Patricia Hill Collins has invoked to describe the condition of black women domestics who lived in intimate proximity with "their" white families but with no illusions that they would ever be actual members.[2]

The antonym to "outsider-insider" is of course "team player." The problem at the institutions in question was, indeed, that over time,

---

[1] Anita Hill, "Insider Women with Outsider Values," *New York Times* (June 6, 2002).

[2] In Barbara Ransby, *Ella Baker and the Black Freedom Movement: A Radical Democratic Vision* (Chapel Hill: University of North Carolina Press, 2003), 422.

under the intense pressure of work, the standing of various team play-
ers relative to one another, and of whole teams to other teams within
their own or competing organizations, had gradually become more
compelling than the work itself or the health of the organizations.
"Warrior cultures" had developed, and understandably so; high levels
of stress sustained over weeks and months at a time probably helped
lock male workers into more or less chronic states of "fight or flight."

Women working in the same environment had little or no stake
in the internal contests, so when trouble was brewing at the FBI, at
WorldCom, and at Enron, their hands weren't as tightly tied by con-
flicting allegiances, and they had no real stake in "the game." They
saw an institution in jeopardy, its original charter all but forgotten;
perhaps because of the "tend and befriend" dynamic they saw that real
human beings—citizens, employees, customers, shareholders—were
being hurt.

Women aren't the only ones who have found their way to the inner workings of an enterprise only to have their outsider identity and
values challenged beyond a breaking point. One thinks right away
of Jeffrey Wigand, whose opposition to nefarious goings-on in the
tobacco industry was the basis for the 1999 film *The Insider.* Yet
the term *outsider-insider* is almost synonymous now with the experience of women who enter previously male-shaped and male-voiced
workplaces.

What may not be immediately apparent is the extent to which the
outsider-insider model applies to the *Enduring Grace* mystics as well.
When we revisit the historical context out of which they emerged
with that model in mind, our understanding of Julian, Clare, Teresa,
Mechthild, and the Catherines shifts in important ways. Once we've
grasped the particular places where women like Julian and Clare felt
compelled to part company with church authorities, and once we've
recognized, on the other hand, how closely their teachings coincide,
point by point, with one another's, we begin to be able to say in newly
concrete ways exactly what it is that constitutes the "spiritual DNA"
of the *Enduring Grace* mystics. We can say, in fact, with regard to
mother-lines of spirit and rivers of spiritual awareness, "*This* is what
the river looks like; these are its various streams."

A little history, then . . . enough, anyway, to establish that the
relatively sudden flowering of female mysticism that began around
the time of Saint Francis and Saint Clare, and the broader spiritual
awakening that accompanied it, did not happen out of thin air. Both
came on the heels of a massive reorganization of the Catholic Church

that coincided in turn with a broad economic and political awakening of the whole of Europe.

Prior to the middle of the eleventh century the focal points of Christianity were its monasteries. (Note the plural—*points.*) To the extent that Christianity was a narrative, it was a story about the war between good and evil, and the monks, seen as warriors of God, were the chief protagonists in that story, far more so than priests. Ordinary Christians received almost no religious instruction.

But even as the highways and marketplaces of Europe were coming to life again, the church awoke to a new vision of itself and its responsibilities to "the children of God." The Gregorian Reforms, so-called in honor of their most forceful architect, Pope Gregory VII, began around 1050, but they continued for almost a hundred and fifty years, and by the time they were completed, the church had been transformed into an elaborately hierarchical organization centralized in Rome. It was the most advanced bureaucracy in Europe—a phenomenally efficient "delivery system" for the word of God—and it was staffed by priests. Priests—university-educated men, their religious authority deriving not from personal sanctity but from scholarship and ecclesiastical appointment—were to be celibate now. They would have much more responsibility toward the laity, and more control over them, but they were at a much greater remove from the ways of life of lay people—and particularly remote from women and families.

Restructured, the church offered career tracks for as many reasonably capable men as cared to show up. The opportunities were virtually unlimited, because the church was poised now to extend its reach to the far corners of the known world. Christianity became, at this point, *Christendom.* That's *dom* as in *dominion, kingdom,* and *dominance,* and in order for the church to be felt as an authentically masterful presence in the world, a crucial shift had to take place in ordinary worship. Lay Christians had to accept that supernatural power was located in the Eucharist, and that priests had control of it there.[3]

Before ordinary Christians could be persuaded to attribute to the Eucharist the full weight of meaning that church authorities wanted them to, they had to be dissuaded from locating supernatural power elsewhere: in a striking cloud formation, or the timely appearance of an eagle, the fingerbone of a holy man, or something as ordinary as rain after a long drought. All of their capacity for awe and wonder

---

[3] Caroline Walker Bynum, *Jesus as Mother: Studies in the Spirituality of the High Middle Ages* (Berkeley and Los Angeles: University of California Press, 1982), 10.

was to be directed now toward the stirring, mysterious drama of a robed man uttering prayers in a language only he understood, elevating the host in clouds of incense, and pulling off in the process the incomprehensible feat of transubstantiation.

Canon law was elaborated during this period, and the sacraments were defined. The penitential system was established, and higher education was brought under the control of church. Advanced theological training was now by definition the preserve of the clergy and, it went without saying, denied to women.

But as we've already noted, administrative overhaul was not the only thing that was happening in European Christianity. Even as decrees were being hurled down from on high, a grassroots religious revival had begun to bubble upward from the villages and cities, an authentic spiritual awakening that in many ways brought back the fervor and the relatively open structures of primitive Christianity. Members of the itinerant orders—Franciscans, Dominicans, Augustinian Canons, and others—were crisscrossing Europe, preaching devotion to Christ crucified and imitation of his life in all things, and their ministries reached out as warmly to women as to men.

All across Europe women mystics began to record their experiences in journals, treatises, letters, and visionary poetry. They encouraged one another, and a body of inspired literature began to accumulate that danced blithely back and forth across the lines of orthodoxy. They did not deliberately and/or collaboratively strategize their way into an oppositional stance within the hierarchical church. But when God comes to visit, you don't keep quiet about it out of fear you might disquiet the bishop, and you don't reword what you actually heard or censor what you saw.

In effect, to put it in contemporary language, these women broke into the lab. They cracked the code. They laid siege to the president's office. In part *because* a certain kind of abdication had taken place, they became insiders. They weren't supposed to—they were laity, after all, not clergy, not *professionals*. They were, in the new scheme of things, amateurs. But amateurs win international mathematics competitions all the time, and when they do there's no quibbling. The proof of their ability is right there in their work, and if the experts have lost, it's because they've let their skills get dull.

Ordinary people knew very well what they were seeing. When a Catherine of Siena or a Clare came into her own, she didn't have to put out an advertisement in the *Corriere della Sera*. Women streamed into San Damiano to join Clare, and wherever Catherine went, half a dozen priests had to accompany her to receive confessions from men and women whose faith in God she had reawakened.

These women agreed with one another on so many grounds that their teachings constituted a distinct new religious voice. It might seem a small thing that this new voice did not speak in Latin, but it wasn't at all. The differences between the insider and the outsider-insider cultures of the newly corporate church crystallized around the use, and non-use, of emerging vernacular languages. In fact, the differences strike me as so important that it seems appropriate to invoke the term *vernacular spirituality* and to apply it in turn to the spirituality of women like Jane Goodall and Helen Prejean.

The *Enduring Lives* subjects are also all outsider-insiders:

- Jane Goodall, when she encounters Cambridge dons contemptuous of her revolutionary approach to primate study and, decades later, directors of American research laboratories who can't imagine why chimpanzees shouldn't be kept caged and solitary in a windowless basement.
- Tenzin Palmo, when she struggles for inclusion in her all-male, all-Tibetan spiritual family, but again, in a subtler sense, when she comes into the context of American Buddhism and feels compelled to utter truths that don't necessarily endear her.
- Helen Prejean, going toe-to-toe with Supreme Court Justice Antonin Scalia over the constitutionality of death penalty laws—she a lawyer's daughter with an insider's disinclination to be impressed by rank or title.
- And I wonder whether it's stretching a point to note that when Etty Hillesum refuses to be spirited out of Amsterdam because of a commitment her more politically oriented intellectual friends simply cannot grasp—to "care and connection"—she is in a position curiously like that of the whistle blower whose commitment to truthfulness and the public won't let her go along with colleagues.

They are outsider-insiders, and like their medieval counterparts, they've been compelled both to challenge the language of their insider colleagues, and even, sometimes, to bend and stretch ordinary language to meet their needs.

Let us look for a moment at what kind of difference it actually made that Julian spoke Middle English, Mechthild spoke and wrote in German, and both Catherines in Italian.

Latin was the language of medieval universities and therefore of learned men, whether they'd studied at Oxford, Bologna, the Sorbonne, or Cologne. If you were a man, knowing Latin meant you were at home, a privileged insider, almost anywhere you traveled. But to be fluent in the language of Cicero, Virgil, and Julius Caesar was to absorb by osmosis the privilege of empire. The meanings of Latin words had been established hundreds of years before and were fixed for all time. Because the language itself had been, in effect, *pegged* in the remote past, it wasn't the best vehicle for the expression of original and/or provisional ideas.

The robust vitality of the new vernacular tongues, in contrast, predicted the rise of independent nation states and a vigorous merchant class, and for that reason anything written in the vernacular carried a whiff of the subversive.

Vernacular languages were only just being sorted out as literary languages, so the first writers in these languages were by definition inventive. When Julian of Norwich set down her *Sixteen Revelations,* she was trying to describe how copiously the drops of blood had fallen from beneath Christ's crown of thorns, she didn't look to Virgil for a simile; she looked out her window and saw drops of water falling thick and fast from the eaves of her house after a rainstorm. An *English* rainstorm: early vernacular writing was redolent of the place where it was written and packed with local color; the Latin root *verna* actually *means* "color."

Because they were alive, vernacular tongues were just messy and indeterminate enough to carry the ambiguities that characterize original thought and expression. But I would argue, too, that those emergent vernacular tongues lent themselves particularly well to a quality in the thinking and writing of the *Enduring Grace* subjects that I'm inclined to call connectivity. (There is, of course, no way to prove a relationship between their preoccupation with connectivity and the newly discovered "tend and befriend" syndrome, but they are certainly compatible.)

Medieval Latin was beautifully adapted to formal argumentation—to Aristotelian logic and categories, and long cherished antitheses like reason *vs.* emotion, sacred *vs.* profane, man *vs.* woman. But Julian of Norwich, Mechthild of Magdeburg, and Catherine of Genoa weren't drawn to argumentation, formal or otherwise. They were enthralled, rather, with flow and fusion—with boundaries that dissolve and beings that melt into one another and antitheses that turn on closer inspection into paradox. Wine, tears, blood, water, light, fire, honey, milk, and divine grace are all but interchangeable in their visionary writings, and that in itself was the outward and visible sign of discoveries each of them had made about the deep, intrinsic connections among love, loss, suffering, courage, wisdom, and unitive awareness.[4] It is almost impossible to imagine how they could have conveyed all of that in Latin.

Latin was a fine vehicle for conveying abstractions; vernacular languages capture the particular beauties of the actual world that's right in front of us, and indeed the women mystics of the Middle Ages were on the whole unimpressed by the idea on which so many medieval sermons were based: *contemptus mundi*. The magnificence of things as they are seems to strike them as forcefully as it did Francis of Assisi when he composed his Canticle of Creatures. On the rare occasions when serving sisters left San Damiano to do errands in Assisi, for example, Clare didn't tell them to travel only in pairs and keep their eyes to the ground, but rather to praise God if they saw a beautiful tree, or flower, or bush—or a human being, for that matter, or a cat, or a dog. After all, it's all God's handiwork!

Glorious as the visible universe is, though, these women concur that it is surrounded and interpenetrated by another that is still more real—more real, however, by *degree*, and not by absolute difference. Two levels of reality seem to have coexisted for them like two versions, almost equally loved, of the same story. And when they experienced, as each of them did, a sudden deepening of the known world and a glimpse of all that hides just behind it, each is emphatically clear that she did not just chance her way into the experience.

Two powerful and complementary disciplines allowed these women to move back and forth between the temporal and the timeless. One was the systematic practice of silent, interior prayer. The other was a sustained challenge to personal desires, prompting them gradually to renounce everything that did not meet their deepest needs, so that finally all of their desires were pointing in the same direction. But once again, and this seems to me very much in keeping with the informality and intimacy of vernacular languages—with, for that matter, the warmth implicit in "tend and befriend"—they departed decisively from traditional ways of talking about this twofold discipline. It is not, for them, *asceticism*. Teresa of Avila is the perfect case in point.

---

[4] The motif of fluidity is particularly visible in the writings of Mechthild of Magdeburg, for whom the Trinity itself is the headwaters of a "love flood" where God enters the world. When the soul is united with God in mystical union, moreover, and it starts to taste God's sweetness, the power of the Holy Trinity flows through soul and body "like mother's milk" (see Carol Lee Flinders, *Enduring Grace* [New York: HarperCollins, 1993], 55).

What *is* interior prayer? "It is intimate conversation with someone you love dearly." And of course you would renounce everything that stood between you and the Beloved. What else matters?

Each of these women would endure at some point in her life excruciating loss and/or pain. In one way or another, and usually several, each was pushed to the very edge of what she could bear, and on that edge each became both other and much more than she had ever been, discovering firsthand the death and rebirth Saint Paul had described when he cried out, "Not I, not I, but Christ lives in me." Emptied of all personal agendas and attachments, each became, herself, a channel of grace. Catherine of Genoa described the process as a long, drawn-out refinement by fire: God binds the soul to himself "with a fiery love," and in the process "so transforms the soul in him that it knows nothing other than God."[5]

Probably nothing sets the *Enduring Grace* subjects apart more definitively from their more conventional fellow Christians than beliefs about God. There is no king here, and no judge; there is rather the Beloved, and something, too, that is more disembodied still, like a presence or a force, both tireless and elemental, that never stops pushing against the human being's resistance. For Mechthild, the Trinity is a "love flood" that never stops looking for a point of entry into this world and asks nothing of us but that we might allow God to be God in our lives. In keeping with their experience of God as all love and all knowledge, and someone whose yearning for us even greater than ours for God, they couldn't swallow the idea that evil has any real substance.

Finally, all of the *Enduring Grace* subjects were compelled on the strength of their visionary experiences to challenge conventional ideas about gender. They had experienced firsthand what Saint Paul had said in his letter to the Galatians—that for those baptized into Christ, "there is no longer Jew or Greek, there is no longer slave or free, there is no longer male and female" (3:28). So the advocacy of women, and the reverent assimilation of everything women know, was not just an incidental aspect of this new paradigm; it was intrinsic to it.

Invite readers to notice in how many ways the subjects of this book sound the same notes and take the same positions that the *Enduring Grace* mystics did. We will not find exact matches between any one contemporary seeker and her medieval counterpart. Reading the stories of Jane Goodall and Tenzin Palmo in the light of Teresa's and

---

[5] Ibid., 141.

Julian's stories is more like sitting in the corner at a family gathering and seeing Grandma's eyes and nose in one child, her cheekbones and hot temper in another, her sense of humor and Grandpa's angular build in still another. No two grandchildren look overwhelmingly alike, yet if you stood ten of them in a row you would know without a doubt that they are a tribe. Those "family resemblances" will be far more meaningful when they are discovered in the context of the stories themselves, but I'll touch on some them now.

The subjects of *Enduring Lives* share their spiritual great-grandmothers' passion for connectivity, blurred lines, and the kind of direct, informal discourse that *cuts through* hidebound ways of thinking. In fact, as one discovers reading Tenzin Palmo, that very phrase, *cutting through*, is a staple in the vocabulary of Tibetan Buddhism. They write and speak in ways that are distinctly their own—vernacular not just insofar as they don't use Latin, but in that it isn't theological either, or even necessarily "religious."

Like their medieval counterparts, whose firsthand encounters with God were a new wine they couldn't bear to pour into old wineskins (and yes, they too will happily seize the odd biblical tag when it's applicable), our contemporary Julians and Teresas are deeply suspicious of language that isn't connected with experience, and they resist the specialized vocabularies that grow up within any field. Etty Hillesum, for example, was unquestionably drawn to many of the ideas of Carl Jung, but she was plainly not comfortable with the technical vocabulary beloved of Jungians and never used one of its terms herself without placing it in the kind of quotation marks that imply a distinct wince. Tenzin Palmo is similarly vigilant where Buddhist teachings are concerned: are those in front of her speaking from experience, be it ever so modest, or are they merely entranced by the sound of the words? And everything Sister Helen Prejean writes or says about the death penalty includes the systematic deconstruction of phrases like *give the family closure* that keep us from understanding what actually happens when someone is executed.

The attraction toward the natural world that has Teresa of Avila sitting down next to a stream when she wants to meditate and talking about silkworms when she wants to say something about the soul becomes, in the lives of many of her spiritual descendants, a defining passion. This is obvious where Jane Goodall is concerned (as it is for kindred spirits like Terry Tempest Williams, Gretel Ehrlich, Julia Butterfly Hill, Starhawk, and Wangari Matthai). From earliest childhood her religious quests have been intimately connected to her study of animal behavior, and the long months she spent virtually alone when she first arrived at Gombe appear now to have been a certain kind of novitiate for her.

But each of the other three women also draws crucial spiritual sustenance from her contact with nature. One thinks of Etty Hillesum, in the last weeks of her life, exulting over the patch of yellow lupine that's somehow managed to bloom in the desolation of Westerbork Camp. Or Tenzin Palmo, at fifty, swimming blue-lipped with cold but deliriously happy in the icy waters of Lake Manasarova, more than fifteen thousand feet above mean sea level. Or Helen Prejean, whose annual reconnection with the forests and meadows of Montana restores her after months on the road and weeks on Death Row.

All of them, too, speak of the still deeper and more radiant version of ordinary reality that can open out and pull us in . . . pulls us *in,* or maybe *out,* for Jane Goodall mulls the possibility that mystical "outsights" rank right up there with insights. For her these tend to occur in natural settings or at least in the company of animals, but for Helen Prejean the likeliest context is Death Row on the eve of an execution. Consistent with her religious tradition, Tenzin Palmo won't talk about the exact nature of her realizations. Etty Hillesum's press in on her when she's walking across a bridge late at night, or lying in a barracks among women crying themselves to sleep, or kneeling in prayer on the hemp mat in a bathroom that is the only place in a crowded house where she can be, for even a few minutes, alone.

Each of them practices a form of prayer and/or meditation that involves the training of attention, and each affirms the need to shed the kind of personal attachment that deadens us to the "inward tug" of . . . well, yes, the inward tug of *what*? No surprise that Tenzin Palmo doesn't talk about God; she's a Buddhist. But Etty Hillesum fights shy of the word too, and Jane Goodall only uses it in the loosest sense when she's sure her reader knows it's just a placeholder for something nameless, formless, and everywhere. Helen Prejean is a Catholic, but she, too, is clearly a bit "allergic" to the word and, when pressed, talks instead about "the loving energy that is at the heart of everything."

Each of the *Enduring Lives* subjects speaks about the necessity to get hold of what Jane Goodall calls "circling thoughts." None of the other three has given meditation the almost absolute priority it holds in Tenzin Palmo's life, but there are plenty of contemporary women who will find a parallel between her teachings on meditation and Teresa of Avila's wonderfully concrete discussions of "mental prayer" and what it requires.

Devastating personal loss struck all four women—the deaths, respectively, of a lover and mentor, a husband, a spiritual teacher, and "my closest friend in all the world," and each wrote afterward a kind of anatomy of grief itself, and it is fascinating to read these side by side. I've alluded to them briefly here, but some readers will want to go to the original sources as well and reflect on both the parallels and the differences between the way each woman comes to terms with her loss and moves afterward into what she herself recognizes, despite her grief, as a new freedom to give herself over more completely to the spiritual calling she has by this time accepted as hers.

Like their medieval forebears, these women all came up hard against conventional assumptions about gender, and each has had her feminist moment—maybe several. Yet none calls herself a feminist, and two have even taken explicit issue with the anger they associate with feminism. When Jane Goodall's biographer describes her as a "natural feminist" though—someone who's tough and independent and goes her own way—he could be describing any one of the four.

If we do accept this rough summary of vernacular spirituality "then and now" as a rough approximation of what it is women can hope to access more directly and powerfully if we align and connect ourselves with the Teresas and Julians of the past and the Ettys and Janes of today, this question almost has to arise: Is it appropriate to label this bundle of values, attitudes, habits, and skills "feminine," as I know some would, or even "the feminine," as still others do?

I have chosen not to. Still, I have argued both sides of this question and will probably continue to do so, because I believe there are useful truths in each position and real risks in settling into either one.

Surely we can see, as I argued in my last book, *Rebalancing the World,* that the values of care and connection are not exclusively feminine. For we all know men and boys (I married one, we've raised one, and those are only the first of many who come to mind) whose capacity for tenderness is unfeigned and constantly evident. And we know women and girls you wouldn't want to be alone with after dark.

A preference for blurred lines and collaborative life ways aren't gender specific, but if we follow the gender scripts that we've inherited, which we know now have both biological and social dimensions, some of us get more encouragement to embrace those values than others, and we've gotten that encouragement for so long that they have become something very like second nature.

But that's a wonderfully telling phrase, isn't it—*second nature?* Because it suggests that beneath even the most seemingly irreducible accumulation of behaviors and attitudes associated with gender habits socio-biologists describe as if they were almost absolutes—there is a *first nature.*

Human nature. The place in consciousness and dim memory where we know that we are one.

This is, of course, the burden of what the mystics among us, and even the mystics-in-the-making, have been saying all along, and it is the reason I keep finding them indispensable to any constructive conversation about gender. Knowing what we do about Saint Francis and Gandhi, on the one hand, and Saint Teresa of Avila and Tenzin Palmo, on the other, are phrases like *the feminine* really applicable? Is Sister Helen Prejean more masculine when she takes over a room with her wit and the force of her arguments, or is she just more fully herself?

One *can*, in fact, talk about the values associated with women's experience without being reductionist or essentialist, and I believe we must develop the ability to do so. Philosopher Sara Ruddick did in her 1993 book *Maternal Thinking: Toward a Politics of Peace,* wherein she outlined a set of skills that she argued are universally associated with "maternal practice"—with the *job,* that is, of bringing up a child from infancy, which has fallen for the most part, and still does, to women. The child needs to be kept healthy and safe, both physically and emotionally. She or he needs to learn how to learn and needs to be socialized, to understand what will be expected of him or her in the culture in which the child is growing up. These objectives, in turn, elicit from the mother, with fair consistency, certain very specific forms of self-discipline. Taken together, they constitute a *practice,* and Ruddick wonders whether the essentials of that practice might not be applicable in the enclaves where life-and-death decisions are daily made in our name—as applicable, anyway, as the practice of law or business or politics.

Might they not, in fact—and she proposes a number of reasons for thinking they could—form the basis for a politics of peace?

Exploring the lives of these four women has allowed me to ask the same kind of question about "vernacular spirituality." What might congressional deliberations over national security sound like, for example, if "tend and befriend" were deemed a plausible response to perceived threats? I invite readers to frame their own similar questions and look for answers.

Like many women of my generation and a bit older, I am enormously grateful that we've been able to construct for ourselves something I really didn't have as a young woman. "A usable past" we've called it—history rewritten as if women had been there. And in fact, thanks to all of our efforts, something like a genealogy actually has formed in my mind's eye that connects all of those courageous, innovative women with one another and with their spiritual great-grand-goddaughters. Only it doesn't look so much like a family tree as a map of a vast river system—a wide network of streams, creeks, canals, and tributaries.

Well, but *of course,* says India, where rivers are not just the visible symbols of divine grace but grace, period, and—lest we think the question will ever be settled for good—*the feminine.* The names of her seven (most) sacred rivers are pure poetry: Kaveri, Ganga (Ganges), Saraswati, Narmada, Sindhu (Indus), Godavari, and Yamuna.

All the rivers are goddesses, but it's probably more accurate to say that all seven are *one* goddess: the Mother . . . Shakti . . . Resilience. The life force itself.

But the most timid, ordinary, discouraged woman is also understood to be an embodiment of Shakti—one who just hasn't yet awakened to the fact.

I know better than to idealize a culture whose record where women are concerned has its own horrific dimensions. But the vast reservoir of story into which India has tipped everything it's ever figured out about the human condition goes on sustaining me, allowing me to believe that there is not only beauty in the values passed down through mother-lines but immense power to heal, redeem, and revitalize.

George Eliot was wrong, you know—unless, as I suspect, the passage in question is a bit tongue-in-cheek—when she said Dorothea Brooke failed to become the Teresa she could have because nineteenth-century England didn't offer her the "coherent social faith and order" that sixteenth-century Spain had offered Teresa. Because, of course, Florence Nightingale had managed in that same period to revolutionize the profession of nursing and become world-renowned for her humanitarian work. And before Josephine Butler challenged the Salt Laws the British government had imposed on India, she shattered Victorian England's willed indifference to both prostitution and the sexual enslavement of children. And then, of course, there was George Eliot herself.

We are never altogether at the mercy of history—not even our personal histories. If there are the dry spells, when we look around wondering "where the women are," they don't trouble me as much as they did before I learned about Saraswati.

Of all the river-goddesses I've mentioned, Saraswati is the one whose provenance is most explicit. She is the goddess of music, art, poetry, and eloquence. She presides over science as well, and any endeavor that requires intuition. She is, says one authority, the goddess of fluidity.

And yet, here's the paradox: Saraswati is also absolutely invisible.

In ancient India she was the uncontested queen of rivers, mentioned over and over in the Rig Veda, India's oldest scripture. And even today, if you were to visit the city of Allahabad, you'd be shown the convergence of rivers called Triveni, where the Jamuna, the Ganga, and the Saraswati meet, making this spot one of India's holiest of holy places. You would, in fact, see only the Jamuna and the Ganga, but never mind, says your guide. We are here on the surface of things, but the river Saraswati flows far, far underground.

Saraswati's invisibility makes her all the more plainly a celestial river, and in that sense the wild card in all important human endeavors. The fact that she is not associated with a visible river probably makes it easier for her to be everywhere at once—in the mind of a mathematician reaching for the equation that's eluded him for weeks; or a young orator trembling before her first public talk; or a musician like the late Ustad Allaud Khan, Ravi Shankar's teacher, who used to go every morning to one of Saraswati's temples, where "she fed me music like a mother cat."

Fine, it's a wonderful concept, but things are getting dire up here. We need visible rivers and water that actually makes things wet. A river like Saint Clare, whose eulogist said of her, "This clear spring of the Spoleto Valley furnished a new fountain of living water."[6]

A river like the beautiful Kaveri, which flows through the Coorg Hills in southwestern India. There is a story about the origins of the Kaveri that gives the credit to a sage named Agastya, whose concern for his drought-stricken region was so great that he walked all the way to the Himalayas and brought home a pot of snow-water—in essence, Ganga herself—that became the river.

But there is another account, and this one's protagonist is a young woman called Kaveri because her father was the sage Kavera, and in this one she didn't *go* anyplace except inward.

"Let me become a river!" she prayed, and she backed up her prayer with such phenomenal penances that her boon was granted.

Granted, but then delayed.

---

[6] Ibid., 25.

Because the sage Agastya has seen her and been so captivated by her beauty that he asks her to marry him. She agrees, but with the condition that if he leaves her for even a short time, she will be free to go.

And, of course, he does. He forgets, or maybe he's called out on an important sage mission, but he leaves, and when he comes back, there she is, shedding one kind of loveliness and taking on another. He rages and weeps, but the metamorphosis has already begun, and soon all you can see of her is the shimmer of the river's surface as its ripples catch the light like a woman's long, wavy, unbound hair, its color shifting continuously like a Benares silk sari.

Once a year Kaveri has the gift that her cousin Ganga has all the time: her waters can wash away any sin, any negativity . . . which says to me that if we look around ourselves in Oregon, or Ohio, or Massachusetts, and the grass is withering and the air is full of dust, we can wish for a river, or we can pray for a river, or we can do as Kaveri did, or for that matter, Clare, and simply become the river.

Call it vernacular spirituality, or maybe *stealth spirituality* is the contemporary equivalent. Because the toxin of "othering" is so insidious, and so invasive, that it has to be pursued everywhere, and flushed out from everywhere, and if sometimes we must travel in disguise to do it, as a scientist or lawyer or filmmaker or politician, so be it. The sometimes subterranean river of women's spirituality hasn't only resurfaced, it has streamed out in every imaginable direction.

To Nazi-occupied Amsterdam, as a young woman who thought she just wanted to write novels.

To the Gombe Stream Preserve in Tanzania, as an English girl who wants to study chimpanzees.

To a cave in the Himalayas, as another Englishwoman, one who was enthralled with the teachings of the Compassionate Buddha.

To Louisiana State Prison at Angola, as a middle-aged American nun who accompanies Death Row inmates to their executions.

Etty Hillesum

"The Thinking Heart of the Barracks"

I try to look things straight in the face, even the worst crimes, and to discover the small, naked human being amid the monstrous wreckage caused by man's senseless deeds. . . . I am no fanciful visionary, God . . . I try to face up to Your world, God, not to escape from reality into beautiful dreams.[1]

On September 7, 1943, a friend of Etty Hillesum's watched her on the platform at Westerbork Camp shortly before she was to board the train that would carry her to Auschwitz, and he described what he saw in a letter to people back in Amsterdam who were as fond of her as he was. He said that she was smiling and speaking gaily the whole time, finding a kind word for everyone she met—"every inch the Etty you all know so well."

As the train gathered speed, a farmer working in fields nearby saw a postcard flutter from a crack in one of the cars and sent it on to the addressee, a friend who had been managing to get food packages through to Etty and her family that summer, and who wouldn't need to any longer. "Opening the Bible at random," it said, in Etty's barely legible hand, "I find this: 'The Lord is my high tower.'" She described herself sitting on her rucksack in a packed freight car, a few cars away from her mother, father, and one of her brothers. They'd left the camp singing, she assures her friend, all four of them. Finally, she thanks this friend for her kindness and care.

I've come to think of the whole body of Etty Hillesum's writings— her diary and seventy letters, all written between the spring of 1941

---

[1] Etty Hillesum, *Etty: The Letters and Diaries of Etty Hillesum, 1941–1943* (Grand Rapids, MI: Eerdmans, 2002), 384. Subsequent references to this book will be made in the form of parenthesized page numbers.

and the fall of 1943—as a note scribbled in haste and flung back toward the rest of us as the bullet train of history carried her swiftly away: a passionate footnote to official versions of what was happening and a fierce corrective to them.

Etty kept her diary in ten exercise books. She is believed to have had an eleventh with her when she left Westerbork, but neither that one nor the seventh have ever been found. She doesn't appear to have written them with publication in mind: on more than one occasion she considered burning them. But when she knew she was going to be deported, she sent them to a friend, a writer himself, asking him to try to get them published if she did not return. He tried during the 1950s but was unsuccessful and left them to his son, who in 1979 found a Dutch publisher for a collection of excerpts. These were published in English in 1984 as *An Interrupted Life*. A couple of years later a small collection of letters appeared under the title *The Thinking Heart of the Barracks*. A complete and unabridged edition of everything she's known to have written between 1941 and 1943 was published in English in 2002 as *Etty: The Letters and Diaries of Etty Hillesum, 1941–1943*.

The complete diary is easily three times as long as *An Interrupted Life*, and it's wonderfully well annotated, revealing, for example, that the writer to whom the diaries had been entrusted was also a former lover and a vivid, complex character in his own right. For new readers the abridged version is probably still the better introduction to Etty, because it establishes a basic "through-line" that gets somewhat overwhelmed in the full diary, but for true Etty-philes, the unabridged edition is an absolute banquet.

It is good to bear in mind that unlike Teresa of Avila's *Autobiography*, which was written from the vantage point of late middle age and had a distinct agenda, Etty's diary was written day by day, and mostly as a therapeutic tool. Had she lived, though, it would certainly have furnished the raw material for a novel she wanted to write and call *The Girl Who Learned to Pray* (alternatively, *The Girl Who Learned to Kneel*), that would document the spiritual transformation she felt herself to be undergoing.

Withdrawal from ordinary life held only sporadic appeal for Etty, and the ascetic's denial of the body none at all. "I am accomplished in bed," she purrs in her first entry. "Just about seasoned enough, I should think, to be counted among the better lovers, and love does indeed suit me to perfection" (4). She had a strong antipathy to organized religion, yet when she experienced the powerful jolt to her being that Mechthild of Magdeburg called "the inward tug of God," she was able to lay hands on everything she needed to answer it: a spiritual practice, a mentor, a body of inspirational literature, and even a ministry of sorts.

If in certain of these regards she wasn't as fortunate as one might have wished—if she lacked a systematic meditation practice, for instance, and the support of a family of likeminded seekers called a *sangham* in Buddhism, and if her teacher was himself still very much a work in progress—it only makes the transformation she underwent during the final two and a half years of her life all the more extraordinary. Slowly, but inexorably, while the world around her was falling into pieces, Etty Hillesum moved into a state of grace. Nothing we know of her reading habits (and we know a good deal) suggests that she was familiar with Taoism. But Lao Tse says of the spiritually awakened that they act with compassion: "And within themselves they can find room for everything. Having room, they live in accordance with the nature of things."[2]

Here is what Etty writes in the last pages of the diary: "Through me course wide rivers and in me rise tall mountains. And beyond the thickets of my agitation and confusion there stretch the wide plains of my peace and surrender. All landscapes are within me. And there is room for everything" (546).

Etty Hillesum didn't exactly follow a religious calling; it was more as if she backed into one, or entered it by a side door. A sophisticated young urban intellectual with writer's block and debilitating mood swings, she sought professional help, and when she began to make the relatively prosaic changes in her life that her mentor suggested, she was stunned by the rapidity with which everything started to turn around. There were depths in her that she'd had no idea existed. Provisionally, self-consciously, she began to call the deepness itself "God," and just over two years later, from the hell that was Westerbork Camp, she would write, sounding remarkably like the Augustine of *Confessions*:

> You have made me so rich, oh God, please let me share out Your beauty with open hands. My life has become an uninterrupted dialogue with You, oh God. . . . Sometimes when I stand in some corner of the camp, my feet planted on Your earth, my

---

[2] Lao Tzu, "Holding to the Constant," trans. Stephen H. Ruppenthal, in *God Makes the Rivers to Flow: Sacred Literature of the World*, selected by Eknath Easwaran (Tomales, CA: Nilgiri Press, 2003), 34.

eyes raised toward Your heaven, tears sometimes run down my
face, tears of deep emotion and gratitude. (640)

She used the word *God* sometimes but wished she didn't have to.
It struck her as a "makeshift construction," primitive and primordial,
and when occasionally she did catch herself talking to God in the
middle of the night ("God, things just cannot go on like this with
me"), she was pretty sure it was just Etty trying to bring Etty into
line (439).

Etty Hillesum was a mystic, but on her own terms. "Mysticism
must rest on crystal-clear honesty," she argued. "[It] can come only
after things have been stripped down to their naked reality" (426).

When we first meet her, Etty is twenty-seven years old, and she
lives in Amsterdam, in a house on the square in front of the
Rijksmuseum that sounds much like households one remembers from
Berkeley *circa* 1967: a haphazard arrangement that had settled over
time into something like an extended family.

Etty herself is working on a translation of Dostoevsky's *The Idiot*
and giving private lessons in conversational Russian. She is an aspiring
poet as well, or novelist, she hasn't decided which. The owner of the
house is a widower in his early sixties, Han Wegerif. Etty does some of
the housework, and she is also—comfortably, and in fact enthusiasti-
cally—Wegerif's lover. She has been so, in fact, for almost five years.
A surviving photograph of Wegerif reminds one somewhat of an aging
Sir Lawrence Olivier. His son Hans, a student, lives in the house, and
so does a German cook, Kathe. Two other people rent rooms.

Born Esther Hillesum, Etty had grown up in Deventer, where her
father, a scholar of classical languages, was headmaster of a *gymnasi-
um*. The family was Jewish, though not particularly observant. People
who knew her father described him as small, quiet, erudite, and witty.
Etty's mother, on the other hand, who'd come to Holland as a young
woman after a pogrom in her hometown in Russia, struck acquain-
tances as lively and extroverted, but unstable, too, and domineering.
The children were talented and extremely bright. Etty had taken a
degree in law, and then entered the Faculty of Slavonic Studies at the
University of Amsterdam. Her younger brother Jaap was a physician,
and the youngest, Mischa, was a renowned concert pianist. But both
young men had been institutionalized several times—Jaap for "schizoid tendencies" and Mischa for full-blown schizophrenia. Because of
this legacy, Etty is determined not to have children.

Leonie Penney-Snatager came to Amsterdam during the late 1930s and knew Etty well. She remembers vividly both the milieu and Etty herself. The neighborhood was, in fact, Amsterdam's red-light district—a kind of Montmartre, populated by students and artists. She and Etty had long telephone conversations and endless visits in "Pa Han's room," where they would turn the heater on and settle into what Etty called "higher gossip." She was like a fairy, Leonie recalls, and "whatever she touched with her magic wand was lifted out of the everyday world" (679n).

Photographs of Etty suggest her intensity, her sharp intelligence, and her irreverence. To the Dutch, she looked something like a gypsy, and she exploited the association, wearing flowers in her hair sometimes and making herself a dress that is "open on all sides to the sun." She had had many lovers and still counted several as friends, and when on occasion she writes about sexuality, she is matter of fact, explicit, and, typically, somewhat amused.

Etty led her life pretty much as she chose, and she was more or less self-supporting. Yet she had no illusions about how far she and women like her had come. "We have set out on a long hard road, we outwardly emancipated women, and I am curious to know where that road will lead us" (118).

When we consider her expressed solidarity with women in general, and her desire to help solve what she calls the "women's problem," it is disappointing that Etty's catalog of heroes didn't include a single woman: Saint Augustine, Dostoevsky, Tolstoy, Leonardo da Vinci, Michelangelo, Kierkegaard, Jung, Shakespeare, Rilke, and so on. How she would have loved Teresa of Avila's *Autobiography*. And for that matter, how she'd have savored Colette, and Emily Dickinson—George Eliot, Marina Tsetsaeva, and Virginia Woolf. Her relationship with her mother was vexed, and she tended to construe the polarities of her own personality in ways that reflected her parentage: discipline *vs.* chaos, Dutch *vs.* Russian, scholar *vs.* chatterbox, man (Alas!) *vs.* woman.

Etty began her diary in March 1941, lamenting the difficulty she has, as a would-be writer, "letting things pour out of me." She declares herself a match for most of life's problems, yet she feels bound up inside, like a tightly wound ball of twine. There is something within her that wants desperately to express itself, but can't: something like "the final, liberating scream that always sticks bashfully in your throat when you make love" (4).

She says nothing, initially, about wanting to find God. What Etty Hillesum wanted more than anything else in the spring of 1941 was to be able to write. She wanted, in fact, to be Holland's greatest writer, and it drove her mad that she didn't even know the words to describe the colors she saw. She was certain that no great work can be undertaken if you can't forget yourself, so she would try to do that; she saw her mental energy to be spilling out on every side, and she wanted to reclaim it, but only so that she could write.

Etty also took very seriously the possibility that her bouts of depression could be related to the mental illness that plagued both her brothers. She herself tended to oscillate between two extremes. On the one hand, with respect to larger, external realities, she felt herself to be "a small battlefield" where the problems of her time were being fought out, and this seemed only right to her: we should all make ourselves available for those struggles. We should accommodate them, pay attention, *care* about them.

After one of these periods, though, there invariably followed headaches, exhaustion, and a grateful retreat to the solitude of her desk, "flowing again in my own narrow riverbed, my desperate involvement with 'Mankind,' 'World History,' and 'Suffering' subsided" (63). Unfortunately, she wasn't particularly productive in either state, and the waste of energy seemed profligate. The one state felt too much like mania, the other suspiciously close to depression.

And she wanted very much to figure out why it was that almost every woman she knew, including herself, insisted on placing a man at the center of her life and deriving every scrap of meaning and identity from that relationship. "Perhaps," she speculates, "the true, essential emancipation of women is yet to come. We have yet to be born as human beings; that is the great task that lies before us" (69).

Religion as such was not in the picture yet, but the conventions of spiritual biography alert us to a possible subtext. Etty would seem to have reached that juncture when with a little luck, a bit of grace, someone quite special might be about walk into her life: a sage; a holy woman; a spiritual mentor.

And in fact, someone had shown up that very month. For Clare of Assisi there was Francis; for John of the Cross there was Teresa of Avila; for a circle of late nineteenth-century proper Bostonians there was Swami Vivekananda; and for Vivekananda himself, there had been Sri Ramakrishna. For Etty Hillesum, lamentably perhaps, there was Julius Spier. Within a few weeks of hearing him lecture for the first time, Etty decided "to deliver myself up to his care."

Girl meets guru, boy meets illumined sage, it's among the oldest stories in the world. Only it doesn't always unfold the way you might think. Sometimes the person who turns up isn't everything one might wish and the story isn't so much "what an amazing teacher!" as "what an amazing student!"

Julius Spier is a problematic character. But if we do not try to see him as Etty did, and recognize in him not merely the greatness she saw, *and* the fallibility, but his endearing qualities as well, a crucial dimension of Etty's story eludes us. For her story is on one important level their story, and their story is its own unusual kind of love story.

Etty sized Spier up on their first meeting as "a man of fifty-four in whom the struggle between spirit and flesh are still in full cry." Jewish, divorced, father of two adult daughters, a successful businessman who had retired early to pursue other interests, Spier had fled from Berlin and was hoping to make his way to London, where his considerably younger fiancée was waiting for him. Spier had trained to be a therapist under Carl Jung. He was the author of a highly regarded treatise on chirology, the reading of palms as a diagnostic tool. Jung himself had written a foreword to the book.[3]

Spier was learned, charismatic, and unquestionably well-intentioned. Contemporaries spoke of his "magical personality"—of his personal warmth, and his uncanny ability to reach even the most discouraged individuals and help them get hold of their own lives. Sometimes it wasn't so much what he said that so effectively galvanized his patients, Etty observed, as the depths from which it seemed to come. He was a sincerely religious man who understood his work as a kind of ministry and his gifts as a sacred trust. By reading palms—"our second face"—he believed he was able to look into people's hearts and see strengths they didn't know they had—to see, in fact, the "little piece of God" he believed everyone carried within themselves. Awakening his patients to their own strength and divinity, he healed them primarily, Etty says, by teaching them "how to suffer and accept."

It was under Spier's influence that Etty came gradually to see her situation and her strivings in religious terms, a shift that was made difficult at first by what she called the "critical, rational, atheistic bit in me." By the time he died, just a year and a half after they'd met, she

---

[3] The book, called *The Hands of Children* and published by said fiancée after Spier's death, is out of print, but there are websites where one can learn more about chirology, which is presently called by its proponents "psycho-diagnostic chirology."

would write: "You taught me to speak the name of God w/o embarrassment. You were the mediator between God and me, and now you, the mediator, have gone, and my path leads straight to God" (516).

Mediator he may have been, but in effect, Spier threw almost as many obstacles in Etty's path as he removed. We could resent him more for this if those very obstacles hadn't also been the making of her.

Along with many other psychoanalysts of the time, Julius Spier believed that a therapeutic relationship could only arise from a physical bond (735). So it was that he invited his subjects/clients/patients to engage in regular wrestling matches with him—fully clothed, but alone in his apartment, with no holds barred. Boldly unorthodox, maybe—illuminating and apparently quite a lot of fun for some, but given that most of Spier's clients were women (he jokes sometimes about his "harem," and you can feel Etty wince as she reports this), and given that he was, after all, their therapist, it is hard to read about those sessions today without feeling a certain alarm. While one can understand his preference for the direct and non-cerebral, and his conviction that there just wasn't enough love in most analysis, it is distressing to learn that he expressed his affection for his female patients by kissing them and lavishing caresses on their cheeks, lips, eyelashes, thighs, and breasts. The women were not to be sexually aroused by his attentions, he told them, only to feel his warm regard for them and be strengthened by it.

It seems significant, and they both certainly thought it was, that the first time Spier and Etty wrestled, she threw him. The second time, too, for that matter. If Etty had in many ways met her match in Spier, so had Spier met his in Etty. Soon after she became his patient she also began working for him. She typed his notes and interviews and organized them, and she also undertook the study of psychology under his tutelage (she balked at chirology) and in a year or so was seeing a few people herself, mostly helping them to prepare for "depth analysis" with Spier.

Analyst and patient, teacher and student, co-workers, sometime lovers, very best of friends. Their relationship would be passionate, mutually instructive, and exceedingly complicated—complicated because of who they were and what they were asking of themselves, but complicated above all else by the fact that they were Jews living within the tightening noose of the Third Reich.

The quasi-erotic wrestling matches aside, the regimen Spier prescribed for his clients resembled traditional religious asceticism more than it did conventional psychoanalysis: a vigorous program of physical hygiene, calisthenics and long walks, cold baths, adequate sleep, healthful food, and breathing exercises. The mind was to be taken in hand just as aggressively. By way of "mental hygiene," Etty was to keep a diary that would allow her to chart her thought processes from day to day. She was to try, in addition, to become more one pointed: Whatever she was doing, she should do with undivided attention.

The ideal, as Spier summed it up, was "to repose in oneself." He was interested in both Eastern and Western teachings on meditation and contemplative prayer, but offered formal instructions in neither. Etty appears to have begun to experiment with prayer—or meditation—or something—soon after they met. In the summer of 1941 she resolved to "turn inward" for half an hour every morning. She would listen to her inner voice and even lose herself. "You could call it meditation. I am still a bit wary of that word" (56). Her intention, she explains, was to turn her innermost being into "a vast empty plain . . . so that something of 'God' can enter, and something of 'Love,' too."

She *listened* at these times so intently, struggling with all her might to fathom the ultimate meaning of things—that the verb *hearken* seemed more apt—a verb that in Dutch *(horchen)* connotes a kind of whole-body listening (90).

She listened for the still, small voice within, but she listened also, with almost obsessive passion, to the writers she loved best. Daily study of inspired literature was for Spier an essential part of mental hygiene. He and Etty both studied the Old and New Testaments, the *Confessions* of Saint Augustine, the *Imitation of Christ* by Thomas à Kempis, and the writings of Carl Jung. Etty's own canon included Dante, Tolstoy, Dostoevsky, Goethe, and Michelangelo as well, but above all other writers—so much so that she identifies him at one point as her spiritual teacher—Rainer Maria Rilke.

The disciplines that Spier recommended worked to tremendous good effect for Etty, allowing her to start re-engineering her own thinking process almost immediately. Soon she was beginning to identify and redress her besetting difficulties: her writer's block, her depressions, and the realization that, as a woman, she was only outwardly emancipated. In fact, she had one more powerful motive for undertaking such an ambitious program. I've given Spier credit for Etty's having gradually redefined her inner work in religious terms, but the context in which they lived was at least as critical.

Etty Hillesum wanted with all her being *not to hate.* "Indiscriminate hatred is the worst thing there is," she believed." It is a sickness of the soul" (18). But for a Jew living in Holland in 1941, not to hate was an almost impossibly tall order.

German air and ground attacks had overwhelmed Dutch defenses early in the war, in May 1940. Surrounded by Germany itself in the East, German-controlled Belgium in the South, and the North Sea to the North and the West, the tiny country could be sealed off with relative ease, and it was. Flat and exceedingly *tidy*, moreover, it was unblessed by the hills, mountains, and forested terrains that sheltered resistance movements in other parts of occupied Europe. And the meticulous recordkeeping for which the Dutch are famous made it devastatingly simple for the Gestapo to locate the citizens it wanted to. In no other Western European country was German control as absolute, and in none other, therefore, despite a courageous underground resistance movement, was it so dangerous to be Jewish.

Yet Nazi administrators knew that in Western Europe they could not address "the Jewish problem" with the same straightforward, uncompromising brutality they did in the East. Jews couldn't be packed into ghettoes to die as they had been in Warsaw because there *were* no ghettoes here—the last one had been closed in the early part of the nineteenth century. Western Jews were for the most part fully integrated into the societies they lived in. They spoke the same languages everyone else did, and they dressed the same. They had the rights and obligations of full citizens, and they had had these for generations. They had intermarried, they taught in the gymnasiums and universities, and they held public office. They were not seen as the threatening "other."

In the fall of 1940, therefore, the first of a series of laws had been imposed that were expressly designed to set Jews apart, stigmatize and impoverish them, and ultimately dehumanize them in the minds of their non-Jewish countrymen. All Jewish-owned enterprises were to be registered, whereupon they were liquidated or confiscated. Jews were dismissed from public office, from professions and jobs, and they could keep only small amounts of money. In January 1941, all Jews were registered (the figure arrived at was around 140,000), and a Jewish Council was created to liaise between Jews and the German authorities. These and subsequent directives were enacted at a pace that was steady and deliberate, in part because it allowed everyone to be "eased" into the new reality by stages but also because the machinery of death wasn't yet in place: Auschwitz was still under preparation.

Etty Hillesum's diary begins, then, nine months after Hitler's takeover, in the wake of an economic restructuring that had left wealthy

Jews poor and middle-class Jews destitute. The process of "othering" was well under way, and its effectiveness led Etty to predict that from this time forward, regardless of the war's outcome, there would probably always be a perceived "Jewish problem" in Holland.

Etty would note each new development in turn—bitterly, apprehensively, but almost parenthetically, too, in the way one communicates things that are utterly beyond one's control anyway, like rain that just won't stop, or insufferable heat. Nothing in the world would have felt more natural than to hate the Gestapo, but Etty was convinced that to do so was to meet them on their level, and that would have been catastrophic for the whole human race. Sounding extraordinarily like Mahatma Gandhi, she writes: "Nazi barbarism evokes the same kind of barbarism in ourselves, one that would involve the same methods if we could do as we wanted. . . . We must not fan the hatred within us, because if we do, the world will not be able to pull itself one inch further out of the mire" (21).

So, all right. Not to hate. Not when your favorite professors are arrested or harassed into exile or suicide. Not when you come out of a restaurant late one winter night and see a terrified family dragged into the street with nothing but the pajamas they'd been sleeping in. Not when you can no longer buy vegetables, and you're put under absurdly rigorous curfews. ("We've been naughty again," Etty writes a friend, "so we must be in by eight o'clock" [559]).

Not to hate when the most terrifying rumors imaginable have begun to filter in from Poland.

How do you *do* that?

Etty was absolutely certain that life is meaningful and beautiful and that there is "something of God" in every human being. That conviction was bedrock to her personality. But unspeakable things were happening, and as a university-trained intellectual, a Dutch citizen, a Jew, and a writer, she saw it as her personal responsibility to bear witness to all these events. She must look upon them squarely, without wavering, and she did.

Was it possible to do this without hating?

In effect, her conundrum mirrored the one that had sent her to Spier in the first place: the disconnect between Etty in her desperate-involvement-with-mankind phase, and Etty in her serenity-at-the-desk-with-flowers phase, and the fear that she might never be able to integrate the two. She'd watched each of her brothers literally break up under certain pressures and slide into a private reality, and now it occurred to her to ask whether her own strong craving for synthesis might not be masking a deep-seated fear of schizophrenia (115).

Etty may not really have thought she was schizophrenic, but she did see "schizoid tendencies" in herself and wanted desperately to overcome them. Repeatedly over the next several months she would express her huge relief at finding that the more faithfully she hewed to her new regimen, the more deeply integrated she felt herself to be. Less than a year after she'd met Spier, she writes that she is no longer conflicted: "Rilke and Marlene Dietrich tolerate each other, as it were, wonderfully well in me" (223).

Eventually she would find in herself the capacity to hold the two halves of her reality and her self in equilibrium, but that ability was the fruit of a considerable and sustained effort—one that began with a discovery she made as soon as she started to keep close track of her own thinking processes and observe how little control she had over attention itself. "If someone makes an impression on me, I can revel in erotic fantasies for days and nights on end" (7).

Etty didn't view such fantasies as wicked or immoral; she just re-alized that they consume an enormous amount of vital energy and, worse, that they "detract from any real contact" (8). They aren't *dirty*, they're just in the way—and absolutely out of her control. Soon she realizes that she can be wrenched out of the moment with equal ease by thoughts that are utterly innocuous—shopping lists, and scraps of old tunes. Even her delight in the natural world is now suspect, because she sees that up to this point she hasn't really known what to do with a beautiful sunset, say, or an opening hyacinth. Foolishly, she's tried to *own* it, to press it to her heart, "to eat it all up," and because of course she couldn't, those transports always ended in pain, and a sense of loss. She would wallow in the pain, try to write verses, and collapse finally, exhausted. She'd thought of this whole sequence as being part of her creative process. But now, "I know it for what it was: mental masturbation" (24). "Over-thinking," mental health scientists call it today, and "ruminating," a habit Buddhists call "monkey mind."

Etty doesn't appear to have studied the Eastern spiritual tradition at all, but she certainly sounds as if she has. Observing the people around her, she sees that many of them play and replay memories of fear, grief, and anger with the same avidity she'd devoted to sexual fantasies, and that because they cannot direct their attention at will, they no longer experience life directly. Like her brothers, they have moved into a private reality, and that has consequences that spread far beyond the individual. "One must not cling to moments of malaise," she decides, "and prolong them needlessly, because in so doing one may prevent the birth of a richer moment" (211).

She would ponder all of this as she lay in bed listening to antiair-craft fire, bombs, and guns. At any moment a piece of shrapnel could tear through the window and take her life. The war feels stunningly, almost majestically impersonal, so far is it beyond any human being's control. But in fact, she realizes, it is not. "All disasters stem from us. Why is there a war? Perhaps because now and then I might be inclined to snap at my neighbor. Because I and my neighbor and everyone else do not have enough love" (307). Yet there *is* love bound up inside us, she adds, and if we could release it into the world, a little each day, we would be fighting war and everything that comes with it.

In effect, it is as if Etty has launched her own campaign—her own war against war. "I can only hate the evil within myself" (307), she maintains. By taking on the "chaos" in her own undisciplined mind, she seeks to confront directly the forces in human consciousness that had given rise to Nazism in the first place.

She speaks playfully about her new disciplines and the pleasure she takes in finding herself "combat-ready" (38). She recognizes that what she is doing is not that far from traditional religious asceticism: so why not go ahead and embrace a monastic life? Yet she mocks herself even as she pictures it: "Sometimes I long for a convent cell, with the sublime wisdom of centuries set out on bookshelves all along the wall and a view across the cornfields—there must be cornfields and they must wave in the breeze" (71).

She reasserts her determination to hold on to both sides of the paradox that is Etty. Running off to a convent would accomplish nothing. She must find peace and clarity in the here and now. "I must fling myself into reality, time and again: . . . feed the outer world with my inner world and vice versa."

The disciplines prove uncannily effective at opening up that inner world. She reads the thirteenth chapter of Corinthians one evening, and like a divining rod, it touches the deepest part of her, "causing hidden sources to spring up suddenly within me." Suddenly she was down on her knees, "and all my released love coursed through me again, purged of desire, envy, spite, etc." (256).

Nothing about a vision of God, we note once again: just a release of love—the love that had been bound up within her at the outset, like a tightly wound ball of twine. Love that was the polar opposite of the hatred she'd vowed not to accommodate. But to *release love* on a daily basis, and nourish the world with it, she would have to come to grips with the way her mind worked. She would have to train atten-tion itself, so that she could refocus it at will whenever it got stuck, whether it was stuck in desire, hatred, fear, or erotic daydreams.

Moving out of the world of fantasy was a particularly tall order, because Etty was very, *very* good at fantasy. It is April 1942, and German soldiers are performing their drills at the skating rink just down the street, and our would-be contemplative has pulled out a length of gypsy material that she'd packed away in a wardrobe. Her friend Liesl will help her make a dress with it, a sundress, "open on all sides to the sun, the wind, and his caresses." The fantasy rolls on: there is the dress, the heath, her own tanned bare legs, and "a small farmhouse with a low-beamed ceiling and the smell of apples and a view over the heath at night" (331).

Presumably, too, cornfields waving in the breeze.

Gradually, as she saw how tumultuous her thoughts are—how *chaotic* to use her own favorite term—she would begin voluntarily to distance herself from the movements of her mind. In fact, the foundation of her spiritual practice was not so much a systematic method of meditation as, rather, an assiduously cultivated moment-to-moment vigilance, and because the diary is written in "real time," we can watch this vigilance developing from day to day until eventually it becomes almost unconscious.

Pained, for example, she describes a nocturnal raid on a locked cupboard (it is 1942 and everything worth eating is rationed) to eat illicit bread and butter with chocolate sprinkles—this *after* she had rebuked one of her housemates because he'd asked for extra food at supper (250).

But there are small triumphs, too. Etty had in the past been rather easily undone by suffering of one kind or another, so she was thrilled now to find that something inside of her has begun "fighting it out" (63). She describes one evening in particular when she was cycling across Amsterdam to meet her brother and fell into a mild depression about some shortcoming or other. Her mind strayed to the recent death of a university professor, a particularly gentle man who had just died in a concentration camp, and her sadness swelled and solidified until it felt like a great stone. But instead of trying to push it out, she opened to it lovingly, because she realized "that sadness, too, was part of my being" (202). Learning to accept even the parts of herself that she had wanted to excise became for her a kind of rehearsal for learning to accept other people as well, in all of *their* unloveliness.

The diary had its therapeutic function, but it was also the place where Etty described her day-to-day life—a narrative richness from which she hoped one day to carve her novel. She continued to give lessons in conversational Russian grammar: she provides cameo portraits of her favorite students, including a Dutch grain importer of splendid character who gives her household a special price on dried beans, and a girl with piercing blue eyes who always wears trousers, doesn't think much of Spier, and disturbs her dreams at night.

She complain about how much she'd like to write and decides the problem is just that she hasn't time. One loves her hyperbole—every writer can sympathize: "I would need hours with a sweeping view over the many hours that follow, all of them for me alone . . . in a hall of time, with many large windows, all of them looking out over Time, and it would all have to be my exclusive domain" (390). She arranges recitals and birthday parties, and describes what a feast looks like in the middle of a war: "Kidney-bean soup, and leek and potatoes, and blancmange with stewed plums. And flowers and the apple pie by way of decoration" (232).

Etty's parents visit her, and she them, and we're given a harrowing peek into the Hillesum household. "Our house is a remarkable mixture of barbarism and culture," she reports flatly. "No human being can flourish here." Hearing a door slam downstairs and her father shouting, "All right then, go!" she adds: " It is sheer hell in this house." Finally, though: "I sprang from this chaos, and it is my business to pull myself out of it" (80–86).

In effect, Etty was trying, in the context of a completely secular and worldly life, to observe disciplines that tradition associates with a monastic withdrawal from life. She sought to be even-minded in pleasure or pain, and she worked so hard at this that it became second nature. There were trees outside her widow, for example, where the stars hung at night, "like glittering fruit in the heavy branches," and the sight of them sustained her as she fell asleep. But one day the branches were cut off, and for just a moment she was all but undone. She caught herself, though, and immediately decided that by merely adjusting her metaphor, she could love the new landscape, too. Now the shorn trees rose up outside her window "like imposing, emaciated ascetics," and even in their new shape, they were beautiful beyond words (307–8).

Over and over the issue of suffering comes up, and Etty reiterates her insistence that suffering must not be avoided. At the core of Spier's therapeutic approach was the insistence that suffering is most acute when we try to hide from it. Teaching his patients how to suffer and accept had nothing to do with masochism or grim resignation, but rather with learning that one can, in fact, resist conditioned patterns of thought and habits, and that doing so will indeed involve some pain or discomfort, but not more than we are equipped to bear. If we do not assume this fundamental human responsibility, he and Etty believed, and learn how to bear the suffering that comes our way, we'll end up trying to push it onto someone else—our children, parents, partners, friends, co-workers. And it's not just a matter of life-altering tragedies: suffering can mean as little as having a slight cold on a chilly morning, or having to make a dentist appointment.

There is throughout all of this, as Etty learns to go against the grain of her own mental habits, a rising note of exhilaration. Nothing comes easily. She feels now "exactly like someone waking up from a general anesthetic" (94), and of course that is a two-edged sword; she feels pain, now, and fear. Echoing Saint Catherine of Genoa, though she surely doesn't know it, she says she feels as if she were in purgatory, on fire, "being forged into something else" (93), and, again, that she feels "like a terrified child being dragged towards a burning house" (102).

There are of course slips and falls; Etty is the queen of recidivism. With characteristic frankness, she recalls a childhood shot through with unsuccessful attempts to turn over new leaves. It would usually happen after she'd raided the refrigerator, she confides, or picked her nose. She would make a fresh start on January 1, "but by 2 January I would already be picking my nose again" (103). Only things are different now.

> A strong, straight pillar is growing in my heart, I can almost feel it growing, and around it all the rest revolves: I myself, the world, everything. . . . Something is being consolidated within me, I seem to be taking root instead of continuously drifting, but it is still no more than the fragile start of a new and more mature phase. (85)

Mystics of every tradition have described a point in their spiritual practice when they suddenly feel they are no longer doing all the work themselves. Sri Ramakrishna describes this experience in a parable of sorts: when the mother monkey is swinging from branch to branch high in the trees, her baby has to hold on tight to the fur on her back or chest. But when the mother cat goes from one place to another, she just picks up her kitten by the scruff of her neck and carries it. During the early stages of meditation, he says, we are like baby monkeys: we have to do all the work. But in the second half, we can go limp, like kittens. It is almost as if someone else were doing the work. It isn't that we don't make any effort, but our own efforts are augmented mysteriously from within. Teresa of Avila says exactly the same thing in her *Autobiography* where she describes deepening meditation, and the consequent flow of grace into one's life, by comparing it to the watering of a garden. One method is to dig down through the hardpan until water bubbles up from the depths—this corresponds to the early stages, when we pay with hard, hard work for every drop of water. As we get more skilled there is a certain effortlessness, and in the final stage it is as if the very heavens opened and grace all but floods the life of the seeker.

"I don't have to . . . tinker with my life," writes Etty, "for an organic process is at work. Something in me is growing, and every time I look inside, something fresh has appeared, and all I have to do is to accept it" (359).

Etty's passion for flowers is a *leit motif* across the whole diary. She always had them on her desk. A red anemone, a handful of snowdrops; violets; yellow roses just beginning to bloom, or hyacinths; tulips; jasmine, lilies of the valley—a spray of orchids or a jug of oxeye daisies. Scarlet cyclamen in a translucent green glass vase. For Etty, flowers were the visible affirmation of the resilience, beauty, and meaning that she insisted lay at the heart of human existence. In July 1942, when panic lay thick in the air, and she was spending her days typing multiple copies of desperate petitions at the Jewish Council offices, she walked several miles home from work—public transportation was forbidden Jews by then—and it was raining, and she had a blister on her foot, but she made a detour nonetheless to buy a bunch of roses.

"And there they are. They are just as real as all the misery I witness each day" (500).

Her desk, with her favorite books, a few pictures, and of course the flowers, becomes her cell and anchorhold. "Here, beside this great black surface that is my desk, I feel as though I am on a desert island. The statue of the Moorish girl stares out into the gray morning with a serious dark look that is carnal and serene at the same time" (175).

And of course, Etty *is* the Moorish girl with the serious, dark look, "carnal and serene at the same time"—as if one *could* be both who was not a statue herself, or a photograph of one.

Throughout this period the central drama of Etty Hillesum's life involved her deepening relationship with Julius Spier. It is the great irony of her story that by accepting Spier as her spiritual director—by "delivering herself up into his care," to use her phrase—she was also doing the one thing she had been determined not to do again, which was to place a man at the center of her life.

Of Spier's extraordinary gifts with troubled people, Etty can't say enough: "He breaks them open and draws out the poison and delves down to the sources where God hides Himself away. . . . The water of life begins to flow again in dried up souls" (411). But she brings her own strengths to the work, finding that the qualities that have served her well in writing and translating have a place here as well—that when someone's words and questions and problems "flutter toward me, a little uncertain," she is able to catch them, try to understand them, and give them form (253). She can keep *turning people back toward themselves*—"catch and stop them in their flight from themselves and then take them by the hand and lead them back to their own sources" (399).

Under these circumstances—the sheer propinquity, the shared excitement at what they are finding themselves able to do for people, and of course, we must never forget, the terrible fears and tensions gathering in around them—Etty and Spier swiftly became intimate friends. His apartment was separated from hers by "three streets, a canal and a bridge," and she walks or bicycles there almost every day. They call each other late at night. "Say, listen to this!" he will say with the peremptory eagerness of a child, and then read something to her that a patient has said—or Rilke, or Thomas à Kempis. She is captivated, and the same time finds herself struggling hard still against the "the sheer weight of his personality."

As we've already seen, Etty threw Spier the first time they wrestled, and it was hard to say who was more astonished. Spier was a large man, Etty quite small. Nonetheless, he was thrown, and not just physically, he admitted, but mentally as well. And nobody had ever been able to do that to him before (6).

Spier told her right away that he was attracted to her, but he also said that they would not have an affair. He was engaged, and he wanted to be faithful to the faraway Hertha—not only out of consideration for her, but also out of his desire to honor the *ideal* of faithfulness as a spiritual discipline. There was, too, his certainty that he was more effective as a spiritual director when he was celibate (Etty refers icily on more than one occasion to "the chastity plan"). And of course there was another factor, which was the crucial difference, fundamental to his work as a psychoanalyst, between chaos and discipline. He valued self-discipline and the freedom that comes with it for his students as well as for himself, and mastering one's sexuality seemed to him the most direct route to both.

Etty's own desire for a sexual relationship ran hot and cold. At first she wasn't even physically attracted to the man, and she didn't want to disrupt her relationship with Han. Yet there was much about him that she did find attractive, including, of course, his expressed determination to remain chaste. Unfortunately (or fortunately), she had embarked on a program that flushed out the sort of self-deception that had fuelled erotic adventures of the past. No sooner has she confided to her diary that she is in very deep, and doesn't see how she possibly *not* go to bed with the man, than she sees with painful clarity what is actually going on.

> Etty, I have something very important to point out to you. You think you are obsessed with his mouth, his eyes, his whole body, and that you cannot rid yourself of them. But make no mistake. You rake it all over time and again in your imagination in order to revel in it. In a way you want him to obsess you and to pursue you physically, because you like it. (34)

"Overthinking" once again. This was, of course, the essence of that "women's problem": the compulsive swiftness with which women reenact the primordial drama. It just feels so comfortable, so familiar, so blessedly simple, to focus one's whole being on getting a man to fall in love.

The relationship was in effect a single extended conversation, barely interrupted by their separation each night and sustained when they weren't together by telephone calls, and letters that they signed with question marks—in token, one guesses, of the questions about identity, self, and God that engaged them so entirely. They had agreed they would not have sex, but somehow, what with the wrestling matches, Spier's Platonic caresses, and Etty's gypsy dresses, things most people would call sex kept happening. It was one of those awful "oh, dear, we mustn't" situations that almost guarantees we will, and since after all that's what diaries are *for*, Etty leaves little to the imagination. One is embarrassed at times, by the sheer melodrama of it all as much as by the intimate details and self-conscious euphemisms. But again, we must bear in mind the context. Considering how desperate things were, people could be excused for having behaved far more foolishly than these two.

And, in fact, for all the slipping and sliding, the two of them actually did want the same thing. Not chastity in the ordinary sense, for the ordinary reasons, but the capacity to love another person self-lessly—unreservedly, but without a trace of the possessiveness that most lovers feel for one another, and this by way of preparing oneself to love all human beings with the intensity reserved ordinarily for one's beloved.

It might be more accurate to say of Etty that she *wanted* to want this. She was, after all, very young, and for all her cold showers and calisthenics, the effort is sometimes just too much. Late one night, she writes, pathetically: "Desire is 'making itself at home' in me, spreading out and taking over my entire inner life and weighing me down like lead. . . . My body feels so young and so lonely and so betrayed" (261).

Yet, once again, no sooner has she described her anguish—the diary works!—than she is almost compelled to see it objectively. It is spring, she realizes, and when you have spring fever it's easy to believe that sexual desire is the very center of your being. But in fact, "no matter how dominant it may appear to be, it is only a part, no more than a part" (262).

There is a passage from Rilke that becomes a talisman for Etty in this struggle in which the poet envisions a time when men and women, "freed of all misconceptions and antipathies," will no longer be drawn to one another as opposites. They will come together, rather, as siblings and neighbors and human beings, "to share the heavy sexual burden that has been laid upon them, simply, seriously, and with patience" (249).

As Etty tried to deal with that burden, and make use of the mental disciplines she'd been working at so diligently, she made a discovery. Cycling home from an evening with Spier, oppressed by the sheer weight of all the tenderness she felt for him and couldn't express, she is suddenly able to pour it out into the night itself: "the great, all-embracing spring night." And as she does this, she herself seems almost to melt into the landscape. For just a moment she slips the bonds of egocentricity, offering all her tenderness "to the sky and the stars, and the water and to the little bridge." Brief as the respite is, it is enough to persuade her that the only way we can transform all of the complex and tender feelings we carry for others is to entrust them to nature, to "let them stream out under the open sky" (345).

By the next evening, she is sure of it: "One must divide one's single great tenderness into a thousand small tenderness's, lest one succumb to the weight of that one great tenderness. A thousand small tender-nesses: for a dog in the road, or for an old flower seller—and finding the right word for someone in need" (349).

The sobering thought that it might in fact be possible to give in to the weight of her own ungoverned emotions forces Etty to wonder more and more pointedly now whether her capacity for love might be so great that no single human relationship *could* satisfy it.

I've already lamented the fact that Etty seems to have known so few women writers, and it's especially sad that she didn't have access to the great women mystics of her own region. She'd have loved the Beguines and in particular, I think, she'd have loved a poem that Mechthild of

Magdeburg wrote in the style of the *chansons* of the Courtly Love tradition. The Lover and the beloved are, in this case, God and the human soul. Delighted, he watches her approach, but he notices that she is carrying something.

"What is it?" he asks, and instead of answering, she poses a riddle, as lovers typically do under the conventions of Courtly Love.

> Lord, I bring thee my treasure!
> It is greater than the mountains,
> Wider than the world,
> Deeper than the sea,
> Higher than the clouds,
> More glorious than the sun,
> More manifold than the stars,
> It outweighs the whole earth!

God declares himself stumped. He is enchanted by her, made as she is in his own image, and adorned by Holy Spirit, and he insists that he has no idea what her treasure is. She stretches out the moment, but finally answers him, playful no longer:

> It is my heart's desire.
> I have withdrawn it from the world
> Denied it to myself and all creatures,
> *Now I can bear it no longer.*
> *Where, oh Lord, shall I lay it?*[4]

Mechthild receives her answer. God will by all means take from her the weight of all that desire. But not right away, because withdrawing desire from the world is only one phase of what she must endure to be fully united with her beloved.

The point that the poem makes, and it is startling, I think, to the contemporary reader, is that desire is the human being's most precious resource. Spend it heedlessly, and we are spiritually bankrupt. And what is true of sexual desire is true, in fact, of all strong feelings. We must become able to bear them—to tolerate and endure them.

Etty Hillesum was absolutely clear on this score. It is a terrible mistake to keep wanting to be rid of our feelings. We have to be able to

---

[4] Mechthild of Magdeburg, "Lord, I Bring Thee My Treasure," in *God Makes the Rivers to Flow: An Anthology of the World's Sacred Poetry and Prose*, selected by Eknath Easwaran (Tomales, CA: Nilgiri Press, 2009), 119.

carry them around with us and draw strength from them, not so that we can bestow them on one man, but because all of God's creatures "have a right to our attention and love" (349).

By learning to love Spier without possessing him—by learning, in the words of Saint Catherine of Genoa, "to love without loving"— Etty came to realize that the only real alternative to hatred is love: not *particular* love, because that is only a way-station, but universal love that seeks nothing for itself. She isn't yet able to act in complete harmony with this insight, but things are unquestionably moving in that direction. The "organic process" she's been so thrilled to feel working within her is moving along steadily.

It would have moved along more steadily still if sex had been the only issue with respect to her relationship with Spier. What made Spier all but irresistible to Etty was that he *got* her to an extent no man ever had before. He loved her intelligence, he loved how hard she was working on herself, he loved the *look* of her, and no, her breasts were not too large at all. And he thought she was funny. She loves to report occasions when she's said something to him on the phone that elicits "his socially unacceptable, liberating laughter" (440). Spier was far more cosmopolitan than most of the people she knew, and he pleased her inordinately when he observed once that most people in Holland didn't understand "the Russian bit in you." He nicknamed her "my wild Kirghiz girl," and sometimes he would half close his eyes and laugh with a deep, warm sound in his voice in imitation of her "Kirghiz laugh" (350).

It wasn't going to be easy to lift this man out of the center of her life. Much of the time she couldn't even remember why she wanted to.

Once again, then, Etty found herself feeling like a battlefield. Her battles were with herself now, and with what she thought Spier wanted of her, and she mocks her own ambivalence, and every once in a while she just can't contain herself.

Take the evening when "the chastity plan" was firmly in place and the two of them were listening to recorded music with friends. Beethoven is followed by a medley of folk songs, and then, arrestingly, a tango. Suddenly, Etty is up and dancing, and she dances with such skill and grace and sensuality that the men in the room are a fair shambles. She dances, someone murmurs, "like a girl who has worked all week in a café and is putting it behind her now" (286). She knows the effect she's having, and she couldn't be happier. This is not ordinary sensuality, but "pure bacchanalian intoxication," and surely *that* shouldn't have to be renounced.

In other words, there is in Etty something one sees rather often in contemporary women who have won through to a measure of sovereignty and self-possession and then try to practice spiritual disciplines. They are *damned* if they're going to hand it all over blithely. Etty is determined not to inflict injury on herself. Whatever she renounces she will renounce of her own free will and for her own reasons.

And in her own sweet time.

It is entirely possible that Etty could have remained in the sort of deadlock we see in much of the diary in the spring of 1942; she is like a plane that can't get clearance to leave the ground and just keeps spinning her wheels on the runway. One remembers Teresa of Avila, who was stalled for nearly twenty-five years, attracted in almost exactly equal measure to, as she put it, heaven and earth.

But everything changed in the summer of 1942, and so did the tone of Etty's diaries. Nazi authority ratcheted down swiftly. In May it became obligatory for Jews to wear the yellow star. As the situation deteriorated, Etty allowed it to almost force her hand. Like so many before her and after, she seems to have determined that "the only way out is in." "The threat grows ever greater, and terror increases from day to day. I draw prayer around me like a dark protective wall, withdraw inside it as one might into a convent cell and then step outside again, calmer and stronger and more collected again" (364).

She can envision times ahead when she might have to wait on her knees for days at a time, "until the protective walls are strong enough to prevent my going to pieces altogether, my being lost and utterly devastated."

June brought still more restrictions. Jews would be under curfew between 8 p.m. and 6 a.m.; Jews could no longer stay in the dwellings of non-Jews; Jews could only buy in non-Jewish stores between 3 p.m. and 5 p.m., and delivery of articles to their homes was prohibited; Jews couldn't enter railway stations or use any forms of public or private transport. Jews could not use public telephone systems. Soon afterward they were forbidden the use of bicycles as well, and greengrocers were off limits.

The effect, of course, was to accelerate dramatically the process by which Jews were being turned into "the other" that Nazi eugenics claimed they were, for now they *looked* different: exhausted from having to go everywhere on foot, pale and thin with hunger and malnutrition, wary and frightened and, of course, displaying on their increasingly worn and ragged clothing a large yellow star. Because she was employed as Wegerif's housekeeper, she herself had been permitted to go on living in a non-Jewish household, but it was surely only a matter of time before that permission was withdrawn.

Etty insisted all along that one must not run away from suffering. Even the hardest truths would have to be accommodated within herself and reconciled somehow or other with her belief in meaning and beauty. It must have seemed to her that someone was taking her up on a rash wager—"Okay, see what you can do with *this*!"

The pivotal date was July 1, 1942. Up until this time the camp at Westerbork, some three hours east of Amsterdam, had been identified as a refugee camp. On this date, however, it became Transit Camp Westerbork, from which over the next two years some 105,000 Jews would be sent to death camps in Poland. For public consumption, of course, and for anyone who badly wanted not to know what was happening, these were described as labor camps. Etty was among those who had no illusions. On July 3, she writes: "I must admit a new insight into my life and find a place for it: what is at stake is our impending destruction and annihilation, we can have no more illusions about that" (461).

The word *maelstrom* is almost always used in the figurative sense, so much so that it can come as a shock to realize that such a thing really exists in nature. A few years ago a popular science journal published a photo essay on certain places in the North Atlantic Sea where under the right conditions an inconceivably powerful whirlpool forms—the tremendous *maelstrom* of North Sea navigational legend. The image seems so apt for what was happening in Holland the summer and fall of 1942: the lethal, downward spirals, deadly at the foaming center. Each individual Jewish life, and every family, was spinning toward extinction, and in fact, toward the end of Etty's diary, she will write repeatedly of the dizziness that keeps overcoming her, and the dizzy spells friends report, exacerbated surely by hunger, cold, and exhaustion, but originating, one guesses, in recurring waves of incomprehension.

"From all sides our destruction creeps up on us, and soon the ring will be closed and no one at all will be able to come to our aid" (476).

"The Jews here are telling each other lovely stories. They say that the Germans are burying us alive, or exterminating us with gas" (484).

Now, more than ever, the impulse to hate would have been almost unimaginably powerful, and this meant that Etty's capacity to resist that impulse would have to be just as powerful. "They are merciless, totally w/o pity. And we must be all the more merciful ourselves" (497).

Etty met the challenge, but only, she believed, because she had built up reserves of mental strength over the course of innumerable small skirmishes with her own thoughts and desires. She'd fought successfully against fantasies, compulsions, extremes of despair and elation, and small tidal waves of self-absorption, and as she began to contemplate life in a prison camp, she took the campaign to the next level:

> My breakfast is at my elbow: a glass of buttermilk, two grayish slices of bread with cucumber and tomato. I have dispensed with the cup of hot chocolate to which I used to treat myself surreptitiously on a Sunday morning, in order to train myself in more frugal habits. *I pursue my appetites to their most secret and hidden lairs and try to root them out.* (435)

She is teasing herself here just a little, probably paraphrasing Augustine or Thomas à Kempis, but she is at the same time perfectly serious. "We must grow so independent of material and external things that whatever the circumstances our spirit can continue to do its work."

She had come to see that any personal desire around which she organizes her life sets a limit to her availability to life. And of course that did not apply merely to chocolate. The greatest single challenge to her independence from material and external things had been her desire for an ongoing and unconstrained physical relationship with Spier. But she had taken that on too, and she is already drawing upon the freedom she'd gained in doing so, one small victory at a time.

There is a moment, for example, in May 1942, when she has been feeling down for several days. There are plenty of good reasons for this, including certain very real physical difficulties, but suddenly she realizes that she has been linking her malaise to Spier—as if anything that was wrong with her must have to do somehow with him and their relationship. No sooner does she catch herself making this mistake, though, than she moves beyond it, and realizes that "parallel with the process of growing toward each other there runs a process of more and more freeing oneself of the other" (385).

Spier was no longer at the dead center of her life and her system of meanings, and yet her love for him and the joy she experienced in loving him were unaffected.

In other words, what made it possible for Etty to go on seeing through what mystics call "the veil of separateness," so that she could spot the small scrap of humanity that is present even within the Nazi officer, was the fact that she had begun to see through the veil of separateness that had seemed to divide her from Spier. Paradoxically, it was as the physical component of their relationship became less and less important that she finally began to feel united with him. There were lapses, to be sure, but Etty was moving steadily into the understanding that the two of them were already one, joined at such a deep level that the urge to possess just didn't make sense any longer.

Freedom really is the byword for this whole period: freedom, most of all, from imagined limitations. Etty becomes more and more inwardly capacious now as she takes in larger and larger truths, and that is no less the case with the most appalling truths as it is with the transcendent ones. Because the reality of death is now a part of her life, she is no longer wasting her energies fearing death or trying to persuade herself she can evade it. She sees now that people who *don't* accept death as inevitable "are left with just a pitiful and mutilated slice of life." What a paradox: "By excluding death from our life we cannot live a full life, and by admitting death into our life we enlarge and enrich it" (464).

Etty is effectively moving away from life as it is ordinarily lived and almost lifting off as she keeps discovering new kinds of freedom; we really are not at the mercy of external events, she realizes, unless we allow ourselves to be. Gandhi had been telling India for some time that evil exists only as long as we support it, and Etty speaks to much the same effect. In order for someone to be humiliated, she reasons, there have to be two parties—one who does the humiliating, and another who lets himself or herself be humiliated. "If the second is missing, that is, if the passive party is immune to humiliation, then the humiliation vanishes into thin air. We Jews should remember that" (434).

The self-absorption that had marked the early chapters of the diary has all but vanished. Etty has moments at a time now when she seems to lose herself altogether in the sufferings of others, and she experiences this very loss as a form of freedom. Walking home one afternoon, aching with exhaustion, she realizes that people in every time and place have walked like this—tired, hungry, cold—and now she is one with them. "A hint of eternity steals through my smallest daily activities and perceptions." She is "at one with millions of others from many centuries, and it is all part of life" (466).

Old ways of construing existence and naming experience no longer seem to apply. It is best to just forget words like *god, death, suffering,* and *eternity.* "We have to become as simple and as wordless as the growing corn or the falling rain. We must just *be*" (483).

Time is becoming fluid for her. She has the curious feeling that everything that is happening has already happened. Place, too, becomes increasingly relative:

> I am in Poland every day, on the battlefields, if that's what one can call them. I often see visions of poisonous green smoke; I am with the hungry, with the ill-treated and the dying, everyday, but I am also with the jasmine and with that piece of sky beyond my window; there is room for everything in a single life. For belief in God and for a miserable end. (460)

She marvels at the contrast between the desolation that is happening all around her and the emergence *within* her of an altogether different way of being in the world. She decides that the only way to prepare for the new age is "by living it even now in our hearts" (497). She is carrying within herself love and humanity that she knows to be indestructible, and that is especially palpable in her relationship with Spier:

> We have embraced a new reality . . . and between our eyes and hands and mouths there now flows a constant stream of tenderness, a stream in which all petty desires seem to have been extinguished. . . . And every encounter is also a farewell. (475)

Curiously, even as Etty has become more and more deeply involved with Spier, her relationship with Han has become in its own way steadily warmer and deeper. His quiet strength is a haven for her, and her enjoyment of their lovemaking has never diminished. In his own way, he too *gets* her. She is wry about her situation: *"I am faithful to everyone."* But she does wonder about her predilection for men old enough to be her father. "My two grey-haired friends. . . . What is it with me?" (249).

She has suffered abdominal distress for some time now, and the complaints intensify as circumstances become more desperate. Inflamed kidneys and bladder, problematic ovaries—the diagnoses shift from week to week, and she alternates among rounds of aspirin, charcoal tablets, and homeopathic remedies, and surely terror itself is at the bottom of the pain. "There is a knot inside that makes it hard to breathe, and I . . . have a stomach ache" (483).

Her gray-haired friends are aging swiftly. She observes a new frailty in each of them, and that in turn elicits new depths of tenderness toward both and, at the same time, a growing detachment from both.

She chastises herself for noticing at a dinner party the taut, chiseled, handsome face of a much younger man when it interposes itself between her and Spier. She begins to see herself as someone who will remain single and, if she survives the war, be something of a wanderer.

And survival has indeed become the burning topic.

In early July the transport of Jews from Amsterdam to Westerbork began: Some four thousand each week. Etty was pressed by several friends to go into hiding. In fact, on two different occasions friends tried to push her into a car and spirit her out of the country, but she refused both times. She didn't want to desert her parents, but more than that, it just felt morally wrong to her that anyone would concentrate on personal survival who could be reaching out lovingly to others instead. She didn't buy the argument that times were so terrible that they obviate our responsibility toward one another. Things have always been bad, she insisted. "One moment it is Hitler, the next it is Ivan the Terrible; one moment it is Inquisition and the next war, pestilence, earthquake, or famine" (483).

There is always an excuse, that is, for looking out for oneself. She acknowledged that others did not agree with her, that some accuse her of indifference and passivity. "They say everyone who can must try to stay out of their clutches." But the argument felt specious to her: "I don't feel I'm in anybody's clutches; I feel safe in God's arms, to put it rhetorically." The Gestapo might break her physically, but they could do no more than that, for she has absolute faith "in God and my inner receptiveness." Ultimately, she confessed, it just wasn't in her nature to "tilt against the savage, cold-blooded fanatics who clamor for our destruction." Her battles would be fought inside "with my own demons" (491), and on that front, she was at long last gaining the upper hand. "It's as if something in me has been compressed into constant prayer," she writes in the summer of 1942. "Something keeps praying inside me, even when I laugh or make jokes. And I am so full of confidence as well" (490).

The diary entries begin to feel a bit choppy now, and disjointed. Spier and Etty considered getting married so that they won't be separated. There was another motive: Etty's mother didn't look particularly Jewish, so if authorities could be persuaded that she wasn't, Etty and her brothers would be reclassified as half Aryan, which might conceivably give them and anybody to whom they were married an exemption from deportation.

Word went out that the Jewish Council would need some 180 more workers. Etty's brother pressed her to apply, and with deep misgivings, she did. Friends intervened on her behalf, and indeed, she was offered the job. Grateful and repelled at once, confused because it had come about so fast, wondering whether she should consider it a miracle—part of God's plan for her (it's perhaps the measure of her desperation now that she's invoking "God"!)—she accepted.

The council's function was ambiguous. Ostensibly its members were to decide who was fit to be sent to the "labor camps" and who wasn't, and who was most needed at home. The Amsterdam headquarters was thus a hotbed of desperate intriguing. Now that the deportations had begun in earnest, council members would also function as quasi-social workers at Westerbork Camp. Located on the Eastern border between Holland and Germany, Westerbork functioned as a depot—a kind of holding pen for human beings where Jews were collected and "processed" before being sent to Poland. Many council members hoped they could use their position to forestall or mitigate the worst horrors, and at the very least pull strings for people they loved—Etty's family certainly hoped she could do this. Ultimately, though, it would become plain, and to many it already was, that the council had been little more than a tool in the hands of Nazi officials.

For a couple of weeks Etty typed petitions at the Amsterdam offices, which she described as midway between hell and a madhouse, but by the end of July she'd had herself transferred to Westerbork itself, the epicenter of the unfolding tragedy, site of continuous arrivals and debarkations and unutterable misery.

She had up until now led a relatively sheltered and comfortable life under Wegerif's roof. Moving to the densely populated camp was in a certain sense a relief. "I am grateful to You for driving me from my peaceful desk into the midst of the cares and sufferings of this age" (499). At the same time, she confesses, "sometimes I feel as if a layer of ashes were being sprinkled over my heart, as if my face were withering and decaying before my very eyes, and as if everything were falling apart in front of me and my heart were letting everything go" (491).

Any misgivings she might have had about being part of the Jewish Council appear to have fallen away once she has determined that being at Westerbork in the way she has assigned herself to be—fully present to what is happening and wholly available to everyone there—will be the hardest thing she's ever done and quite probably the calling that she has been getting herself ready for all this time. She has decided that Westerbork would be, for her, what the monastery had been for mystics of the past. People close to her saw what she was doing and remonstrated: She shouldn't kid herself that there are "spiritual advantages" to be garnered in such a place. "You grow a 'hard shell' around you, that's all" (495). But Etty swears that a hard shell wouldn't fit. She would remain open to everything, she insisted, including even the anguish of knowing that she and other Jews are being used by the Nazis to make everything happen in an orderly and seemingly lawful fashion. Bitterly, she acknowledges this: "Nothing can ever atone for the fact, of course, that one section of the Jewish population is helping to transport the majority out of the country. History will pass judgment in due course."

Etty lived at Westerbork that summer and part of the fall, traveling back and forth between there and Amsterdam every few weeks and using the opportunity to carry letters, medicines, and food for others. Spier himself, meanwhile, remained in Amsterdam, waiting to be called up. His own health was deteriorating rapidly. For this whole period, from the end of July until the middle of September, there is no diary. Etty had said repeatedly that words didn't even exist to convey the full weight of what was happening, and it may be that living at Westerbork had made that so clear that she just put down her pen for the time being.

When she does resume, beginning a new exercise book, it is September 15. It is the day Spier was to have reported to Gestapo authorities for removal to Westerbork, but he never reported because he had died that day in his bed.

Etty wrote several entries over the next twenty-four hours, and there is a distinctly feverish and disjointed quality to them: she is, once again, so *dizzy*. She can't sleep, and nothing in her body feels right. She has been determined all along to accommodate suffering within herself in whatever form it took, but she wonders now what her capacities really are.

> Perhaps, oh God, everything happening together like that was a little hard. I am reminded daily of the fact that a human being has a body, too. I had thought that my spirit and heart alone would be able to sustain me through everything. But now my body has spoken up for itself, and called a halt. (514)

From now on, she would have to do everything by herself. She stood beside Spier's bed, and gazed upon the "childish, worn-out husk" that was left of him, and knew that she could not comprehend the change. This was a mystery, and she would carry it as such, uncomprehending. In the diary, she addresses him one last time:

> All the bad and all the good that are to be found in a man were in you—all the demons, all the passions, all the goodness, all the

love. . . . You sought God in every human heart that opened up before you—and how many there were!—and found a little bit of Him in each one. You never gave up, you could be so impatient about small things, but about the important things you were so patient, so infinitely patient. (517)

There remain a thousand things she had wanted to ask him, but she feels herself at the same time to be unprecedentedly strong. It is as if she has assimilated him into herself—quite literally. She will put all his likenesses away and never look at them again, because "I want to carry you in me, nameless, and pass you on with a new and tender gesture I did not know before."

Etty would remain in Amsterdam until mid-November. After a few weeks at Westerbork, she came back to Amsterdam and stayed there until the following June. By now her body really had gone on strike. Intestinal hemorrhage, stomach ulcer, and anemia were among the diagnoses, but she conceded, too, that her doctor was probably right in thinking she had given full reign to spirit at the expense of body and that she was now paying the price—though when the malaise stretched out into months, and she wanted nothing more than to be back in the camp, her distress was acute.

She did resume writing in the diary now. Sitting again at her desk, she looked back across the two months she'd spent at Westerbork that summer and realized, gratefully, that the chasm that had once stretched between her two ways of being in the world no longer existed. In the barracks, in the midst of all that misery, her love of life had been confirmed. "Life in those drafty barracks was no other than life in this protected, peaceful room. Not for one moment was I cut off from the life I was said to have left behind. There was simply one great, meaningful whole" (527).

Even now, barred from returning to what in effect had become her religious community, the convent she'd once imagined for herself, she continued to be at peace. The contending forces in her life and personality had declared a truce, and all the separate currents in her nature pointed in one direction.

In her first diary entry after Spier's death Etty looked back at the past two years and realized that whenever she had shown herself ready, "the hard was directly transformed into the beautiful. And the beautiful was sometimes much harder to bear, so overpowering did it seem" (514). She had developed a kind of inbuilt circuit breaker. No sooner did a wave of fear or anger rise up now than there arose, without her consciously willing it, an opposing wave of courage or compassion. Bone-shaking terror would give way to feelings of absolute security. Her diary is filled with these instances. In May 1942, she catalogs the horrors that are taking place in houses very near her own: a son imprisoned, a father taken hostage, a boy sentenced to death. She *knows* all of this because she refuses to look away, and yet, uncannily, even as she is confronting it, she finds in unguarded moments that she is resting against "the naked breast of life, and her arms around me are so gentle and so protective," and her own heartbeat—low, regular, soft, constant, "as if it would never stop" (386)—feels in itself like yet another guarantor that life is both good and meaningful.

At the beginning of her diary Etty had lamented the absence of a *tune* in her life—a thread, or an underlying theme. But by now all the old anxieties—Could she write? Should she marry? Was she schizophrenic?—have slipped away. She has her calling now—the tune, the underlying theme that had eluded her before. People come to her, "bundles of human misery, desperate and unable to face life" (519), and she knows what to do.

She listens. Sometimes she sits and puts an arm around someone, but mostly she just listens, looking steadily into the person's eyes, flinching from nothing, taking everything in. Friends decide she must have nerves of steel, and she swears she doesn't. She can do what she is doing because she has reached the point in her own life where nothing is alien to her. "Not one single expression of human sorrow" (543).

The women and girls of Westerbork couldn't bear to think or feel, they told her—they were afraid they would go out of their minds if they did. And as she lay awake on her plank bed and heard them all around her, "gently snoring, dreaming aloud, sobbing and tossing and turning," an immense tenderness came over her, and she knew what she was there to do. She who had feared once for her own sanity would think and feel *for* them because she could. She would be "the thinking heart of the barracks" because she had acquired the strength to take in the most wrenching truths and yet remain certain that life is full of meaning and beauty.

She seems almost to have been using her days at Westerbork to temper the steel of that conviction. She felt more powerfully than ever the connectedness of all humankind, and she wanted to proclaim it: "But first I must be present on every battlefront and at the center of all human suffering. Then I will surely have the right to speak out" (531).

If she could look straight into the eyes of the eight-months pregnant wife of an epileptic man who was being transported to Poland, and if she could then look that same day, and just as unwaveringly, into the eyes of the bully who was pushing him onto the train . . . and if she could then *still* swear that life is meaningful, then and only then, she maintained, would her words carry weight.

Her mental strength during this period was phenomenal. But her body kept giving out. From her sickbed in Amsterdam, impatient to be back at Westerbork, she writes, "I feel like the sole of a shoe which has been walked on for so long that it's completely worn out. . . . There is an iron band round my skull. . . . I really do not want to be a sick, dry leaf dropping from the stem of the community" (543) and "I shall have to wait a little longer to gather up all their tears and fears" (545).

Etty often alluded to pregnancy as a metaphor for the work she felt herself called to do at Westerbork. There is precedent for this usage among other mystics—Teresa of Avila comes to mind—but it has special force where Etty is concerned, because in December 1941, she realized that she was pregnant. Years earlier she had watched her brother Mischa being carried off by force to a mental institution, and she had vowed that day that she would never have children. Her resolve had grown even stronger now that Jews were being hunted down, imprisoned, and murdered. Twenty quinine pills, a bottle of cognac, quantities of hot water, and vigorous calisthenics had their desired effect, and her relief was unmixed.

"It feels to me as if I am occupied in saving a human life."

A few days afterward, without alluding to the abortion, Etty asserted that "the only certainties about what is right and wrong are those that spring from sources deep inside oneself" (175). Immediately afterward, she added: "Oh God, I thank You for having created me as I am. I promise You to strive my whole life long for beauty and harmony and also humility and true love, *whispers of which I hear inside me during my best moments*" (175).

She had ended the pregnancy, and she stood unequivocally by her decision, pledging herself, though, in almost the same moment, to another kind of gestation. She would nurture in herself the spark of divinity that Meister Eckhart called the "God seed," and she would nurture it in everyone around her as well. Her ideal in relationships would be to carry "the other" within herself. "Not just one, but many. . . . Draw them into your inner space and let them go on growing and unfolding there. . . . That is the fundamental thing" (281). Even among her co-workers at the Amsterdam offices of the Jewish Council, she sees now and then "in each one of them a gesture or a glance that took them out of themselves. . . . I was the guardian of that glance" (518). And still more explicitly:

I feel as if I were the guardian of a precious slice of life, with all the responsibility that entails. I feel responsible for that great and beautiful feeling for life I carry within me, and I must try to shepherd it safe and sound through these times, towards better ones. . . . There are moments when I feel like giving up or giving in, but I soon rally again and do my duty as I see it: to keep the spark of life inside me ablaze. (498)

She had come to believe that the special gift women possess is the capacity to carry life as it moves from formlessness to form: physically, but figuratively too, and to that end then she would expand her interior space deliberately and systematically, dismissing extraneous thoughts and defying personal desires so as to more fully accommodate the needs of others. At times it feels as if someone else were doing the work. "Sometimes it is as if there were a great workshop inside me where hard laboring is being done, much hammering and who knows what else. And sometimes it is as if I were made of granite inside, a chunk of rock ceaselessly lashed and hollowed by powerful currents" (402).

Toward the very end of the diary, racked by illness and exhaustion, she writes in short patches, recording thoughts as they surface. She describes herself lying awake all night trying to take into herself and *accommodate* the terrible suffering that winter had in store for the world.

Finally, she realizes that she can't do it. The enormity of what is happening is simply beyond her. Her body is in revolt. She has asked so much of it that she's probably forfeited all say in the matter, even as she has earned the right to say—with Jesus Christ, with Francis of Assisi, with Catherine of Siena: "I have broken my body like bread and shared it out among men. And why not, they were hungry and had gone without for so long" (549).

The tone of the last entries of the diary gives the impression of someone very near the end of her rope. In fact, Etty would live another thirteen months, the last three of them at Auschwitz. She had begun another volume of the diary—friends saw it—but it probably went to Poland with her.

There are seventy-one letters though—fifty-five of which were written after the last diary entry. And reading them one forms quite a different impression than we get from the diary. Written to friends, family, and in some cases for a wider public audience, the letters are altogether free from the unrelenting self-absorption that shaped the diaries—which had been undertaken in the first place, we must recall, as a kind of spiritual therapy. In her correspondence Etty's immense generosity and good humor are manifest, as are her courage and her merciless powers of observation. Her public face is confident, warm, and steady. Should there be any doubt as to whether Etty had the makings of a great writer, they are settled by the letters.

What does she do all day at Westerbork? The members of her Amsterdam household want to know, so she tells them. She finds blankets and warm clothes for new arrivals or people being shipped out; she is juggling five mugs to bring coffee to hundreds. She helps people find a place to sleep, she is setting up a lending library, she visits people in the infirmary, and she listens to the life stories of old ladies.

As was mentioned above, friends at both Westerbork and Amsterdam begged her to go into hiding. One of these was Werner Sterzenbach, a member of a resistance group that helped prisoners escape Westerbork and found hiding places for them in Holland. Wouldn't Etty allow him to hide her so that the resistance movement could use her literary talents? She refused, saying she didn't want to desert her parents, who were by that time in Westerbork, and that she was committed to helping people in the camp. Sterzenbach escaped Westerbork the same month that Etty was transported to Poland.

Klaas Smelik, the writer to whom she would entrust her diaries when she knew she was leaving, describes an unsuccessful attempt he and his daughter had made to "kidnap" Etty and hide her at their home outside Amsterdam, and another when she was leaving Amsterdam to return to Westerbork. Convinced she didn't really understand the danger she was in, Smelik grabbed her. She wriggled free, he recalls, stood about five feet away from him, and stared at him for a moment before saying, "You don't understand me." When he admitted he didn't, she said, "I want to share the destiny of my people." At that point he knew there was no hope: she would not allow herself to be rescued (761).

No, she would stay at Westerbork and use her position with the Jewish Council to be of service to everyone who came into her sphere. And if remaining with the council meant that her parents wouldn't be called up until the last transports left, so be it. History could pass whatever judgment on her that it liked, and she might even agree.

In two long missives that were published illegally in the autumn of 1943, she paints a searing picture of Westerbork Camp. Like a war photographer skilled at conveying the full horror of a military campaign through the smallest, most ordinary images, she describes what she sees and lets the images speak for themselves:

- "If the barbed wire just encircled the camp, then at least you would know where you were. But these twentieth-century wires meander about inside the camp, too, around the barracks and in between, in a labyrinthine and unfathomable network. Now and then you come across people with scratches on their faces or hands." (583)
- "There was a little old woman who had left her spectacles and her medicine bottle at home on the mantel—could she go and get them now, and where exactly was she, and where would she be going?" (585)
- "There were children who would not accept a sandwich before their parents had had one. . . . And two others whose mother lay unconscious on the floor. Why wouldn't she answer them?" (585).

The official pretense was still that the transports were taking prisoners to labor camps. But when trucks come in from Amsterdam loaded with the aged and the infirm, and trains take them away in a matter of days, what is anyone to believe?

Etty herself was shipped out September 7, 1943, on the same train that took her brother Mischa and her parents. Her family was killed immediately on reaching Auschwitz. Etty, who had been certain she wouldn't last more than three days in a camp, lived another three months. She was killed November 30, 1943.

I'm not sure how well this foreshortened account of Etty Hillesum's last two and a half years reflects what may be the most striking element of her story—the mounting claustrophobia we feel watching history close in around her. "Get out!" we want to shout. "Run for your life!" Because I wanted this account of the period to reflect that sense of mounting urgency, I've kept digressions to the minimum, but I promised myself that once the story itself was told, we would revisit certain waypoints.

I want to return briefly to the vexed business of Spier's place in Etty's life. For all his drawbacks, and without always seeming even to know what he was doing, I would maintain that Spier did serve Etty's best interests in a crucial regard. He helped her understand the limitations of an exclusive romantic relationship, and he nudged her toward a way of loving that would be more like the Greek *agape* than *eros,* and I believe that she thought he was right. She hints from time to time at the possibility that she'd intentionally, if unconsciously, fallen in love with men she knew she would outlive. Etty was well aware that this behavior amounted to a kind of high wire act: "If this man did not have so strong a sense of responsibility and so profound a love of mankind and did not work daily on himself, he might easily unleash natural disasters in the helpless individuals who entrust themselves to him" (562).

One gathers that he *did*, in fact, unleash a disaster here and there, and if Etty had been any less experienced than she was—any less street smart, strong, and self-possessed than she was—she might have been one of them. Ultimately, she was probably as much his teacher as he was hers. At the conclusion of one of her first sessions with Spier, she leaned forward and traced a horizontal line across the middle of his face. Forehead and eyes lay above the line ("incredibly wise, age-old grey eyes"), his mouth below ("his full, sensual mouth"). She described to him the conflict that she saw between the two halves of his face and added that she herself felt almost crushed under the weight of that struggle.

"That's because it's your own conflict too," he replies.

It is a defining moment. Looking at one another, each could be looking into a mirror, because in each of them there coexisted a worldly sensualist and a clear-eyed seeker of truth—an Etty A and an Etty B, a Spier A and a Spier B. On any given day, any of four combinations might occur, and they did. When Etty the idealist waltzed into the rooms of Spier the truth-seeker, all was well. There was much talk of Thomas à Kempis and the almost infinite spiritual potential of psychology. But if Etty the sensualist dropped in on Spier the ascetic, or if, on the other hand, she was feeling particularly otherworldly and he drank one more glass of wine than he should have and got silly, the dissonance was severe and *noted*. There were, of course, also times when both of their inner idealists took the night off and the "chastity plan" was scuttled altogether—or scuttled just long enough to leave both parties sexually gratified without violating Spier's definition of fidelity to his fiancée.

It shouldn't surprise us that Etty and Spier were both great admirers of Saint Augustine, who has won hearts down the ages by asking in the *Confessions,* "Lord, give me chastity, give me continence . . . but please—not yet."

Etty's attitude toward her sexuality was more complicated than either Spier's or Augustine's. The complications had to do with the fact that she was a woman and only, as she put it, "outwardly emancipated." She did not, as yet, have a sturdy sense of self. There is a famous passage in Augustine's *Confessions* in which pleasures of his past come and pluck at his sleeves and ask, "Are you really leaving us behind? We were so close! How can you?" It's generally assumed that Augustine is talking about old mistresses and the pleasures he'd enjoyed with them. Reading Etty Hillesum's diary reminds us that in fact the disembodied voices that plague a spiritual seeker aren't solely or necessarily those of sexual partners at all, or even "sins" in the ordinary sense. They can also be representations of self—often all we have known of self—and identity.

The formation of identity is much more far-reaching in Etty's life than sex. She wanted to become so innocent of private designs on life that she could in effect "nourish the world" with her love and become "a balm for all wounds." Yet she also wanted, and had wanted for a long time, to become fully emancipated and fully human. Defying the gender stereotypes of her time and place, she had worked steadily for years and years to cultivate the sort of richly faceted identity that few women of her time achieved. She had strong opinions on literature, art, politics, and human nature, and she expressed them effectively. She loved work, friendship, flowers, trees, travel, and as we've already seen, she loved love itself. All of these different ways of engaging with life had powerful claims on her. Like many contemporary women, she savored her *multiple* identities: as a writer in the making; as Russian scholar, and for that matter as *Russian*; as woman, and as lover. Once she got past the initial thrill of taking up Spier's regimen and seeing it work so effectively, she began to realize that more was at stake than just her bad habits.

"Repose in yourself!" Spier had counseled her. Well and good. But which self? Was everything about her except her very deepest self expendable? And what if she peeled all those layers away and put them to one side, and found that nothing was left? And could she be certain that Spier himself wasn't drawn as powerfully to her various "personas" as to the real Etty, whoever that turned out to be?

The resistance is real, and understandable, but over the course of time it relaxes as each of the various identities is subsumed by the "organic process" that is taking place within her. She'd begun her diary agonizing over the difficulties she was having putting words onto the page. Yet only a year later, still writing obviously, she has decided "that it is possible to create, even without ever writing a word or painting a picture, by simply 'molding' one's inner life. And that too is a deed" (318). She cherished her Russian lineage—her "Dostoevskian streak"—even though she feared the madness, addiction, and suicide that seemed to come in the bargain. But by the summer of 1942, when Nazi persecution was gathering impetus, she had come to prize the tremendous intensity of feeling that she possessed, and associated with being Russian, solely in terms of the pact she had made with herself early on in the Nazi occupation: eager as she was to affirm the inherent meaning and beauty of life, she would not permit herself to do so without at the same time recognizing the full depravity of what was going on around her. Westerners, she had decided, tend to evade deep feelings, while the Russian "bears his burden to the very end, buckles down under the full weight of his emotions and suffers to his very depths" (453). It was the Russian half of her personality that would uphold that part of the assignment she had imposed upon herself: to be an unblinkered witness to history, but one who would not give way to hatred.

But the most important "reworking" of her sense of who she was had to do with her conflicted relationship with her own body and embodiedness in general. Just a few pages into her diary, around the time she is remarking on her own skills as a lover, she observes, "It is difficult to be on equally good terms with God and the body."

Indeed.

And it's the femaleness of her body to which she is particularly attached. When she complained to Spier one day of pre-menstrual depression, he urged her to bring herself under control. She was willing to try, but not altogether, because she knew that during the days just before her periods her mental processes seemed to work quite differently—"wilder, more fanciful, less inhibited—more languid, slower, underlying sadness, too" (350). This is, of course, nothing that any number of traditional cultures wouldn't have confirmed for her ten times over, but Amsterdam in the early 1940s, especially the circles Etty moved in, was anything but traditional.

In effect, as we've seen, Etty Hillesum had effectively transmuted the idea of bearing children into the understanding that, as a woman, it would be her calling to "carry" within herself the New Age that Rilke had conjured up. But there was another equally important regard in which she managed to reconcile her genuine reverence for the body and for embodied ways of knowing with her desire for spiritual awareness and the freedom that comes with it.

The solution to the dilemma came all unbidden with the astonishing discovery that there was something her body wanted even more than it did good food or sex.

It wanted to kneel.

Etty wrote part of an autobiographical novel she called *The Girl Who Learned to Kneel* (the title kept shifting: in moods of discouragement it became *The Girl Who Could Not Kneel*). It went against the grain, "and yet every so often I have a great urge to kneel down

. . . to listen to that hidden source within me" (103). While she refers to meditation a few times, she was clearly more comfortable with the notion of prayer, and she connected prayer almost always with the physical act of kneeling and with an inclination to *hearken*. She kneels in order to *listen*, and it's difficult to believe that this young woman who lived just a few blocks from the Rijksmuseum could have managed not to associate the posture with Medieval and Renaissance paintings of the Annunciation.

> The desire to kneel down sometimes pulses through my body, or rather, it is as if my body had been meant and made for the act of kneeling. Sometimes, in moments of deep gratitude, kneeling down becomes an overwhelming urge, head deeply bowed, hands before my face. It has become a gesture embedded in my body, needing to be expressed from time to time. (320)

And again, "Sometimes when I least expect it, someone suddenly kneels down in some corner of my being" (518). Ultimately, she decides that kneeling in prayer is her most intimate gesture, "more intimate even than being with a man" (547).

There is an evening when Etty comes home from a day spent with Spier and finds herself making love with Han in the same warm and tender way she always has, even though she knows she is no longer in love with him, and she can only conclude, wryly, that "bodies have their own laws." But over time I think she decided that those laws have more to do with spirit than she had thought. If kneeling in prayer comes at least as naturally to the body as lovemaking, then the desire to know God may be as inalienable to human nature as the desire to procreate, nurture, work, laugh, look for food, and make art.

Ultimately, Etty would seem to have reversed the position she'd taken early on in the diary: one *can* be on equally good terms with God and the body.

When Etty first began writing the diary, she describes her desire for "a tune": a thread, or medium, a calling that would make sense of her existence. By the end she has found it, and what she has found is so quiet it is almost intangible by ordinary standards. Harvard Medical School psychologist Kaethe Weingarten calls it "compassionate witnessing," and explains that when we do it, we turn "unwitting witnessing of violence and violation into something deliberately chosen." To be a compassionate witness, she adds, one must possess a set of capacities: awareness, safety, empathy, and compassion, but a fifth, as well, that she calls "Aidos" after the Greek goddess of "reverence and righteous shame." All of these capacities, she notes, can be developed.[5]

Compassionate witnessing means making oneself completely available to another. It means standing before "the other" with heart and eyes and ears wide open, ready to hear the person out no matter what. By bearing witness to another human being who has endured terrible trauma, Weingarten believes, we can set that person on the first steps toward being healed.

"My heart is a floodgate for a never-ending tide of misery," says Etty (524), and it's useful to remind ourselves what a floodgate is—that it presumes a body of water that never stops flowing. The floodgate adjusts the flow when it is raised and lowered, making certain there will always be a reservoir, but that the village itself won't be flooded. If there was a trick to what she did, given she insisted she did not have nerves of steel, it was that she learned to rest in something she believed lies at the heart of nature and that she describes quite simply as "ebb and flow." Because she had learned how to let go of the merely personal, she could fully receive the sorrows of others without holding on to them—she knew in effect how to lift the gate and let the grief flow on out of her, as she did the night on a bridge in Amsterdam when she allowed all of the thwarted tenderness she felt for Spier to pour out onto the natural world. Everything could circulate *through* her. Joy, grief, anger, despair, and, of course, love, above all, must be able to circulate through ourselves and one another and all of life. The imagery of uninterrupted flow is crucial to her. At the very beginning of her diary, and then again at the very end, she exults in the feeling that her "inner traffic jams" are moving again. Love has to circulate; it can't stop, can't be caught in time.

She had fully absorbed the insight that lies at the core of contemplative traditions everywhere: the mind is conditioned to go after pleasure and run away from pain. If we want stillness of mind—"so that something of 'God' can enter us"—we must learn how to hold off those conditioned responses. We must be able to experience something pleasurable without trying to hold onto it, and we must be able to experience the most intense forms of suffering without going to pieces or trying to pass it on to someone else. What unifies her desires, then, or at least integrates them, is the necessity of finding her way to a depth where consciousness flows continuously back and forth between the

---

[5] Kaethe Weingarten, *Common Shock: Witnessing Violence Every Day* (New York: Dutton, 2003), 163, 168.

poles of awareness of suffering, on the one hand, and unquenchable faith in meaning and beauty, on the other.

Etty is absolutely aware of the magnitude of the transformation she's undergone, so that now when she wakes up parched in the middle of the night and takes a sip of water, all she can think about is how much she wishes she were back at the camp and able to give all of her people water.

There is a passage from the *Katha Upanishad* that describes beautifully what she is undergoing: "When all the knots that strangle the heart are loosened, the mortal becomes immortal. When all the desires that surge in the heart are renounced, the mortal becomes immortal."

Finally, a last reflection on Etty's personal terror of "splitting off." It's probably important that we recognize not only that "doubling" was a recurring theme in the life and work of Dostoevsky, but that it is a staple of Western literature this past hundred years or so, particularly with regard to victims of trauma. No one has treated the theme more powerfully in recent years than Australian novelist Pat Barker in her World War I trilogy. Over and over, characters who have in the course of the war either witnessed or performed unspeakably terrible acts find themselves slipping into fugue states that might last hours or even days. Unable and unwilling to integrate the memory of what has happened into their sense of who they are, they have simply split in two. "I didn't do it. I wasn't there. That must have been Andrew." A psychiatrist whose job it is to rehabilitate victims of "shell-shock" and send them back into combat realizes at one point that the "stiff upper lip" that is expected of combatants is the same thing as the "detachment" a colleague assumes when he is treating patients with electro-shock therapy.

I've suggested that there may be no more urgent concern for humanity today than the phenomenon of "othering." But how interesting it is to consider that my ability to "other" someone to the degree that I am able to kill them may be directly related to my ability to alienate myself from myself as well. Both states are surely maladies, but they may also be understood as *maladaptations*. I've wanted all along to open this book with the story of Etty Hillesum. She was vivid, improvisational, earthy, irreverent, and inclusive, and as such she stands in direct line with the vernacular spiritual tradition I described earlier. She is in these same regards quintessentially modern as well.

But it mattered to me also that her story forces us to look squarely at what I've described as the definitive event of twentieth-century history: the seventy million human beings who were murdered in Europe and Russia, by state order, between 1914 and 1945. Etty Hillesum lived and died in a context we might well think of as the Ground Zero of the mid-twentieth century, but in a very real sense the story of every contemporary spiritual seeker has to be read and assessed against that background.

There are organisms that biologists call *extremophiles* because they are able to live in situations that would seem to be uninhabitable. Bacteria that live in the depths of the sea, for example, or inside chunks of granite, or on the rods of nuclear accelerators. Reading Etty's diary is like watching an extremophile in the very process of adapting to an impossible setting. Metaphorically, it is as if her lungs were adjusting, from one day to the next, to air that contained dwindling levels of oxygen.

In terms of her spiritual development, Etty really did seem to pull what she needed out of thin air. Her upbringing had been turbulent, she'd had nothing in the way of a genuinely religious grounding, she had a confessed "psycho-allergy" to organized religion, and her chief mentor was himself problematic, but there was that within her that kept managing to turn straw into gold, and I realize that this is another of my reasons for wanting to place her here at the beginning of the book. She embodies spiritual hunger itself—religious*ness* as opposed to religion—as a force in consciousness that *will* be expressed. Teresa, Julian, and the like lived within a comfortably closed system of meanings, but Etty, like most of us today, never had that luxury.

And that, of course, makes her triumph all the more dazzling. Because while most of us can't even imagine what it would have been like to get out of bed every morning and walk out the door with a yellow star on our sleeve, there she was—not just getting up, but imposing what some would call "mortifications" on herself, the most effective of which was the simple refusal to give in to hatred. Her trajectory argues that there is no situation within which it is impossible to have a spiritual practice. She was an extremophile, but that only makes her one of an entire "tribe" of contemporary men and women

All the while I was studying Etty Hillesum, very basic questions about human heroism kept crossing my mind, so it was timely that somewhere in the process I got hold of a book called *Climbing Free: My Life in the Vertical World*, by Lynn White, an outstanding female athlete during the 1980s and 1990s. I was intrigued by what seemed to me distinct parallels between her and all the women in this book, though maybe Etty in particular, and I want to introduce her here by way of recognizing that while my familiarity with women like Mech-thild of Magdeburg provided a kind of key to the unfolding of Etty and the others, it is also true that certain contemporary figures have been just as helpful.

Lynn White is about five feet tall and weighs 100 pounds. She has broken rock-climbing records all over the world, but she is probably best known for having free-climbed the face of El Capitan, in Yosemite National Park, in less than twenty-four hours—*through the night!*—a feat she accomplished in 1993, and which is considered by many to constitute the most challenging vertical rock climb ever accomplished. Lynn is so short that she can't reach nearly as far as most male climb-ers can, but her fingers are so small that she can get purchase in crack systems they can't. She had only been climbing for a few weeks when she experienced something for the first time that would determine the direction of her life.

> I had never climbed anything as demanding as this before. The combination of controlling every position of my body and of forcing my mind to shut out . . . the very real fear of falling created an interesting result: a feeling that I was simultaneously acutely aware of both everything and nothing. Everything, be-cause twenty-five years later I still recall the kaleidoscope of crystal patterns in the rock in front of me as I moved over it, and nothing, because at the time I was so immersed in the passage of movement that I felt no sense of time, gravity, or existence. The only sound I heard was the flow of my breathing.[6]

Quite by coincidence, and in a context that couldn't have been more different from Etty's, Lynn Hill had found her way to a place in consciousness that was much like the one Etty inhabited for most of that last two and a half years. The effort to be simultaneously aware of everything that was going on around her and yet resistant to the panic and rage that could at any moment have engulfed her had allowed Etty, too, to become so focused that she seems almost to have been lifted up out of herself for days at a time, moving about in an semblance of serene well-being that baffled her as much as it did everyone else.

We will see this phenomenon again. The point of bringing Lynn Hill's experience into the picture is not to argue that she is a mystic,

---

[6] Lynn Hill, *Climbing Free: My Life in the Vertical World* (New York: W. W. Norton and Co., 2003), 36.

but rather to suggest that there is something in the human personality—latent in every one of us perhaps, and fully manifest in some—that gravitates toward difficulty as if it were ice cream, turning toward the virtually impossible as flowers do to sunlight.

It isn't that everyone who possesses this quality is a mystic, but I do suspect that every mystic possesses it, and I would guess that it is intimately connected with another quality. In individuals who have placed themselves in these situations and come through, not once but over and over, something like faith arises—not so much a faith in God as in "what is." One finds it written between the lines by naturalists like Gretel Ehrlich, Terry Tempest Williams, and Julia Butterfly Hill (though, by all means, in certain men as well, like John Muir): the conviction, borne of personal experience, that the most dire, adversarial wilderness situation can turn out to be "the teacher."

Here is Lynn Hill's recollection of a moment during an earlier ascent of El Capitan, a little before midnight, when she was about three-quarters of the way up the sheer granite face:

> I began to truly see the meaning behind big-wall climbing. The wall was like some living entity that was testing our mettle by throwing up new challenges, new unknowns, that we had to overcome. . . . Because up here there was no turning back and no room for panic. Dealing with a space flake that was about to break off the wall and squash you, or making it through a pitch in the inky dark, were all parts of a journey of self-discovery and self-reliance.[7]

What a gift . . . to be able to look squarely at the utterly impossible thing that is looming up in front of you and instead of running away to recognize it as somehow familiar and something you've dealt with before and are pretty sure you can again. "Climbing by Braille," White calls it—allowing yourself to be placed *in extremis* and even colluding with circumstances to get you there because that's where you come to life.

What does *come to life* mean in those circumstances? Maybe it means exactly what it does on the level of the simplest life forms as they evolve into greater complexity. Challenged by a sudden drop in temperature, or oxygen, or moisture, the organism has to wake up and reorganize itself into something whose structures are more complex and versatile. I've said "wake up," but Etty Hillesum's formulation is

---

[7] Ibid., 101.

probably closer to the truth when she describes a process that seems to have a life of its own: "Something in me is growing, and every time I look inside, something fresh has appeared, and all I have to do is to accept it" (359).

Jane Goodall

"I've Blurred the Line"

Nobody had ever told eleven-year-old Valerie Jane Goodall that she couldn't look at the newspapers, and nobody took them away from her in May 1945, when Allied troops began to open up the Nazi prison camps in Eastern Europe. She would never forget the photographs she saw during that period—of walking skeletons in gray rags, and bodies stacked haphazardly, like piles of brushwood. For the rest of her life she would buy books about Nazis and the Holocaust, trying to understand how one group of human beings could have done what they had to another. She would struggle much as Etty Hillesum had struggled to reconcile her knowledge of what had happened during World War II with her bone-deep conviction that this world is both beautiful and coherent.

Years later Jane Goodall is the world's foremost primatologist and easily the most widely known ambassador for the global environmental movement. Because it is becoming more widely recognized today that threats to the environment are invariably threats to human beings as well—and their political, social, and economic stability—her work is also understood to have powerful implications for world peace. In 2001, she received the Gandhi/King Award for Nonviolence, presented by the World Movement for Nonviolence at the United Nations. She lives at that level of celebrity where the air starts to get thin—not far from Angelina Jolie (who, indeed, puts in an appearance in the movie *Jane's Journey*), a stone's throw from the Dalai Lama. For three hundred days of the year Dr. Goodall is in and out of airplanes, hotels, and lecture halls. When she isn't in a hotel, she is in somebody else's home, making nice over breakfast whether she feels like it or not. She has lived this way since 1986 in support of the causes closest to her heart, and the array of causes just keeps growing.

I consider all of this as I sit in an auditorium in Marin County, California, where Dr. Goodall is about to speak. I have never seen her in person, and as I wait, I'm aware of a fluttering sensation right around my solar plexus.

. . . And here she is, the good doctor herself. Her carriage is perfect: one can easily picture her at eighteen, when she made her debut at Buckingham Palace. Her gray-gold hair is still thick, still pulled back and lifted up into the gently arching horsetail one remembers from the *National Geographic* documentaries. She wears a black turtleneck and slacks with black leather flats, and she is all but enveloped in a soft gray shawl with long white fringes that ripple whenever she moves. She will explain in a moment that a group of Dakota Indians had given her the shawl that morning during a naming ceremony. A beadwork pendant and heavy silver pin gleam against the black, and topping it all off, she is wearing huge sunglasses. These are explained in the first couple of minutes. "I've gone Hollywood," she jokes, fingertips on the frames. In fact, she has an eye infection that doctors had promised would be gone in a week. "But it's been seven weeks now, and I'm well sick of it."

There is something borderline fanatical about the desire people have to be in her presence, and even touch her, and that can't be easy for her; her health is compromised by recurring bouts of malaria and pneumonia. Yet it is also evident, watching her sit for hours signing books and greeting hundreds of admirers in turn, that the attraction goes both ways. She has said that knowing about all the people around the world who support her work makes for "a warmth around the heart" that has sustained her through hard times.[1]

Pachamama Alliance hosts tonight's event. The organization's stated purpose is to preserve the earth's tropical rainforests by empowering the indigenous people who are their natural custodians. The theme for the evening is *Reason for Hope: The Reunion of the Eagle and the Condor*. A Pre-Columbian myth, my program tells me, holds that two great peoples inhabit the North and South American continents. The people of the Eagle, in the north, are very cerebral, inventive, and materialistic, while to the south, the people of the Condor live on the level of spirit and the heart. These two ways of being in the world have traditionally been at odds, but ancient prophecies hold that one day the two populations will come together and the gifts of each will together make up a whole human being.

---

[1] Jane Goodall, *Through a Window: My Thirty Years with the Chimpanzees of Gombe* (New York: Soko Publications Ltd., 1990), 257.

It would be hard to think of anyone whose lifework more perfectly embodies the convergence of Eagle and Condor than Jane Goodall. She has spent more than forty-five years saying the same thing that mystics like William Blake and Francis of Assisi did—that all of life is one profoundly interconnected whole—only her language is not that of a poet/seer but of a highly skilled ethologist, a rigorously trained specialist in animal behavior.

Throughout her scientific career she has argued that science and religion are not incompatible but simply two different windows onto reality—two modes of knowing, one of which is achieved through mastery over something or somebody, while the other comes with openness, and connection. These latter windows, she says, are the ones "through which the mystics and holy men of the East, and the founders of the great world religions, have gazed," and these days, she is finding them more and more to her taste.[2]

Goodall fully believes that an ambient power, sacredness itself, is all around us, all the time: "an unseen, intangible Wind" that will strengthen and support us if we allow it to.[3]

Jane Goodall appears not to have taken the time to think through in a systematic way the relationship between her religiousness and the rest of her life until theologian Phillip Berman approached her in 1996 with a proposal that was both modest and intriguing. She had contributed an essay to his 1984 book *The Courage of Conviction*. How would she feel now about a joint venture—a series of interviews, in which the two of them might go more deeply into the themes of that essay? All she would have to do was to answer his questions and edit her replies.

She agreed, and the interviews were carried out, and somewhere along the line, Goodall's imagination caught fire. Joint venture gave way to solo flight, and the result was *Reason for Hope: A Spiritual Journey*. If it took even more time to write than she thought it would, and if the experience of writing it was in certain ways more harrowing (how eager are any of us to revisit the past?), producing *Reason for Hope* allowed her to put together the more comprehensive view of her life and work that her previous books only hinted at. It also has allowed her to set the record straight on a couple of points.

Not that *Reason for Hope* is the last word on Goodall's long, full life. Her mother Vanne ("my incredible mother") had been working

---

[2] Jane Goodall, *Reason for Hope: A Spiritual Journey* (New York: Warner Books, 2000), 175.
[3] Ibid., 10.

for years on Jane's biography. Four years before her death in 2000 Vanne turned the project over to Dale Peterson, co-author with Jane of a previous book and someone who had himself been "chimp-bitten" decades earlier.

Peterson has nearly two thousand letters in hand, dating all the way back to Goodall's childhood, and he drew on these to write a comprehensive biography, *Jane Goodall: The Woman Who Re-defined Man*.[4] But meanwhile he published a two-volume autobiography in letters called *Africa in My Blood* and *Beyond Innocence*. To read Goodall's letters alongside *Reason for Hope,* moving back and forth between the two narratives, is a fascinating exercise and offers a much more three-dimensional picture of Goodall's development than either of the two works does by itself. The letters Goodall wrote as a teenager, for example, are so uniformly sunny and exuberant that if the mature Goodall weren't here to tell us, we would have no idea that there'd been a markedly different subtext, for she went through quite a prolonged and serious spiritual struggle. When she was just sixteen, she wrote that her love for Jesus was so strong and her conviction that he was close at hand so powerful that she felt herself to be "haunted by the agony of the Crucifixion."

And on the other hand, though Goodall does speak in *Reason for Hope* about her love for her second husband, Derek Bryceson, and the anguish of losing him to cancer only four years after they'd married, the full weight of that loss comes through far more keenly when we read a letter she wrote to him in the fall of 1974, from Stanford, where she was teaching. It had been raining this particular morning, but now it had stopped, and she'd come out into the wet garden with her tea. She sees a hummingbird: "I so much wish you were here to share the hummingbird, my darling, for I love you so very much. For always. For ever. . . . Oh, how super. It is a pair of humming birds. . . . It is raining again. I love the rain."[5]

Goodall has been in the public eye since 1962, when *National Geographic* editors asked her to pose for photographs washing her hair in a stream. She could have refused, but she knew that funding for the research at Gombe would probably depend in large part on her willingness to give up a measure of privacy. Like a great many people who live in that kind of spotlight, she's learned to deflect it, too, and to seem much more forthcoming than she actually is.

---

[4] Dale Peterson, *Jane Goodall: The Woman Who Re-defined Man* (New York: Houghton, Mifflin, Harcourt, 2006).

[5] Jane Goodall, *Beyond Innocence* (New York: Houghton Mifflin 2001), 243.

Spiritual autobiography is a tough genre, but *Reason for Hope* eludes many of the usual pitfalls. Long before she was a scientist, Goodall was a poet, and her sensitive use of language is one of the great strengths of everything she has written. But she is a scientist, too, and even when she's writing about herself, she writes with a certain objectivity as well. The questions she is answering because Berman has raised them are clearly questions she's asked herself, as well, because as a life scientist she is genuinely curious.

Where *does* she get her energy and endurance?

Why *is* she so peaceful?

How *does* she manage to do the work she does without being regularly overwhelmed with despair—or anger at the powers that be and the forces that prevail?

What grounds *does* she find for hope?

To answer these queries, Goodall looks thoughtfully and gratefully back across the whole length of her life. There is nature, and there is nurture, and Valerie Jane had been blessed several times over in both regards.

"God was as real to me then," she writes of the child she'd been, "as the wind rustling through the trees in our garden."[6]

There have been, then, in this particular scientist's life, a considerable number of experiences for which she knows no scientific explanation. She builds no massive theological edifice on these, and she doesn't insist the reader believe them. But she isn't willing to pretend they didn't happen just to protect her reputation for objectivity. Her mother, she declares, was a psychic, and she'd seen evidence of this on many occasions. A night during the war, for example, when Vanne was taking a bath and suddenly burst into tears and cried out "Rex! Rex!" Her husband ran in and asked what was wrong, and she said she didn't know but knew it had to do with his brother Rex, an RAF pilot. Later they learned that Rex had been shot down over Rhodesia at that very time and died.

On a night not long after Jane's own husband, Derek, had died, moreover, and she lay sleepless and almost paralyzed with grief, he was suddenly there with her after all, his arms around her, his voice in her ear telling her "things I should know, things I should do."[7] And even though she couldn't retrieve any of the things he'd told her, the sense of his presence remained with her for some time. And she doesn't believe for a moment that she dreamed him into existence.

---

[6] *Reason for Hope*, 10.
[7] *Beyond Innocence*, 162.

But the real focal point of Goodall's spirituality is not the occasional eruption of the supernatural in everyday life. Most of her deepest and most restorative spiritual experiences have taken place quietly and unspectacularly, when she is alone in nature.

At the core of her commitment to the environmental education organization she founded in 1991, Roots and Shoots, is her sense that children who do not enjoy the closeness to trees, rivers, animals, and birds that she did may be crucially handicapped. She says as much with real force to her Marin County audience: "This connectedness with the natural world needs to be nurtured in every child. Without it, something in the psyche is broken."

Of course, restoring that connection is not only in the best interests of children or their spirituality. If the natural world is to be preserved at all, even imperfectly, children growing up today must have vastly different assumptions about life than their parents have. "*Nothing* I've done to help people understand chimpanzees, and nothing we've done to protect them or the environment will matter if we don't raise a generation of children to be better stewards than we've been."

What were the factors in her own background, Goodall wonders, that had allowed her to engage so fully with the natural world? Chief among these is the succession of enthusiastic mentors who supported her and her dreams through every stage in her life, but who could have had no idea what kind of influence they were having or where it might lead. Typically, and I think this is what she wants everyone to understand, none of them was doing anything more than to live up to their own ideals.

The general outlines of Goodall's story are probably familiar to most readers. But like all the life stories that intrigue us most, hers will always remain somewhat open to interpretation. My own reading has been shaped by long immersion in the stories of women who were similarly courageous, resourceful, determined, and "connective," but who lived out these qualities as religious reformers, healers, visionaries, and spiritual counselors—as mystics, in short. I believe that Jane Goodall would be very much at home in their company. The course of her life, that steady, stepped expansion of empathy and sphere of influence that eventually embraces the whole of life, mirrors that of Saint Catherine of Siena and others: "a falcon's rising gyre," in Dale Peterson's words, "that turns beyond innocence through experience into wisdom, and on to focused dedication."[8]

---

[8] In ibid., 13.

The arc of Goodall's life resembles that of saints Teresa, Clare, and the like in one more important way. The saintly legends around those individuals, and the careful sculpting of their stories to emphasize obedience, purity, and self-abnegation, have long obscured the truly radical critique of religious institutions and doctrine that was implicit in their testimony. Just so, the insights Jane Goodall has gleaned into the intelligence, the behavior, and the emotional lives of chimpanzees *haven't* just delighted generations of children and they *haven't* just revolutionized primatology; they have challenged in fundamental regards the way we think about what it means to be human. Ultimately, in fact, Goodall's study of chimpanzees would draw her into virtually the same deep inquiries that preoccupied Julian, Teresa, and their sisters in spirit. She loves to say, with a triumphant little gleam in her eye, "The line that is supposed to separate chimpanzees and human being—it is no longer sharp. It is *blurred* now."

But the full significance of her lifelong campaign to "blur that line" really becomes apparent only when we take the whole of her remarkable life into account, and particularly when we consider it in the context of the extraordinary revolution that has taken place this last century with regard to—and I use this word in very broadest meaning—anthropology.

There is a photograph of Valerie Jane taken when she was just eighteen months old, snuggling into the furry shoulder of a toy chimpanzee that is easily as big as she is. Jubilee, named after the first chimpanzee born into captivity at the London Zoo, is still around today, quite bald because his fur was rubbed away decades ago, but a presence nonetheless and a reminder that while you and I were snuggling teddy bears and Chatty Cathy's, for Jane it was always chimpanzees.

The passionate intensity Goodall would bring to everything she did was evident from the beginning: "Let's polish all the brasses!" she would cry out as her best friend walked in the door, or "Let's take all the fleas off Rusty!"

She was outgoing as a child, and energetic, but loved to be alone. The well-developed interior life that would make the solitude of a Tanzanian forest feel like home was evident early on, and so was her capacity for long, steady observation: She was just four the afternoon she sat waiting for four hours in a chicken coop, oblivious to the panic her disappearance had caused, so that she could see how chickens lay eggs.

The circumstances of her early years were unusual, and yet there seems to have been an almost perfect fit between the child and her setting: the organism, she might say as a biologist, and its environment. Within that environment, no one element was as crucial as her mother, Vanne.

Jane was about two the night she brought a handful of earthworms to bed with her one night and tucked them carefully under her pillow. Vanne intervened on the worms' behalf. Not a word about dirty sheets or horrid messes, just, "Jane, worms can't live under pillows. They'll die unless they're put back in their *own* bed." And while we might expect the story to end with Vanne's offering to scoop them up (and get *rid* of them!), it doesn't—the child herself ran outside and placed them carefully back in the garden where she'd dug them up.

Nothing that lives is beneath us, her upbringing taught her; no creature is just a thing. Decades later, when she was a graduate student at Cambridge, the papers she turned in to her tutors kept being handed back with certain pronouns circled in red. She was not to refer to chimpanzees as "he" or "she," but "it." Stubbornly, she kept writing "he" and "she" back in, and eventually her preceptors acquiesced.

Goodall believes that field biologists are best equipped to grasp what's going on among animals when they've experienced something similar themselves. Her descriptions of a remarkable chimp she named Flo are very much to the point. Her affection for Flo and her offspring, and her understanding of the family dynamics, are unquestionably a reflection of her own background.

The only truly stable social unit among chimpanzees is a mother and her offspring. Unless they leave the community altogether, which does happen, daughters tend to remain close to their mothers and so do their children, forming something very like a matriarchy within an otherwise male-dominated society. Flo was a middle-aged chimpanzee when Jane first met her in 1963. She was phenomenally popular among the males. She was also a terrific mother—vigilant, tender, playful, and generous. Observing Flo and her offspring over several decades, Goodall was able to watch her daughter Fifi absorb these same qualities and exercise them as a mother herself. It has been a spectacular mother-line: confident, resilient, and good-natured in ways that distinguished Clan Flo from other families in the same community. (A measure of the strength Flo passed on to her daughter Fifi is the fact that while most female gorillas are able to bring perhaps three children to maturity, Fifi raised eight and had her ninth in tow when she vanished in 2005.)

In Jane Goodall's own upbringing, Vanne Goodall was as pivotal as Flo was in Fifi's. "I come," Jane loves to say, "from a long line of strong, compassionate women." (Sometimes she'll say "self-reliant" rather than "compassionate.")

The stuffed chimpanzee Jubilee was a gift from Jane's father, who would be a benign but for the most part remote figure in her life. Mortimer Morris-Goodall was a telephone-cable testing engineer who worked in London until England declared war on Germany in 1939. Goodall enlisted immediately and was sent overseas, and Vanne Goodall brought five-year-old Jane and her younger sister, Judy, to her mother's home in Bournemouth, a resort town in Dorset, on England's south coast. There, as things turned out, they would remain, for while Jane's father survived the war in Europe, the marriage, like so many others of the time, did not.

The Goodalls divorced in 1946. Mortimer became a professional racecar driver and all but disappeared from his daughters' lives. If there is sensed deprivation on that score, there is no evidence of it— no public expression of loss or even wistfulness. The war itself had already taken her father away, Jane reminds us, for nearly seven years. She barely knew him, and her childhood in the Victorian brick house called Birches was so very rich and satisfying that feelings of deprivation don't appear to have loomed particularly large.

Birches was a child-centered household and, for all practical purposes, a matriarchy. There was Danny, the grandmother (called that after Jane's mispronouncing of *Granny*); the girls' mother, Vanne; two aunts; and, throughout the war, two women who had been evacuated from London. The house itself was roomy, peaceful, and packed full of books: a library of philosophical and religious works, because Danny's late husband had been a distinguished Congregational minister, but shelves full of children's books, too, bought used because there was never enough money to buy new ones. The Doctor Doolittle books and the Tarzan series were Jane's hands-down favorites, and she pretends never to have quite gotten over the fact that Tarzan married the Jane he did. "She was a *wimp*," she laughs, clearly savoring the word. "I always knew I'd have been a far better mate for him."

There were trees one could climb—and love, and even name— hedgerows where wild animals nested, paths that wound steeply down to the English Channel sea, and all manner of perches and "hides" where a budding naturalist could sit for hours at a time watching birds, foxes, rabbits, and hedgehogs without interruption. And in fact, nobody *did* interrupt her. She appears to have had a good, long tether.

She loved to be alone, but she was sociable too, if, as older sisters tend to be, a bit managerial. The summer she was twelve she organized the Alligator Society for herself, her sister, and their two best friends. Membership requirements included the ability to identify ten birds, ten dogs, ten trees, and five butterflies. Jane's "society name" was Red Admiral, after one of the indigenous butterflies. The constitution stipulated that when the four members set out together, they would walk in a row, as if they were an alligator, with Red Admiral at the head and, bringing up the rear, her sister, Judy, or Jim, a.k.a. Trout.

The atmosphere at Birches was imbued, Jane recalls, with Christian ethics. Ethics, but not dogma. Jane never felt pressured to choose between faith and reason. As a teenager she read the Bible from beginning to end and concluded that much of it was simply not to be believed. On the other hand, she loved it for its inspiration and poetry. Church attendance was optional, but bedtime prayers and informal examinations of conscience were not. "Let not the sun set upon thy wrath" was a Bible verse her grandmother loved; her own favorite, though, cherished throughout her life, was "As thy days, so shall thy strength be."

When she was ten years old, Jane was enrolled as a day-student at the nearby Upland School for Girls—which placed her, yet again, in a single-sex environment. School came in a distant second to Birches itself, but she wasn't unhappy there; she made friends easily, and she loved literature and history. Biology, interestingly enough, she called "bilge," and she barely scraped by in it.

Money was always in short supply. Jane took riding lessons, as most of her friends did, but she paid for them herself by shoveling out the stables, grooming the horses, and, eventually, giving lessons to other children. She became an accomplished horsewoman.

Clearly, Jane Goodall knew herself to be the undisputed hero of her small, untroubled world and the protagonist of her own narrative. She would never be elbowed aside because she was a girl. Nobody else's education would be deemed more important than hers just because he was a boy. She was never bullied or even "put in her place" by a brother, and she doesn't appear to have been told to "make herself pretty" for boys. And, of course, there was no father at hand, either—no one to adore her as a resident father would have, but no father, either, to be head of the family. Jane never saw her mother ("my amazing mother!") defer to a man or place him at the center of her universe. The center of Vanne Goodall's universe was occupied entirely by her two girls.

Of Goodall's grandmother we know that, like all the women in the family, she was easily moved to tears—"kinking," in the dialect of her native Yorkshire—but we also know that at tea time during the war she would help the little girls draw Nazi leader Hermann Goering on their bread and butter with sugar syrup so that they could behead and devour the director of the Luftwaffe as ruthlessly as his planes were bombing England.

Still, the old lady was very much a product of the Victorian age. When a gloriously bawdy letter arrives from Gombe describing Flo's marathon couplings, Danny exacts a promise from her granddaughter that henceforth there would be no more descriptions of "that certain behavior."

Reading the letters Jane wrote as a little girl, one senses that she had very little contact with boys or men, beyond her uncle Eric, a physician who came to Birches on weekends. Her first serious crush was not on someone her own age but on a charismatic Congregationalist minister who arrived in Bournemouth when she was seventeen. Trevor Davies was intelligent, warm, witty, and happily married. Jane could not have placed her affections (which she made no effort to hide) in a safer place. Interestingly, when she wrote *Reason for Hope* in 1996, Goodall recalled being just fifteen when she met Davies, adding that "in those days one could still be a child at that age." But in fact he came to Bournemouth in 1951. That means she was seventeen when he arrived and eighteen when she wrote in a letter dated August 1952, when the Davies have just come for tea: "I sat in a little arm chair beside HIM. . . . I wore my white dress—*AND he*!! Said how nice it looked—him *not* her! We talked about everything under the sun—and oh! He was so wizard."[9]

She does sound like a young fifteen year old here (she even saved his cigarette butt, his matchstick, and his tea leaves), but in fact she was a *very, very young* eighteen, unfolding, as many gifted girls do, given half a chance, in her own sweet time. Being "madly in love" under such circumstances, as she insisted she was, allowed her to remain as long as she liked on the threshold of romantic experience: deliciously aquiver, but suspended—safely—in mid-motion.

In fact, what Goodall would gratefully recall thirty-five years later wasn't so much the crush itself as the daunting spiritual impasse Davies had enabled her to resolve. Goodall's connection with the natural world had become her primary spiritual support, for she had

---

[9] Jane Goodall, *Africa in My Blood: An Autobiography in Letters* (New York: Houghton Mifflin, 2000), 34–35.

lost access early on to the religious faith that had sustained her family for generations. Her vivid awareness of World War II—the Holocaust, the dropping of the atomic bomb—had made it all but impossible to accept the idea of a benign and all-powerful God. "I had pushed religion out of my mind." But Davies's sermons were so powerful that they began to bring the mysteries of Christian belief to life for her, and they were at the same time so well reasoned that she was able to begin thinking about God in new ways. She prayed now, and she felt the presence of Jesus vividly, and "in the fervor of adolescence, I did my best to let the Holy Ghost creep into my being."[10]

She would go to Stalinist Russia! She would organize small groups of believers, and of course she would be tortured for her beliefs!

Sympathizing much later with the ardently religious girl she'd been, Goodall would observe in *Reasons for Hope* that by imagining herself a hero she had been able to fight off deeply oppressive worries about how she was going to perform in "real life."

"In the meantime," she notes dryly, "this poet-martyr was about to leave school."

Jane finished school at eighteen, and while friends who weren't nearly as gifted as she was were going off to university, she was not. There was no money for tuition, and although scholarships were available, they required a facility in foreign languages that she would never have. ("I hadn't learned Chimpanzee yet," she deadpans today.) She had really only ever had the one dream, and that was to go to Africa and study animals and write books about them. Without a university degree it was hard to imagine how the dream might be realized.

But Vanne had an idea: If Jane were to become skilled at secretarial work, she could go anywhere in the world. Even Africa. And once she was there, well, who knows? And what fun it would be in the meantime to live in London while she studied typing and shorthand at Queen's College. Jane appears to have liked the idea, but she was clearly feeling just a little fragile, too. One of my favorite of all the letters, because the fragility is there between the lines and because Vanne is depicted in such heroic colors, is one she wrote that summer to her best friend, Sally. Did she remember Isabel Abbay? Well, Jane had failed to phone her after she'd promised to, so when Isabel called she'd really had to make an appropriate social gesture. It was arranged that the girls would go to see the film *Quo Vadis*, and beforehand Isabel would come to the house. Jane's mother had helped her improvise a ping-pong table on trestles. "The first back-putting-up thing she

---

[10] *Reason for Hope*, 24.

said was she wouldn't deign to play with us because we weren't good enough, then that the table wasn't proper, & then that Queen's College . . . was inferior to her place.

"Ma squashed her wizardly, though, and made her go quite pink."[11]

The episode is comical enough on its own terms, but it is wonderfully telling when read in the context of normal primate behavior. In Goodall's master work, *The Chimpanzees of Gombe,* written in 1986, she would note that the overwhelming factor for establishing the rank of a Gombe female—more critical than any variable but extreme sickness or advanced years—is "the nature of her family" and the rank of her mother. "For a high-ranking, aggressive female will almost always support her daughter during agonistic interactions with other females."[12]

Again and again, at pivotal moments in Jane's life, the supportive presence of Vanne Goodall would prove as crucial as it had here, in a game of ping-pong.

The next few years were transitional and relatively sunny. Three months were spent in Germany to see whether the language barrier could be broken (it couldn't). In the spring, Jane enrolled at Queen's Secretarial College in South Kensington. A year later she finished the course and worked for a few months for her aunt Olly, a physiotherapist. A boring clerical job at Oxford came next, its tedium offset by a lively social scene, and she was back in London by the summer of 1955, working at the BBC, where she chose background music for documentary films.

British comedian Ian Carmichael made a series of charming films during the 1950s full of pretty, silly blondes with ponytails, full skirts, and wide belts clasped around improbably small waists, with armies of bright young men in pursuit. Those movies form a natural backdrop to letters Jane wrote home during this period. A giddy succession of Brians, Keiths, Jims, and Davids parades through her life, each of them "madly in love" with her, and she reacts much as might be expected considering how little contact she'd had with boys or men as she grew up. "Oh, mummy, it was a *hoot!*" Or "Oh golly, it was *smashing!*"

The reader may wince, but Goodall's timely discovery of her inner *femme fatale* was not, as we'll see, the worst thing that could have happened to her.

---

[11] *Africa in My Blood*, 36.

[12] Jane Goodall, *Chimpanzees of Gombe: Patterns of Behavior* (Cambridge, MA: Harvard University Press, 1986), 439.

In fact, Goodall was nobody's butterfly. At night she took courses at the London School of Economics, one of them a philosophy class taught by a woman who was a Theosophist. Jane was cautiously intrigued, particularly by the concept of "circling thoughts, the constant flow of thoughts that keep us from being more aware of what's going on around us." Detachment from circling thoughts would be a recurring theme in her spiritual life. Meanwhile, her menagerie kept growing: turtles, a gerbil, cats, dogs. . . . Would-be boyfriends helped build cages and walked the dogs.

Jane was twenty-two years old and had been out of school for four years when she received an invitation from a school chum: would she like to visit her in Kenya? Abruptly, at this point, the pace of the story quickens. The low-paying job with BBC was chucked that same day, and Jane came home to Bournemouth so that she could work at a nearby resort and save for the price of her ticket. By March 1957, she had saved what she needed and was on board a ship to Africa.

Goodall reached Kenya in April, and by the end of May, tipped off that "if you want to know about animals, you should meet Louis Leakey," she went to his office at Nairobi's Coryndon Museum and asked for a job.

In fact, Leakey did have an opening. He had lost his secretary not long before when his wife, Mary, found out he'd been having an affair with her—quite a serious affair, that almost broke up the marriage. None of this, of course, did he convey to the wide-eyed young woman before him. After marching Jane around the museum while he explained the exhibits and peppered her with questions in turn, he decided that she did indeed know a good deal about animals, and he offered her the job. A few weeks later he also invited her to join his family on their annual expedition to the Olduvai Gorge in Tanganyika. In previous digs they had found simple stone tools at Olduvai, but they were still looking for the remains of the human beings who'd made and used them—an effort that would be rewarded two years later with the discovery of Australopithecus robustus, known to the family as Dear Boy.

The summer at Olduvai was transformative for Jane. "The child I had been had dreamed the life I was now living." The work was grueling, but there was time to walk about on the Serengeti Plain as well and encounter gazelles, giraffes, miniature antelopes called dik-diks, a rhinoceros, a lion, hyenas. . . .

As she worked, and watched, absorbing the wealth of story and information that emerged around the Leakeys' campfire every evening, time seemed to fall away. She would dig up a bone, or a tusk, and realize as she held it that it had belonged to a creature who once had run here, and walked and slept and propagated, and for a few seconds she could almost feel its body heat and smell its rich scent, and when this happened she understood that she was linked with that creature through the process of evolution, much as the young woman she had become was linked with the little girl she had been when she had first dreamed of Africa.

Leakey was bent on knowing everything that could be known about our Stone Age ancestors. Fossilized bones and artifacts could tell one quite a lot about what they must have looked like, what they ate, how they hunted—but they revealed very little about behavior, because, as he observed, "behavior doesn't fossilize." At what point in the evolutionary continuum, for example, do we declare a primate to be human? Is it, as was commonly believed, when he or she begins to use and fashion tools?

This was why he was so interested in our nearest relations, the great apes—the family that includes chimpanzees, orangutans, and gorillas—but in particular, the chimpanzees, found only in Africa. If we could study the common behaviors of chimpanzees and human beings, he reasoned, we would know a great deal about our "apelike humanlike common ancestor."

There had been sightings of chimpanzees on the eastern shore of Lake Tanganyika, six hundred miles south of Olduvai. This was particularly intriguing because our first human ancestors had probably lived on the shore of a lake. The terrain was terribly steep and rugged, and there were no guidelines for such a study, and it would be dangerous: chimpanzees are about four times as strong as human beings, and there was really no knowing what they might do to a human being they thought was invading their territory.

Jane wondered what kind of scientist Leakey would find for such a monumental task. By the end of September he had begun to drop hints that she herself was that kind of scientist, and Jane wrote her mother about the plan that had begun to take shape.

Up to this point things had moved along with remarkable speed, yet almost three years would pass before Jane actually arrived at the Gombe Stream Reserve in July 1960.

If we were to think of Jane Goodall at this stage in her life as a questing hero, her meeting with Leakey could be compared to Odysseus's with Tiresias, or Prince Arthur's with Merlin. For Louis Leakey was one of those mysterious liminal figures in whom opposites seem to coexist in a state of continuous excitation, like electricity crackling between two poles. The son of a British missionary to Africa, Leakey had grown up in the highlands of Kenya among the Kikuyus. He had learned to track and hunt from Kikuyu boys his own age, and when it was time for them to undergo the arduous circumcision rite that marked their passage into manhood, he underwent it along with them. He spoke fluent Kikuyu and till the end of his life claimed that he would often dream and even think in Kikuyu. His initiation name was Son of Sparrow Hawk.

Leakey was also something of a trickster figure—like Coyote, or Kokapeli, or Raven—who loved to get around institutions and formalities. By sheer force of will he had shoehorned himself into Cambridge as a young man, where he graduated summa cum laude, and just so he would shoehorn Jane first into the Gombe Stream Reserve and then into graduate school at Cambridge, where she was one of only eight individuals to enter without having received an undergraduate degree first. He was a brilliant if unorthodox scientist, and he was deeply religious as well, baffled always at why so many scientists rejected religion. Strong willed, described by those who knew him as very much an alpha male, he was also a passionate nurturer who fretted over the physical well-being of his assistants as well as their finances. He loved to cook. Goodall recalls still how often the Leakey home was permeated with the fragrance of Louis's freshly baked bread.

Back from Olduvai, it became painfully evident that Leakey's enthusiasm for mentoring Jane was not as straightforward as she'd assumed. Leakey was sixty-two at the time, but he looked even older, and she was shocked by his infatuation with her. A long letter home describes the situation and how she dealt with it; clearly, the succession of Brians, Keiths, and Davids has schooled her in the fine art of discouraging an unwanted suitor without destroying his dignity or an otherwise valued friendship. Jane knew very well how much she owed to Leakey, and her affection for him ran as deep as her gratitude. She would convey her own sense of their relationship by dubbing him, in her letters, her Fairy Foster Father—FFF for short.

What probably helped clear the air even more was Vanne's arrival in Kenya. She came to visit Jane in September 1958, and she and Leakey became fast friends almost at once. In fact, Leakey asked her soon afterward to co-author his book on the early origins of human beings, called in its American edition *Unveiling Man's Origins*. He announced in his preface to the book that Vanne had written the first twelve chapters; one wonders how many readers he thought would fail to notice the book is only thirteen chapters long.

The idea of doing research on wild chimpanzees by actually living among them for long stretches of time was Louis's, and so was the idea of sending an untrained young woman to do the job. Leakey believed that the chimps wouldn't feel compelled to challenge her as fiercely as they would a man, but he also believed that women are better observers than men. Her lack of academic training was, in his book, an advantage: Her impressions would not be distorted by prejudice. When he began discussing the scheme with the British district commissioner of the area where she would be working, he was told she would have to have a companion. Thinking aloud to Vanne, he mused that it would have to be someone with whom Jane was relaxed, who would not compete with her, and who would leave her to do the study as she thought best. On cue, and happily, Vanne offered to accompany Jane to Gombe.

In December 1958, Leakey secured the official permissions for Jane's study of the Gombe chimpanzees. Raising the money would take considerably longer. Jane, meanwhile, went back to England with her mother to study zoology, bringing with her a mongoose and a bush baby, and leaving behind with friends the bat-eared fox, the vervet monkey, the cocker spaniel puppy, the hedgehog, snakes, spiders, the rat, and the fish tank that had shared space in her apartment in back of the Coryndon museum.

In England once again, Goodall did not wither away for want of Africa; she fell ravenously, rather, on all that she had missed. She holed up in London to learn everything established primatologists could teach her about chimpanzees, which turned out to be very little, but her evenings were spent in coffee houses with young people who shared her passions for music, poetry, philosophy, and religion. A handsome young actor came courting, and they had just announced their engagement when Leakey wrote, in mid-May 1960. He had found the funds; the project could go ahead. Within a couple of weeks Jane and her mother were flying back to Africa; of the engagement, we hear no more.

More complications, more delay. Dramatic political upheavals were taking place throughout Africa during this period, and it wasn't until mid-July 1960 that Jane and her mother were able to board the motor launch that carried them the twelve miles from the town of Kigoma to the Gombe Stream National Park, where the extraordinary second phase of her life would unfold.

Goodall recalls little of that first evening. She remembers stepping out of the boat and heading directly up into the forest, and she remembers an odd feeling of detachment that gave way, by the time she'd cleared the first hill, to an overwhelming sense of the excitement and magic of what was happening. London, Nairobi, parties, jobs, and boyfriends fell away, and she was once again the nine-year-old girl who has never wanted anything in the world but this.

"As a child I had dreamed of living in the African forests, silently moving from tree to tree, surrounded by animals—invisible animals, perhaps, but surely ever present."[13] One would love to know what her mother was thinking, too, as she watched her long-legged, ponytailed daughter lope up the steep hillside as if she'd been there all her life. If Vanne Morris-Goodall gloated just a little bit at that moment, she had every right to, because her plan had worked. It had taken six years, but here was Jane, doing what she was born to do, and here—What a bonus!—here she was, too. Vanne had probably already begun taking notes for the novel of high adventure she would publish a few years later called *In the Rainforest*.

The first three months at Gombe were disappointing: One sighting the first day, and then virtually nothing. Jane wasn't permitted to move about in the forest by herself—she had to be accompanied by a government-appointed game scout and, to keep her prestige high among the local people, a porter to carry her haversack, so that wherever she went, she was a crowd. The chimpanzees kept their distance.

Yet the time was anything but wasted. Helped by her African assistants, Jane learned to find her way around the Reserve. Her skin toughened; she developed a resistance to the tse-tse fly; she became surefooted on terrain that was steep and slippery. She became, in her own words, "increasingly arboreal." She learned to spot the animal tracks and tunnels that threaded through the forest and how to negotiate them—on hands and knees for the most part.

Much later, writing her definitive scholarly work on chimpanzees in the wild, Goodall would reflect on the different levels of commitment that various researchers had brought to their work at Gombe. Recalling how unrewarding her own first three months had been, she remembered that her persistence had two sources: her desire to know everything about chimpanzees, and her desire not to let Louis Leakey down.

One comes almost to assume, following Jane Goodall's life story, that she will handle each apparent impasse with the same indefatigable

---

[13] Jane Goodall and Dale Peterson, *Visions of Caliban* (Athens: University of Georgia Press, 2000), 68.

resolution, but it is useful to pull back now and then and realize that this is a woman possessed of incredible determination. Teresa of Avila used to say that determination is the preeminent quality anyone must have who wants to find God. In fact, she used to call for "a very determined determination." She would surely have found in Jane Goodall a kindred spirit.

Vanne would stay at Gombe for five months. She had brought with her some basic medical supplies, and with these she set up an informal clinic at the camp, dispensing aspirin and dressings for minor wounds to the local fishermen and their families. The "White Witchdoctor" was immensely well liked, allowing Jane to focus completely on her research and building up a fund of good will that would last for years to come.

Two months into their stay Jane and Vanne were leveled by malaria, and weeks passed before Jane was well enough to leave her tent. When she finally did go back up the hill, stopping repeatedly to recover her strength, she went by herself. This was a violation of protocol, but she was desperately anxious to see whether she could see any chimps. Her funds would run out in a couple of months, and she had learned almost nothing.

That morning would turn out to be the turning point of her study. She came upon a group of chimpanzees at unexpectedly close range. They gazed at her, and eventually they moved away, but they didn't run this time, and they didn't scream. It was as if she had served some kind of apprenticeship and won a tentative acceptance by the community she'd come to study.

Or perhaps it was just that she had come by herself.

From that day on, Goodall arranged to move around by herself most of the time. It would still be months before she could get within fifty meters of most of the chimpanzees, but as long as she didn't come too close she could follow them now as they moved from fig tree to waterfall, up into the trees at night, and down again in the morning. One chimpanzee in particular, a gentle fellow Jane would name David Greybeard, was comfortable with her presence much earlier than the others, and she believes that his acceptance helped calm their fears.

Goodall wasn't foolish or foolhardy. She had watched the chimps closely and determined that when she behaved in certain ways they were visibly more comfortable. Birute Galdikas emphasizes that Jane's approach was not to hide, as many behavioral biologists traditionally did, but on the contrary to be fully visible. She was confident they would get used to her. She never followed them when they moved away from her. She always wore drab clothing, and she tried to stay low. The chimps just seemed to be more comfortable if she did. In fact, she observed, "looming" is intrinsic to the charging display by which the great apes assert dominance over another. Much later, when Goodall learned about Koko and Michael, two gorillas who had been taught American Sign Language, she wrote and asked their teacher to ask Koko how she wished human beings to behave around her: should they sit or stand? Koko was unequivocal. She preferred that human beings lie down![14]

Goodall came to feel completely at home in the forest. Up at 5:30 every morning, she typically stayed out until after dark and spent the evenings typing up her observation notes by kerosene lamplight. After a while she had a small tin trunk carried up to her favorite observation post, "the Peak," in which she kept coffee powder and sugar, a kettle, and a blanket so that she could spend the night there when the chimpanzees were sleeping nearby. That's *blanket* in the singular, and that's, as far as I can gather, without a tent and directly on the ground—unlike the chimps themselves, who build themselves comfortable aerial nests before bedding down.

A banana for breakfast, a handful of raisins for lunch, days on end of solitude: the regimen was almost anchoritic. Her routine varied little, and once her mother had gone back to England, she was alone most of the time. She was developing the capacity to sit for hours on end in uncomfortable positions. It would rain sometimes for an hour, two hours, and as the chimpanzees themselves sat hunkered over in cold, wet misery waiting it out, she, too, would drop down inside herself, insensible to the chill and wet, as oblivious to the passage of time as the chimpanzees. Goodall had tried at various times since her theosophy class in London to "suppress circling thoughts," but it had been a while. Now, though, she began to feel the old mystery steal over her—"the cessation of noise from within."[15]

She was unaccompanied now for days and weeks on end, yet she doesn't seem to have felt herself to be alone at all. No more, probably, than Charles Dickens might have felt strolling through the neighborhoods of London enjoying the various "street people." The behavior of Flo, Evered, David Greybeard, Goliath, Fifi, and Madame Bee was for Goodall endlessly enthralling. A fellow scientist visiting Gombe asked her once why she didn't take a bundle of paperbacks up to the Peak with her, and she was nonplussed. "Think about everything I would have missed!"

---

[14] Ibid., 287.
[15] *Reason for Hope*, 79.

In the fall of that first year, a biologist named George Schaller, who had been studying wild gorillas, stopped at Gombe. Gorillas, he told her, do not eat meat, and they don't use tools. So if she were to observe chimpanzees doing either of these things, demonstrating their close kinship to human beings, all of her waiting and watching that year would be justified. The significance of the use of tools is obvious enough, and the significance of meat-eating was directly related, for many scientists believed that the desire for flesh and the subsequent development of hunting techniques and tools may have been a crucial factor in the transition from pre-human to human being.[16]

Just three weeks later, looking through binoculars, she saw a group of chimpanzees perched in a tree eating what appeared to be a baby bushpig. A week after that she watched while David Greybeard and his friend Goliath pushed blades of grass into red termite hills, carefully withdrew them again, and popped the blades of grass into their mouths. When they'd left the clearing, she hurried to the termite hill herself and pushed a blade of grass into a termite hill. When she brought it up, it was laden with termites. A few days later she watched another group doing the same thing, only this time they were using twigs and stripping the leaves off first. They were not merely *using* tools, they were *making* them.

Louis Leakey could not have been more thrilled. To his protege's triumphant cable he responded: "Ah! We must now redefine man, redefine tool, or accept chimpanzees as human!" He knew now that he would be able to get the funding necessary to continue the study.

By discovering that chimpanzees use tools and eat meat, Goodall did indeed blur the line that was supposed to have separated chimps from human beings. But even as she was making her discoveries and documenting them, researchers working with chimps in captivity were blurring that same line in other ways. The ease with which captive chimpanzees were acquiring American Sign Language and then teaching it to one another was rapidly dispelling the idea that language is something only human beings possess. The distinction had to be refined. Chimpanzees can learn and use language; it's *spoken* language they lack, and that would seem to have more to do with the way human beings and the chimpanzees have adapted to their particular environments than it does with any inherent, fixed limitation on the part of the chimps. In the human being, that is, certain ways of processing and communicating information have developed that did not

---

[16] *Africa in My Blood*, 227.

develop in chimpanzees only because they would have been useless for them in their African forest homes.

The upshot of findings like this is that human beings did *not* descend, as some had thought, from chimpanzees. Rather, we have a common ancestor that we don't share with any other primates except the relatively recently discovered bonobo monkeys. And that ancestor undoubtedly looked very much *like* a chimpanzee.

By slow degrees, the chimpanzees came to accept the presence of this almost-ape, so oddly pale and smooth skinned.

Goodall's relatively matter of fact and even rapturous descriptions of how she spent her days don't begin to convey how strenuous they must actually have been, or even, at times, how dangerous. When she tells us that Goliath "stomped on my head," on one occasion, "and could have killed me," the point of the remark isn't to underscore the riskiness of a follow, but rather the very real differences in chimpanzee temperament.

In 1966, colleague and friend Roger Fouts visited Gombe with his wife, Debbi, and he gives us a considerably better sense than Goodall does of what it was actually like:

> It was . . . the most grueling physical challenge of my entire life. We climbed straight up rocky hills, holding on to vines for dear life, crawled on our stomachs under impassable brush, and hacked through a dense sea of thorns with our bare hands. We slid, stumbled, fell, and cursed. All of us were bleeding from the arms, legs, and head. Debbi was bleeding from the sternum as well, where she had gouged herself on a sharp rock that broke her fall as she slid down a ravine.[17]

Scientists are always striving to close the distance between themselves and the phenomena they are observing, and typically that means developing instruments that increase our visual or auditory powers: more powerful telescopes, or microscopes, or recording techniques. But Goodall dealt in a revolutionary way with the gap that is supposed to separate human beings from animals: she placed *herself* there. Soon she was able to write home triumphantly, "The hills and forests are my home. And what is more, I think my mind works like a chimp's, subconsciously."[18]

---

[17] Roger Fouts, *Next of Kin* (New York: HarperCollins, 1998), 375.
[18] *Africa in My Blood*, 186.

Simply by watching, with unwavering attention, she determined what the chimpanzees' vocalizations and their gestures meant. She became sufficiently "chimped" that she could move about with them and experience the environment much as they did. Sitting near them by a stream, for instance, and noticing that they seemed wary and tense, she understood why: the noise of the water made it difficult to hear the sounds of other animals that might be approaching. Threading through the maze of paths in the forest, having to decide quickly at each turn which way the chimpanzees *might* have gone, she amazed herself by how often she chose the right track.

Again, fellow primatologist Roger Fouts is helpful. That first harrowing day that he spent following a group of Gombe chimps, it seemed to him that in the heat of the chase, his ordinary mode of mental processing was briefly suspended. He writes, "I was going on adrenaline now and all of my sensory neurons were firing in unison for perhaps the first time in my life."[19] In other words, most human activities are characterized by a sequential mode of thinking, which is fine for most of the things human beings do. But other mammals process data in a more holistic fashion, allowing them to process several kinds of information at once, which comes in handy when you're tearing through a forest pursuing, or pursued by, another creature and you have to assess your situation and weigh your options simultaneously. Fouts makes this point in support of his argument that it isn't accurate to say human beings are more intelligent than chimpanzees. Rather, he argues, human intelligence has adopted sequential ways of organizing experience, characterized by left-brain dominance. The price we've paid has been the ability to think holistically—like a chimp.

In February 1961, Goodall was privy to a kind of celebration, or performance—a rain dance, she called it, or perhaps a rain festival. Huddled at the bottom of a natural amphitheater, while the rain poured down and thunder rolled and lightning lit up the sky, she watched, astounded, as one male chimpanzee after another took a star turn, "huge and black on the skyline, flinging themselves across the ground in their primaeval display of superiority and power."[20] Silent, the females and children watched, and at the very end, everyone slipped away but one powerful male she called Pale Face, who stood for a long moment at the top of a ridge and gazed directly at her, as if delivering a silent *envoi* to the last member of his audience.

---

[19] Fouts, *Next of Kin*, 377.
[20] *Africa in My Blood*, 172.

Her greatest achievement was probably the simple fact of habituation itself, for finally the chimps accepted her presence. They didn't run away, and they didn't stop what they were doing when she showed up. To this momentous breakthrough, the particularly gentle male she had named David Greybeard was the key. In May 1961, he turned up at Jane's camp and spent the night in the palm tree near her tent. The palm nuts were ripe, and he'd apparently decided that neither she nor her co-workers were a tremendous threat. He spent a couple of days there, watching Jane and the others from his nest in the tree, coming down from time to time to pick up bananas she left out on a table. He left, and when he returned, other chimpanzees came with him. The ice was broken: Goodall could observe the chimps at close quarters when they came into camp, but she could follow them, too, settle down nearby when they stopped, and record everything they did. In fact, if she happened to be following David Greybeard, he would wait for her to catch up along the trail just as he would wait for his friends.

Louis Leakey had wanted Jane to enter the forest unburdened with theory, and in retrospect she believes he was absolutely right. She claims to have worked without a hypothesis.

And yet, surely, none of us is really ever working without a hypothesis. Jane knew very well that some domestic animals are sweet natured and eager to please, and that others are like a pony Mary Leakey had asked her to ride in a show that first summer in Kenya, so obdurate they will walk backward just to humiliate the rider. She knew that dogs, too, have highly individual personalities and a wide range of mental capacities. So why on earth wouldn't chimpanzees, our closest relatives, be at least as gifted and as diverse in their gifts?

It might not have occurred to her to call it a hypothesis, but Jane Goodall's conviction that chimpanzees are endlessly interesting *as individuals* was just that, and it was not, in fact, one that all of her colleagues shared. Believing that chimpanzees would reward many times over the closest, most scrupulous observation they could be given, she gave herself over completely to that work. She had no other agenda, no axe to grind, no turf to defend. In retrospect, she recognizes that there was a religious dimension to what she was doing. For the long stretches of time she spent with the chimps—the silence, the watching, and the sheer companionship—gave her "a peace that reached into the inner core of my being."[21]

---

[21] *Reason for Hope*, 78.

Naturalist Sy Montgomery took her cue from Jane Goodall and spent six months following three emus around in their homelands in South Australia. She emerged from the experience forever altered. Confident that her fascination with them was to a very real extent reciprocated, she characterized her relationship with the birds as "a privileged trust unlike any other," that existed entirely on their terms, and she was grateful to Goodall for inspiring her to think such a connection possible. "Jane's strength is that she relinquished control. Today this strength is honored, not as a passive act, as the men before her might have seen it, but as an achievement—one that allowed her to see and inspired her to stay."[22]

The possibility that relinquishing control might actually be a strength or an achievement hasn't been proposed terribly often in the history of Western science, but the idea did come up regularly during the Middle Ages, when clerics had to figure out some way of accounting for what was almost an epidemic of female mysticism: why were all these *women* having visions, healing the sick, and bringing souls to the straight and narrow? A recurring explanation had to do with the idea of divine grace as something like water, which flows, and can therefore only enter spaces that are empty and low. It's *because* women have "gentle hearts" and "frailer minds," one hagiographer explains, that the flow of wisdom from heaven isn't impeded, as it is in *hard* men.[23]

Montgomery's formulation doesn't depend on such extreme gender stereotypes, but it does point in the same general direction. Challenging the conventional notion that scientists should not be emotionally involved with their study subjects, she insists that, in fact, all of Louis Leakey's proteges, the so-called Trimates—Goodall, Dian Fossey, and Birute Galdikas—related to their "subjects" exactly as she did to the emus she accompanied. "For they do love them. It is a love as deep and passionate as the love one has for a child or a spouse or a lover; but it is a love unlike any other. The bonds between the women and the individual apes they studied are complex, subtle, and almost universally misunderstood."[24]

She goes even further. Toward the end of her consideration of these three very different field biologists—Fossey and Galdikas be-

---

[22] Sy Montgomery, *Walking with the Great Apes: Jane Goodall, Dian Fossey, Birute Galdikas* (Boston: Houghton Mifflin, 1998), 128.

[23] Lamprecht von Regensburg, cited in Emilie Zum Brunn and Georgette Epiney-Burgard, *Women Mystics in Medieval Europe* (New York: Paragon House, 1989), xiv.

[24] Montgomery, *Walking with the Great Apes*, xix.

ing Goodall's "daughters" in a sense, as "strong and compassionate" as Goodall's mother and grandmother and fully aligned with her spiritual mother-line—Montgomery proposes that the Trimates be viewed as modern shamans and suggests that Leakey himself (Son of Sparrow Hawk) envisioned their task not only as scientific but as a vision quest. "Theirs was a profoundly sacred journey to the brink of the chasm that modern man has carved between himself and the animals and, once there, to peer over its edge and perhaps, if they dared, to cross."[25]

Montgomery is undoubtedly right about Leakey and the Trimates: the level of empathy they have brought to their work is, in fact, love. But *love* can mean a great many things. I suggest that the term *attentive love*, as defined by philosopher Sara Ruddick, probably gets us closer to understanding Goodall's feelings for her subjects. I wonder, too, whether it might not shed some light on the phenomenon of mother-lines—both biological and spiritual.

The idea of attentive love was central to the work of French philosopher-mystic Simone Weil and was developed further by philosopher-novelist Iris Murdoch. Ruddick sees it as the key to what she calls "maternal practice." Mothers everywhere seek to protect, nurture, and train their children, but also to socialize them—train them to be acceptable, that is, within their group or culture. Attentive love is the faculty they exercise to accomplish those objectives.

Love becomes attentive love, Ruddick explains, when it joins forces with a passion to know and understand someone else. In the special case of mothers the someone else is often also experienced, in a certain sense, as an extension of self.

For Weil, Ruddick observes, "the capacity for attention is integral to a religious quest for blessedness." Ruddick herself shies away from that application. For her, what is interesting is the balancing act mothers perform when they try with all their might to understand someone they love unconditionally. Attention is, in that context, very closely related to empathy, she notes, except that empathy implies that "in the other's experience you know and find yourself," and what a good mother must do is to be able to *know* the child without necessarily finding herself in the child at all. We must be able to look at the child without appropriating him or her into what Murdoch calls "the greedy organism of the self." It seems to me that over the course of her career, Jane Goodall moved steadily toward this ideal, achieving a finer and finer balance between scientific objectivity and love. By

---

[25] Ibid., 261.

extension, presumably, we should strive in all our relationships to love "the other" and at the same time allow others to be freely and fully themselves, even when that means allowing them to walk right on out the door! Saint Catherine of Genoa said that she was compelled to develop such a skill during the purgative segment of her spiritual journey—the capacity, she called it, "to love without loving."

As we consider the phenomenon of mother-lines and what it might mean for Western culture if we took them seriously, we would do well to reflect on Sara Ruddick's examination of attentive love, for of the various kinds of wisdom that might be understood to flow down through those mother-lines, it may be the most critical. It certainly seems central to Jane Goodall's story—not only to her experience as daughter and as mother, but to her scientific work as well. Over the course of her career, as we'll see, she would move steadily toward a finer and finer balance between scientific objectivity and bone-deep affection.

Goodall's discoveries that first year were groundbreaking; if she'd done nothing else for the rest of her life, her place in the history of science was secure. But, of course, nothing she'd reported would be taken seriously until she was credentialed as a scientist.

On the strength of her discoveries and his own reputation, Louis Leakey was able to get Goodall admitted to Cambridge University's graduate program in ethology, the study of animal behavior. So it was that she left Gombe in December 1961, for her first of three winter terms at Cambridge, during which she would do the course work for her PhD, her work there punctuated by lecture tours to the United States under the auspices of the National Geographic Society.

She smiles wryly today about the way she was greeted when she turned up at Cambridge. The students and faculty weren't actively hostile, she recalls, but "supercilious." "I'd done it all wrong, you see. I'd named the chimps: I should have assigned them numbers. I'd imputed vivid personalities and emotions to them whose existence I couldn't prove, and of course I was the wrong sex!"[26]

But, she laughs, she was just twenty-seven, and her mind hadn't been biased, and she'd always been obstinate. "And I'd had a teacher who'd convinced me beyond any doubt that animals have emotional lives, and my teacher was my dog Rusty."

Rumors circulated meanwhile that the Gombe chimpanzees only knew how to fish for termites because Goodall had taught them!

[26] Jane Goodall, speech, April 17, 2004, San Rafael, California.

But Goodall's accomplishments in the field spoke for themselves, as did the several prestigious awards she'd already received. She was several years older than most entering graduate students, and far more widely traveled, and she had no driving interest in becoming what she called a scientist with a capital *S*. She was proof against a certain kind of intimidation to which most graduate students are painfully susceptible. It couldn't have hurt, in addition, that in Africa, as in England, men young and old had tumbled over one another for her attention. She'd had her first serious love affair in Kenya with a young man who was, improbably enough, a "white hunter." In socio-biological terms, she knew herself to be, indisputably, an alpha female.

"Supercilious" is a magnificently dismissive choice of words.

By working toward her degree at Cambridge, Jane Goodall was acquiring the credentials she needed for her work to be taken seriously in the scientific community. But hearsay alone would not suffice: the chimpanzees would have to be photographed as they fished for termites, ate meat, and did all of the other remarkable things she had observed them doing. No small task, as it turned out. Jane couldn't pull it off, nor could her sister Judy. Once again, Louis Leakey had a solution.

To Jane he wrote that he had located someone who was perfect for the job—a Dutch photographer who'd been filming animals on the Serengeti Plain.

To Vanne he wrote that he had found a husband for Jane.

Hearing from Leakey that Hugo was already clambering around a mountainous forest with his equipment to see how much he could carry and how fast he could move, Jane was won over to the idea of the man even before he arrived. But shortly before van Lawick arrived at Gombe, David Greybeard and a few of the other male chimps had begun to come calling for bananas. The photographer was met with the news that David Graybeard had for the first time taken bananas from Jane's hand—"So gently, no snatching."

Even for a photographer as experienced and indefatigable as van Lawick, getting clear pictures of the chimpanzees in their densely forested habitat proved to be almost impossibly difficult. One really couldn't run and climb and crawl on one's belly through underbrush and carry heavy, expensive equipment at the same time. Not for long anyway, and especially not in the rain, and rain trumped the shooting anyway. You could easily get up there with all your equipment and *no rain* and see no chimps, either.

On the other hand, if you just sat there in camp doling out bananas, here they came, singly or in small groups, and after they'd eaten the fruit, they often stayed around, bickering and making up, grooming one another head to toe, making noisy displays, turning somersaults and chasing each other around trees, courting, exploring the resources of the camp (sweaty shirts are in their own way quite tasty!), and engaging in petty theft. And there one could be, camera and notebook in hand, learning the most extraordinary things about chimpanzee interactions and capturing their every movement on film.

It wasn't a particularly difficult choice.

The banana-feeding project brought its own headaches. The excitement sometimes got out of hand. When mature male chimps begin hurling rocks or branches about, it doesn't much matter if their intent isn't really hostile. Jane and Hugo had a good-sized cage built that they could run into when projectiles started flying, but the setup posed potential dangers to the chimps as well. As they became habituated to humans, they might start turning up at the homes of nearby fishermen who would probably not be nearly as tolerant as the researchers were. In addition, there would come a time when the local baboons found out about the bananas, and they began showing up as well.

And, of course, there was a more fundamental objection to the project. Luring the chimps into a human environment with ripe fruit was a violation of scientific protocol. The observer had altered the normal behavior of her subjects, and that in turn brought into question the value of her observations.

Even her closest mentors were alarmed, Louis Leakey among them. But once again, Jane stood her ground. She acknowledged that the banana-feeding operation disrupted normal chimpanzee interactions. But the follow itself was a disruption, as was the very presence of Jane and her cohort. Habituation itself had already differentiated the chimps of Gombe Stream from other chimps living in the wild to a degree that meant the data in question was irretrievably "contaminated." If someone came along with a way to observe chimpanzees in the wild that had no effect on the chimps or their environment, well and good, but in the meanwhile researchers would simply have to recognize the limitations of whatever methods they used.

Whether she knew it or not, and I rather suspect she did, Goodall's attitude toward field biology was right in line with the Heisenberg Uncertainty Principle, which states as a universal law of science that whenever we take a measurement, we disturb the thing we are measuring. In order for me to know something is there, I have to bump into it, and when I do this I knock it off its course, by however infinitesimal a measure that might be. Scientists can choose between big bumps and slight ones, but "no bumps" isn't an option.

The question would come up again and again: during a polio epidemic in 1966, for example, when six chimps died. As soon as they realized what the disease was, Jane ordered vaccinations not only for herself and Hugo (she was several months pregnant), but for the chimps who were coming into camp. "Why did you interfere?" she was asked later, and her reply was unapologetic: we've already interfered with the lives of these creatures in so many negative ways—like destroying their environment and giving them our diseases—surely we can rationalize a measure of positive interference as well!

Within a few months the banana operation was moved up the hill, well away from the lake shore, and Hugo had had boxes built that dispensed the bananas one or two at a time and could be operated by remote control. Gradually, the chimps figured out that on some days there just weren't any bananas, and the squabbles and stampedes dissipated.

At least they did among the chimps. Jane's colleagues were never entirely won over to the banana-feeding regimen.

Empathy as a mode of knowing, understanding as an expression of love—these lay at the heart of Goodall's scientific practice, and everything that Sara Ruddick says about the way attentive love manifests itself in maternal practice can also be seen in Goodall's story. First, Ruddick maintains, mothers are required to hold close, for the growing child needs this kind of protection. At the same time they must be prepared to let go, relinquish control, and even welcome change.[27] Second, maternal practice gives rise to a preference for concrete rather than abstract thinking. We deal always with a particular child, and not with children in general.[28] Third, the concept of attentive love, says Ruddick, "implies and rewards a faith that love will not be destroyed by knowledge, that to the loving eye the lovable will be revealed."[29] Fourth, mothers encourage the values of attentive love in one another by telling each other stories.[30]

Goodall has always insisted on studying each of the Gombe chimps as unique. Focusing always on "the particular chimp" has allowed her to perceive and document behaviors that no one had observed before. She "sorted out" her feelings toward the chimps over time. Early on, she spoke about them as her friends, but she moved away from that

[27] Sara Ruddick, *Maternal Thinking: Toward a Politics of Peace* (New York: Ballantine, 1989), 89.

[28] Ibid., 93.

[29] Ibid., 119.

[30] Ibid., 98.

as she recognized that the word *friendship* implies a particular kind of reciprocity that chimps do not render. They tolerate her presence most probably *because* they know they can get away from her. Theirs is a limited, qualified version of affection, and she accepts that, gratefully, without illusion. This heightened objectivity would prove something of a lifesaver later on, for love could very well have been destroyed by knowledge in the 1970s, when the "Gombe wars" shattered some of Goodall's most cherished beliefs about the nature of chimps.

Ruddick's final point—the usefulness of storytelling to preserve and pass on "what mothers know"—goes right to the heart of Jane Goodall's greatness. When mothers counsel other mothers indirectly, through an accumulation of narrative rather than through direct instruction (which hasn't necessarily been invited), it's because it's a very gentle and respectful strategy that encourages the other woman to trust her own observation powers and intuition. "Here's what happened to me, and wasn't I surprised," as opposed to, "Here's what you have to do." Just so, Jane is saying to other ethologists, trained and would-be-trained: Go have your own experience. Watch as closely as I have and tell us what you see. She is credited, as an ethologist, with having revived a commitment to empiricism itself that had been core to nineteenth-century science and had fallen into disrepute by the middle of the twentieth. "One of the maladies of the field today," says primatologist John Mitani, "is the studies are too methodologically rigorous. People don't watch the animals anymore. You have an idea and go out to test your idea—and you have blinders on."[31] Ethologist Konrad Lorenz calls for a return to what some would call amateurism in field biology, and for "men whose gaze, through a wholly irrational delight in the beauty of the object, stays riveted to it."[32] Sounds a lot like attentive love, doesn't it? Only how amazing is it that as late as 1981 it was still assumed that those loving observers would be men!

Stories, then. A stream of enchanting vignettes and stories was emerging at Gombe, and collectively, they make up not so much a scientific record as an ongoing saga. Goodall has made the beguiling observation that if chimpanzees collected stories and retold them around a campfire, as human beings always have, Flo and Humphrey and David Greybeard would be memorialized for their deeds, just as Penelope, Achilles, and Beowulf were for theirs. But, in fact, her sketches of the chimps work in exactly this way, forming narra-

---

[31] In Montgomery, *Walking with the Great Apes*, xix.
[32] Ibid., 128.

tives that stretch across several generations, like William Faulkner's *Yoknapatawpha County* novels, or John Galsworthy's *Forsyte Saga.*

It's all there—high drama, low comedy, stirring battles, and wrenching pathos.

How wonderful it is to learn that the first thing a group of chimps does when the chimps come upon a tree full of ripe figs is to hug and kiss one another and chuckle in mutual delight.

On the other hand, how magnificent it also is to watch the adolescent male Fagan "work the system" once the banana boxes have been installed and equipped with remote-control devices. One of only two young chimps who figured out how to unscrew a nut and bolt that then released a handle, allowing the banana box to fall open, he also learned how to do it on the sly, with one hand, looking in the other direction, and faking the other chimps out completely until at last, after they'd wandered off, he released the handle and ran, soundlessly, to claim his reward.

Generations of children have grown up now knowing that little Flint died of grief not long after he lost his mother, Flo. They know that four- and five-year-old chimpanzees *play,* just as human children do, and that they even do some of the same things—spinning around to make themselves dizzy, chasing one another, tickling one another, carrying their younger siblings around like dolls, and imitating their elders in comical attempts at charging displays.

Just about every element of traditional narrative turns up in Goodall's books and films except romance. Among chimps, sex is "public, promiscuous, and unprovocative."[33] When a female comes into estrus, her genitals swell up and turn bright pink, and the entire male contingent can think of nothing else. She might have sex twenty or thirty times a day. Indeed, observed one day at the peak of estrus, the legendary Flo was mated at least fifty times.

The beauty of Goodall's emphasis on story is that it makes for a wonderfully balanced picture of her subjects. She is superb at rendering the tender back-and-forthings of the Gombe mothers and their offspring, for example, but never sentimental. Her interpretations of chimp behavior are grounded in a clear understanding of evolutionary biology. Watching Melissa fish for termites alongside her daughter Gremlin, for example, she sees that Melissa repeatedly crowds Gremlin away from her workplace and takes away tools that Gremlin

---

[33] Dale Peterson and Richard Wrangham, *Demonic Males: Apes and the Origins of Human Violence* (Boston: Mariner Books 1997), 11.

has prepared. Gremlin throws a tantrum. Melissa embraces her but takes away the twig anyway. Callous mothering? Not at all. Because Melissa is still fertile, she needs all the food she can get—especially protein. And she is way too old and heavy to pick the fruit from slender branches overhead where Gremlin can clamber about with ease.

Insightful as she is where mothers and daughters are concerned, Goodall is no less responsive to the exuberant, over-the-top behavior of male chimps. She gets an enormous kick out of watching a cheeky young male climb or connive his way to the top of the heap—like Mike, who became *capo da capo* at the precocious age of twelve by banging empty kerosene cans on the ground as he ran up and down the camp. (Televised congressional debates have never looked quite the same since I took in the mental picture of Mike with his kerosene cans.)

Goodall fully accepts that chimpanzee males are bent on dominating one another and females, and that most of the females are preoccupied with mothering. She recognizes that, in the broadest sense, this highly gendered behavior probably does maximize the chances that one's DNA will be replicated. (Though, in fact, it's not nearly that simple. We know now, for instance, that the alpha male doesn't enjoy the reproductive success that some of his less aggressive counterparts do. Having to keep defending a title appears to take a lot out of a guy.) But she underscores the broad range of behaviors, too, noting that certain female chimps, Flo among them, will occasionally display in much the way males do, and that, for that matter, certain male chimps are consistently more solicitous toward infants than others and can have a real knack for easing tensions within a group. The variety of maternal styles among chimps intrigues Goodall, and so does the effect that those differences have on offspring, rendering them confident and outgoing or fearful and tentative.

The stories Goodall tells are never of an individual chimp in isolation from the others; each is described as a unique individual in the context of his or her birth family and the other members of his or her community. What kind of mothering did she receive? How many siblings did she have? What was her relationship with them? And if the chimp in question was a male, what kind of hierarchy did he have to fight his way into?

Birute Galdikas, whose immersion in the world of orangutans mirrored Goodall's involvement with chimps, says of her mentor's approach, "Jane held that the social structure of a community of chimpanzees could only be understood in light of the different temperaments and personal histories of a particular group of individuals. But this point was lost on scientists accustomed to dealing with anonymous animals and generalizations."[34]

The individuals determine the nature of the group, and the group in turn shapes the individual. Like country villages and neighborhoods everywhere, Goodall argues, each chimpanzee community has its own character and history. With that argument, and with her trust in empathy as a reliable channel for scientific knowledge, Goodall joins the ranks of contemporary life scientists whose rejection of the Aristotelian view of things (dualistic and hierarchic) coincides with an approach that is remarkably Franciscan (relational and egalitarian).

The mountain of data that was accruing now at Gombe vindicated Leakey's gamble many times over. At least ten more years of observation would be necessary. Funding would have to be found for a permanent research station, and more staff would have to come on board.

Meanwhile, as Leakey had intended, Hugo and Jane had fallen in love. She was visiting her family in England at Christmas 1963 when she received a cable: "Will you marry me love stop Hugo." In the spring of 1964, in London, the two were married.

London was at that moment the epicenter of a youth revolution scored by the Beatles and the Rolling Stones, costumed on Carnaby Street, and filmed by Richard Lester. It seems doubtful that the van Lawicks noticed any of this, but a clay model of David Greybeard topped their wedding cake, and blown-up photos of the whole Gombe clan presided over the reception. One could hardly *get* more 1964 than that.

Adding to the quasi-magical ambience we love to associate with weddings, Louis Leakey's Fairy Foster Child would now have a title: Baroness van Lawick.

The baron and baroness quickly captured the public's imagination. In a Volkswagen bus fitted out with beds, a refrigerator, and so on, they dashed across the Serengeti filming hyenas, vultures, and wild dogs. They were flown to the United States to give lectures, and they came to the San Diego Zoo's fiftieth anniversary celebration, where they were photographed cutting a cake that was fifty feet long. Together, they began to turn the Gombe Stream Reserve into a world-class research center staffed by Africans as well as Americans and Europeans.

Hugo coped with what Jane called "the horrid financial side of things." He designed and oversaw the construction of the problematic

---

[34] Birute Galdikas, *Reflections of Eden* (Boston: Little Brown, 1995), 387.

banana boxes and the expanding facility itself, taking pictures all the while and dealing manfully for the time being with the discovery that he, too, had acquired a title through marriage. To a great many people in all parts of the world the talented wildlife photographer would now be known primarily as Mr. Jane Goodall.

In 1967, their son was born, a beautiful little boy with white-gold curls called Grublin, or merely Grub, for his less-than-elegant methods for getting food into his mouth. Now that she was a mother herself, Jane felt even more closely attuned to the mothers of Gombe. Indeed, having a child was the logical extension of her empathic exploration of chimpanzee behavior.

The letters of this period are uniformly high spirited, but they give the impression, too, of tremendous *commotion*. The young woman who had spent her days alone following chimpanzees through the forests of Gombe and her nights writing up her reports by lantern light was now at the center of a vortex. She was wife; she was mother; and she was author and co-author, turning out books, articles, and a staggering volume of correspondence. She was the head of a rapidly expanding research center like none other in the world, and soon she held an appointment to visit Stanford University in California twice yearly.

The Taoist sage Lao Tse had something to say about such times:

> Open up the openings,
> Multiply your affairs;
> Your whole life
> Will become a burden.[35]

Most of us recoil at such a churlish reading of human existence, because the places where we open out to life—love, marriage, childbirth and parenting, profession, community, politics, intellectual and artistic endeavors—are surely the places where life's richness pours in. Well and good, says Lao Tse, only that very influx has a way of closing us off to something else: a state of mind, a way of being in the world ("the constant," he sometimes calls it, because it is always within us) that is the only thing that meets our deepest needs.

Jane Goodall had experienced something very like Lao Tse's "constant" during her early years at Gombe, and she would find her way back to it much later, as we'll see. But in the eventful years she was entering now, it would be almost nowhere in sight.

---

[35] Lao Tse, *God Makes the Rivers to Flow: An Anthology of Sacred Poetry and Prose,* selected by Eknath Easaran (Tomales, CA: Nilgiri Press, 2009), 35.

Jane was thirty years old when she married Hugo van Lawick; he was twenty-seven. She'd been at Gombe for four years, and the *National Geographic* articles for which Hugo shot the photographs had already made her an international celebrity: "The Beauty," as one journalist identified her, "and Her Beasts." She married, that is, at the very moment when the pace of her life was accelerating exponentially.

Funding for the research at Gombe was always touch and go, and Hugo's dried up almost immediately, sending him back to the Serengeti, where he focused on jackals, hyenas, and wild dogs, the "innocent killers" of a book published under that name in 1970. During the late 1960s, Jane accompanied him on most of these expeditions; Dale Peterson believes she probably wrote most of *Innocent Killers*.

But from 1970 on, Gombe and the chimps exerted an increasingly strong pull on Jane. Stanford University professor David Hamburg had become a scientific adviser to Gombe in 1968, and that connection gave rise in 1971 to a joint research project between Gombe and a newly established undergraduate degree program at Stanford in human biology. Jane would give the program a primate studies dimension by offering a series of lectures at the university twice a year, and Stanford students would come to Gombe for field study. Plans were undertaken to establish the Stanford Outdoor Primate Facility—Gombe West—on the Stanford campus.

A letter written to the president of one of the funding organizations for the project underscores the tremendous significance Goodall attached to these new developments. The language is formal and businesslike, yet you can sense her excitement, too, at the opportunities and vistas that are opening, and we are reminded that her genius for field biology was never narrow in its focus. The young girl who had been obsessed by the deepest, most searching questions about human nature and the meaning of existence is still very much in the picture: "My own ultimate goal, as you know, has always been that out of a thorough understanding of chimpanzee behavior should come a furthering of our understanding of our own behavior."[36]

Hugo's work, meanwhile, continued to keep him out on the Serengeti most of the time. It was perhaps inevitable that the marriage would begin to fray at the edges. There were differences from the beginning, Goodall would recall much later, which, like so many couples, they'd hoped to get beyond but really couldn't. The raising of Grub, meanwhile, presented its own challenges, and not just

---

[36] *Beyond Innocence*, 151.

because he was easily as strong minded as either of his parents. He could have been the most compliant child on the planet and his early years would still have challenged his parents. Gombe itself was the problem. Grub was endangered even before he was born by the polio epidemic that killed and injured a number of chimpanzees, and which Jane herself could easily have contracted. He didn't escape malaria, and in fact the chimps were a huge potential threat. To forestall the unthinkable, a cage was built. It was capacious enough, and it was painted an attractive sky blue. But it was a cage nonetheless, and you have to wonder how it felt to be Grub, sitting behind bars with his picture books and construction toys, watching the chimps cast long, hungry looks at him.

From the beginning Grub's passions were not "upstairs" in the forest, where the chimps were, but "downstairs," at the edge of the lake. He fished, he swam, he paddled inflatable boats around. He was a consummate water baby, accompanied always, when he wasn't with one of his parents, by watchful sitters, for in certain parts of the lake there lurked water cobras, sleek brown snakes with a black band around the neck and a bite for which there was no anti-venom.

The maternal strategies of chimps like Flo and Melissa actually matched up well with emerging theories of child development, and Jane followed their lead: Keep your baby close to you until he's at least three years old; breastfeed him; discipline by distraction, not confrontation; be playful, be physical, be patient.

Be patient, and then be patient some more.

Writing to her mother in the summer of 1968, Jane describes the trials of a pregnant Flo. Like any pregnant female, she needs her naps, and her two children are ruthless in their demands. Little Flint insists on being carried and Fifi *will* be groomed, pushes Flo to make her sit up, picks up her arm, whimpers, pushes "until poor old Flo, in self defense, had to laboriously sit up and do as her terrible daughter demanded." Two paragraphs later Jane is at her own wit's end: Grub has hold of her arm, he's screaming, he's climbing all over her, "just like Flint!"[37]

The child is a wonder, "chattier than ever"; he can spend hours untangling fishnets on the beach, and he loves to sweep the floor.

The child will *not* do his schoolwork; he looks down his nose at his mother's cooking; and he still does not like chimpanzees.

The child is all but continuous with oneself; you seem to share one nervous system. Yet, even as you are feeling his toothache as if it were

---

[37] Ibid., 88.

your own, or his loneliness, you come up hard against his imponderable otherness.

Birute Galdikas spent the better part of two weeks within the van Lawick-Goodall family circle when they were all in London in the fall of (probably) 1970 while she was still waiting to get started on her own work with orangutans in Indonesia. She had come to visit with Louis Leakey, who was installed in Vanne Goodall's flat, along with Jane's family. Eager to make herself useful, and very much in awe of Jane, Birute helped take care of Grub, and while she had no particular interest in small children at the time, Grub struck her as "one of the sweetest and most perceptive children I have ever met."

Her impressions of Grub's father were more pointed—and a bit sad. A palpable warmth circulated among Jane, her mother, her sister Judy, and Leakey, who "played the role of a doting, cherished uncle." Hugo, in contrast, was elegant and poised but seemed "distant, aloof, and preoccupied." Dian Fossey was in town, too, and she came to dinner several times, clearly as star-struck as Galdikas. There is a moment during one of these evenings when Leakey, Jane, Dian, and Birute are visiting over drinks and Leakey notices Dian has finished hers. Over Fossey's embarrassed protests, Birute goes to the kitchen to get her a refill, and there in the kitchen is Hugo, alone, "with a moody expression on his face and a drink in his hand."

By the time Galdikas recorded all of this in her 1995 book *Reflections on Eden*, she had seen her own first marriage deteriorate under pressures not unlike those that were eroding Jane's.

With the arrival of Stanford students, beginning in 1972, Gombe became a small village. Counting African staff and their families, British and American students, more than a hundred people were supporting a study of fifty-four chimpanzees and the resident troops of baboons. Jane was a full-time administrator now. Her "urgent file" seemed never to get smaller.

The difficulties were real and had been from the beginning. As early as 1968, for example, there were conflicts between researchers who'd come to study chimpanzees and others who were there observing the lakeside troop of baboons. A chimpanzee researcher might come to the dinner table elated at having gotten to watch "his" chimp catch and kill a baboon baby, blithely unaware that the baby in question was little Huxley, beloved of the fellow scientist to his right.

Jane was determined that the Gombe Center would reflect a radically collaborative approach to scientific research—and to that end she brought everyone together regularly to air personal grudges and grievances and look for solutions. The evenings would be genuinely convivial. All were encouraged to share what they'd seen that day, and if they felt like putting it into verse, that was all the better. Goodall herself did so at least once. There were skits, music, parties, and even a weekly film. Hers was a distinctly "tend and befriend" approach to joint scientific research.

All was well. Quite magnificently well.

Except that it wasn't. Even as she wrote this glowing description of Gombe itself, seismic waves were rippling through her personal life.

A few months earlier, in March 1973, Jane had traveled to the capital of Tanzania, Dar es Salaam, to meet with government officials. The government had been delaying clearances on American and European students coming in to study, and in a broader sense it was timely to enter a closer working relationship with the Tanzanian government. The visit was a great success. Jane was invited to become a visiting professor at the University of Dar es Salaam, and the new director of parks, Derek Bryceson, was sure he could do something about the clearances.

Jane describes her visit in a happy, longish letter to Vanne.

"Here I am at the Kilimanjaro [Hotel], and funnily enough, Hugo and Grub are in Nairobi." Between meetings, which have been very fruitful so far, she is working on the book on wild dogs that she's co-authoring with Hugo. She's had dinner with Derek and others. There was lunch the next day at Derek's ("glorious") home by the sea—where she met his wife also, who was laid low by injuries to her arms and by hepatitis. After lunch there was another meeting with Derek and others, and it was punctuated by a comic interlude involving a couple of drunks. By that evening, together again, or still, the two of them are regaling a friend with the story and finding it even funnier in retrospect.

"We were quite weak with laughter."[38]

She continues with the same letter the next morning. The ocean view out the hotel window is marvelous; she describes it in detail, and as if talking to herself writes, "I should do some more of the dog book now. But I don't think I shall. Somehow I don't feel like it."

Vanne would not have had to draw heavily on her gifts as a psychic to guess what was happening.

Derek Bryceson was twelve years older than Jane. Born in China, schooled in England, he'd been an RAF pilot in World War II. Shot

---

[38] Ibid., 229.

down by enemy fire, his legs had been so badly injured he'd been told he wouldn't walk again. In fact, he did learn to walk—"with a stick," as Goodall puts it, "and will power." He'd studied agricultural science at Cambridge and came to Kenya to farm. Just three years later he met Julius Nyerere, then a leader in the movement for Tanganyikan independence. The two became close friends, and eventually Bryceson moved to Dar es Salaam, where he was the only white member of Prime Minister Nyerere's first cabinet. He was elected and repeatedly reelected to the young nation's parliament, for a long while "the only freely elected white person in post-Colonial Africa." His love for Africa matched Jane's own, and as Tanzania's director of parks, he was in a position to be immensely helpful to Gombe. In *Reason for Hope* she would speak of his strong and forceful character, his wonderful sense of humor, and add that "he was honest to the point of brutality."[39]

(Over time, Goodall was able, ruefully, to see a pattern in her choice of partners. She remarks in *Jane's Journey* that both her husbands had been jealous and possessive; it's impossible to imagine that she could be leading the life she does today, and loves, if she were still married.)

Toward the end of May, there is another letter, this one to longtime supporters of Gombe. The director of parks has just visited Gombe, such a VIP, Jane explains, that she had felt she should go meet him at Kigoma herself and escort him back. She'd had a stretcher ready to carry him up to "top camp," but he insisted on walking. "He is a marvelous man," and happily enough, more chimps appeared that day than had been sighted for the past five months.

In August another letter home has Derek at Gombe now, lecturing the students on Tanzania and its people, and helping Jane organize the program she has set up to train Tanzanians to do field work. "He has great wisdom, and all the students love him, and so do the staff." Jane is looking forward to taking Grub to Dar es Salaam "for my lecture at the University." (Of course, Jane. Why ever else, Jane?) In a postscript to the same letter, Jane and Grub are in Dar es Salaam, where Grub is having a fabulous time playing in the tide pools, ecstatic that he's not having to look over his shoulder for predatory baboons or chimpanzees.

A week later, another letter, this one to Bryceson himself. The letter survives, though it says in part that she trusts he will destroy it, or bring it to Gombe, where they can destroy it together, because, "there

---

[39] *Reason for Hope*, 97.

is always a risk." He is "Derek, beloved" now, to whom she writes, "You know—it is easier to think things than to carry them out."

And yet, months pass—it is February of the next year—before she can write to her mother and say that she and Hugo have talked. That he had come to Gombe and asked if she would come away with him. "We covered everything & decided, quite calmly, how it wasn't any good."[40] Hugo has said that he needed someone on safari with him, and Grub, fully in the picture, has suggested that since his mother "couldn't look after things properly," he thought it would be a good idea if his father got another wife. She and Jane could, in effect, spell one another. Grub had grown up among Tanzanian fishermen, who often did, in fact, have several wives. His only immediate concern was whether Hugo would still be welcome at Bournemouth, which indeed he would be.

Jane and Hugo were divorced that summer. Derek obtained his divorce later that year, and he and Jane were married in February 1975.

The decision to end her first marriage had not come swiftly or easily. Had she not met Bryceson, things might have hobbled along the way they were for several more years. She appears to have hoped that Hugo, too, might have found somebody else—that would have made everything so much easier. Even so, she might have continued to "waffle," as she put it, if something hadn't happened to vanquish her inertia. In January 1974, she flew with Bryceson and Grub to a camp where Tanzanian rangers were being trained to help with the research at Gombe. There was a crash landing from which, miraculously, everyone walked away unhurt.

"You know," she wrote Vanne, "you suddenly realize that it could happen (death, I mean) at any moment. So [you do] what is best to do with the life entrusted to you."[41]

For several months after their marriage, Jane and Derek commuted every few weeks between Gombe and Dar es Salaam. Grub's birthday party in March was spectacular: a scavenger hunt and sack races, apple pie, chocolate cake, new fishing gear, and a huge box of Legos. Derek has brought some Tanzanian whiskey along. ("It was super over the cake!") At Gombe, a mongoose comes to call regularly now, and a civet, and a genet. Jane has a bad bout of malaria around the first of April, so Derek takes her to Dar es Salaam to recover by the sea, where they adopt a new dog. Grub, meanwhile, is "very perky" and applying himself well to his schoolwork.

---

[40] *Beyond Innocence*, 241.
[41] Ibid., 240.

But the peace of Gombe was shattered forever late on the night of May 19, 1975, and the research center itself was changed forever. From Zaire, across Lake Tanganyika, came a band of forty men, followers of Laurent Kabila (he would be president, later, of the Democratic Republic of Congo), who kidnapped four American students and held them for ransom over the next two and a half months.

The situation was impossibly complex. The official position of both the Tanzanian and the United States government was that no one should negotiate with the kidnappers. But Dave Hamburg, with whom Jane had set up the Gombe-Stanford liaison, flew out and determined along with the families of the students that the only way to guarantee their safety would be to pay the kidnappers. As a Tanzanian government official, Derek's hands were tied, and over the ensuing months resentment built against both him and Jane for their perceived inertia. One of the parents took out a loan, and at last the students were released—first one, then two more, and finally, late in July, the fourth.

Gombe was cleared of all Americans and Europeans the day after the kidnapping, and for the next couple of years Jane herself would only be able to visit the research center by special permission and for short spells. Fortunately, the Tanzanian field staff she'd been training were able to step into the breach; the ongoing observations were only interrupted for a day. She traveled to Stanford as usual that fall but was told by several people once she got there that it would be better if she left "until things die down." Hurt and angry, she dug in instead, sought out her detractors, and confronted them, one by one. Vanne came to lend support, bringing Grub along with her, and so did Derek. By the time the quarter was over, she believed she had laid most of the rumors to rest, but her relationship with Stanford was over.

In fact, no American foundations were willing to support the Gombe research now, in part because American students couldn't come to Gombe, but also because there was no longer a senior scientist in residence. It was in this context that the Jane Goodall Institute was set up by friends and benefactors who wanted to release Goodall once and for all from dependence on outside grants. The money would come from private contributions and from the revenues of Goodall's own lecture tours.

If the work at Gombe were to continue, Goodall's life was going to be every bit as peripatetic in the future as it had been so far, and that undoubtedly affected the decision she made now about Grub and his education.

Grub's schooling had been spotty all along—a patchwork of correspondence courses and tutoring, a brief spell at an elementary school on the Stanford campus, and quite a lot of parental handwringing. Jane had always hated the blithe manner in which the British overseas packed their children off to go to school "back home," but clearly she could not continue her own work, with all the travel it required, and provide Grub with anything like the quiet, child-centered stability she'd experienced herself as a child. By the fall of 1976, Grub was nine and old enough to go to England for school. Vanne was delighted to have him come stay at Birches. Jane would join him for Christmas and Easter, and he would come back to Africa for the summers. He loved Birches; he would be happy there. But the separation was all that Jane could bear.

"*I ACHE for Grub!*" she wrote to her mother, and to Grub, "*I keep looking for you.*"[42]

The mid-1970s were relentlessly difficult for Jane. With regard to her marriage, her parenting, and the tremendous responsibility of creating and sustaining the Gombe research center, she was virtually pummeled. On top of everything else, some of her most fundamental assumptions about her beloved chimpanzees were overturned.

Goodall's research into the social and emotional life of chimpanzees had been shaped from the very beginning by an experience she has described over and over. She had broken the ice with David Greybeard not long before, and she was following him for some hours on this particular day when after a while he stopped near a stream, sat down, and gazed back at her. "Serenely self-assured," he didn't appear to mind her presence at all. She saw a ripe red fruit from an oil nut palm and offered it to him on the palm of her hand. He glanced at her and took the fruit, but dropped it and took her hand instead and held it for just a few seconds. He didn't want the fruit, but "he knew I meant well."

David Greybeard was a particularly winning character, but over her first ten years at Gombe, Goodall's impressions of the social and emotional lives of chimpanzees kept confirming the glimpses he'd given her of beings that were in certain crucial ways "nicer" than human beings.

Across the mid-1970s, however, Goodall was forced to come to terms with dark new revelations about her beloved chimps: they were capable of infanticide and cannibalism; and they made war as well as love.

The empathic tenderness of a David Greybeard was real, and it belonged in the official record. But room had to be made as well

---

[42] Ibid., 180.

for the ruthless bloodlust of Passion and her daughter, Pom, who between them murdered and ate at least three infants and quite likely five others; and whole chapters had to be given over to the episodes of inter-communal violence that escalated steadily through the early 1970s, culminating in what could only be called war—a war that was fought unto the death, by 1977, of everyone who was on the "other" side. No less remarkable than the war itself was the question of how, in just a couple of years, an extended family had split and become "us" and "those others."

To the known repertoire of gestures and facial expressions by which chimpanzees communicate love, lust, fear, grief, anger, joy, and sheer goofiness, a new one was added that signals a degree of ostracism so severe it constitutes a death warrant.

As early as 1971, observers had noted that the chimpanzees were consistently approaching the banana-feeding station now in two sub-groups. One came in from the south, the other from the north. One contingent appeared to have broken away and laid exclusive claim to the southern end of the territory they had all shared. The southern subgroup, called Kahama after the valley it mostly inhabited, was smaller, but it was headed by two powerful males who, between them, could intimidate the alpha male of the northern Kasakela subgroup.

Gradually, through 1973, researchers watched tensions mount. Males from each of the two subgroups were observed patrolling the territory where their respective ranges overlapped. In January 1974, six adult Kasakela males came upon a young Kahama male, Godi, who was by himself. They attacked him brutally, undoubtedly killing him.

Over the next three years four more of these attacks were witnessed, and at last, late in 1977, it was clear that the Kahama community had been annihilated.

Chimpanzees fight one another, Goodall notes, and wound one another, all the time, particularly "during the frenzy of a charging display." But they rarely inflict serious injuries. In these encounters limbs were twisted, strips of skin torn off, and blood drunk with cupped hands from a victim's wounds—behavior that's ordinarily only seen when a chimpanzee is trying to kill a large prey animal *of another species.*

And that was the baffling issue. The Kasakela chimps weren't just brutalizing members of their own species; they were killing friends, and probably cousins, with whom they had hunted and played and slept. What mechanism—what quirk in the brain—was powerful enough to override the inhibitions that would normally prevent such behavior?

The answer, says Goodall, is that the Kasakela chimps had done what human beings do all the time. They had "pseudo-speciated"—though Goodall herself prefers the phrase "cultural speciation."

On the face of things, the phenomenon that psychologist Erik Erikson was the first to call "pseudo-speciation" seems benign enough. It is the transmission of individually acquired behavior from one generation to the next, forming what we think of as cultures.

Haven't the best things in life arisen out of the formation of new cultures? Unfortunately, Erikson notes, pseudo-speciation is also the basis of radical "othering," allowing us in effect to dehumanize one another on the basis of cultural differences. And it doesn't take generations to accomplish this; we can do it in no time at all and do it with simple, eloquent gestures.

Chimpanzees, it turns out, do much the same thing. They "de-chimp-ize," to use Goodall's term. In November 1975, between a group of Kasakela males encountered a female who was from another community and who had an infant. The Gombe war was well under way, and the mood of all the males was martial and highly agitated.

Surrounded by the Kasakela chimpanzees, and cut off from her own group, the female was seized and stamped on hard. After a while she approached a couple of the Kasakela males, extending her hand in the way chimps do who are declaring their submission. They ignored her, and she tried to leave, but they cut her off. Half an hour later, she approached one of the senior Kasakela chimps in the same conciliatory manner, actually touching his leg.

Like a brahmin priest appalled by the effrontery of an untouchable who'd brushed against him in the street, he pulled back from her touch, grabbed a handful of leaves, and *scrubbed* himself where she had touched him, exactly as he'd have done—for chimpanzees are remarkably fastidious—if he had accidentally fouled himself. Had they been children on a playground, his meaning would have been crystal clear: Don't get your cooties on me! By scrubbing himself so vigorously, he was telling her unequivocally that there was nothing she could do to change his mind, she was "the other," and he owed her nothing.

Immediately after this, three males attacked her savagely. She escaped, finally, bleeding heavily, but meanwhile her infant had been captured. One of the males seized it and ran through the trees, "smashing the infant against the branches and trees as he ran."

Pondering the mysterious dynamics of pseudo-speciation, Goodall speculates that by the very act of withdrawing from the larger community and claiming exclusive rights to a piece of the territory they'd previously shared with the Kasakela chimps, the Kahama males might have unwittingly forfeited the right to be treated as kin and sealed their own doom. In effect, it was *they* who had pseudo-speciated! In retrospect, she admits that it was painful for her to take in this new information. But because the evidence was indisputable and overwhelming, she accepted it. As a responsible scientist, she felt she had to.

Remarkably, though, many of her colleagues felt differently.

Goodall's report on the darker side of chimpanzee nature had emerged at an awkward moment, in that the whole issue of human aggression had become intensely politicized. Anthropologist Richard Dawkin's popular book *The Selfish Gene* had come out in 1976, arguing that virtually all animal behavior, human beings included, can be traced to the organism's drive to perpetuate its own DNA. For males of nearly all species, he argued, aggression is therefore "adaptive." Even earlier, in 1972, anthropologist Colin Turnbull had shocked readers of his widely loved book on the Mbuti Pygmies, *The Forest People,* with a devastating portrait of Uganda's Ik, the Mountain People. In *The Forest People* Turnbull described a subsistence people whose relatively nonviolent culture grows out of a longstanding, reverent knowledge of their environment. The Ik, on the other hand, a tribe of hunters who had lived in a no-less-timeless, intimate connection with their mountainous region, had been displaced from their tribal lands shortly before Turnbull arrived to study them, and within only a few years their culture had disintegrated to the point of nonexistence. The Ik lived in stunning depravity, and Turnbull concluded from the experience that culture is far more fragile than we assume and far more dependent on external circumstances. We can nurture all we like, but nature abides, and nature is red in tooth and claw. (Interestingly, Turnbull was himself a deeply religious man—a follower of the Indian woman saint Anandamayi Ma when he first came to Africa. He would end his years a vowed Buddhist monk.)

So polarized was the debate over nature and nurture, and so heated, that Goodall's findings on chimpanzee aggression elicited extreme responses. Scientists who should have known better were claiming that violence and aggression are learned behaviors found only among human beings. One colleague urged her not to publish her findings because they would be used by "irresponsible scientists and writers" to argue that human aggression is inborn, and war, therefore, inevitable.

The debate over the relative importance of nature and nurture goes on full strength today. Goodall is obviously someone who believes in the efficacy of nurture, but she also believes that if the human being's capacity for cruelty is rooted in our pre-human past, we need to know that. If we pretend otherwise, we risk being blindsided by the truth, as indeed we have been, over and over and over again. She is not pessimistic, but she refuses to wear blinders.

There is, of course, a wonderful irony in the fact that Goodall was now under heavy fire for displaying the very scientific objectivity that her research methods were all along supposed to lack. One hardly wonders that she raised no strenuous objection around this same time to the creation of the Jane Goodall Institute. Some have criticized her for allowing her own name to be attached to it, but considering what was going on at the time it seems quite understandable. She would go her own way, and for good reasons.

In the rocky aftermath of the kidnappings, Derek Bryceson proved an indispensable friend to Gombe. Without his intervention, Goodall believes, the research center would probably have closed down altogether. Their marriage was inordinately happy; they were wonderfully well suited to one another, and not least because of the commitment they shared to Africa itself—the wildlife, the land, and the people.

But in May 1980, Bryceson fell ill, and in June he was diagnosed with incurable cancer. By October, he was dead.

Goodall was devastated—stunned, in fact, and bitterly angry. She'd grown up believing there was nothing she couldn't do if she wanted it badly enough and worked hard enough, and up to this point that had proven true. She'd also grown up believing that mind can override matter. She had tracked down every promising alternative cure known, and still the cancer had killed her beloved partner in exactly the time frame his doctors had said it would. She said later that she had no regrets, because those last months had been far more bearable for the fact that they had clung to hope. But when in his final days Derek looked at her and said to her that he simply hadn't imagined that such pain was possible, one senses that something in her simply broke and stayed broken for a considerable stretch of time.

That Christmas, Goodall's mother, Vanne, would undergo emergency surgery to replace a valve in her heart. Jane was in England at the time to see Grub, but at first she couldn't bring herself to visit her mother in the hospital. She wrote to her explaining that while she'd been thinking about Vanne, her recent experience with "cut open people" had been so terrible that she feared her mother might absorb her residual "bad feelings" and have a setback. A woman whose name is almost synonymous with courage had been brought very low indeed.

Following Derek's death, Jane visited Gombe a number of times: in February 1981, again in May, and then for a longer period that summer with Grub. With each visit she was able to draw more deeply on the place itself (the chimps were not very much in evidence) to assuage her grief.

In a chapter in *Reason for Hope* that she calls "Healing," Goodall describes a day she spent at Gombe sometime in May 1981, which she regards as a kind of spiritual watershed. (I suspect that she is off by one year, and I'll explain why in a moment.) She woke early on this particular day, had a banana and a cup of coffee, and headed by herself up the steep slopes behind her house. Within minutes she heard rustlings and was able to follow Flo's daughter, Fifi, and Fifi's offspring—Freud, Frodo, and Fanni—for the rest of the day. She'd brought her notebook, pencil, and binoculars, but she wasn't really there to observe. She needed their company. The follow was delightful, and she felt unusually attuned to the chimps. It began to rain with gathering force, and the temperature dropped swiftly. "Soon, turned in on myself, I lost all track of time. I and the chimpanzees formed a unit of silent, patient, and uncomplaining endurance."[43]

The weather shifted, and the sun came out. In the distance, lightning still flickered against a storm-dark indigo sky, raindrops glistened like jewels on cobwebs, the chimpanzees wet brown-black coats gleamed next to the brilliant green new leaves. In the breathtaking beauty that now surrounded her on every side, Jane experienced for just a moment that suspension of *self* and that awareness of truth and unspeakable beauty that mystics of all traditions have struggled to articulate. An "outsight," she calls it—in which for just an instant she knew "timelessness and quiet ecstasy."

Thinking later that evening about what had happened to her in the forest, Goodall was certain that the experience would remain with her always, " a source of strength on which I could draw when life seemed harsh or cruel or desperate."[44] That night she was too wound up to sleep, and as she lay there, realizing that she was at the mercy of "circling thoughts," she tried to still them. Suddenly, a string of vivid pictures came before her mind's eye of loved ones who had died: her grandmother, uncle, and aunt; beloved dogs; Flo, whose body she had found years earlier in a streambed; and finally, Derek. She wept and wept and wept, but when she woke she knew that she could cope with her grief now, because the Gombe forest had given her "the peace that passeth understanding."

---

[43] *Reason for Hope*, 172.
[44] Ibid., 173.

Goodall has not kept journals; her letters are the only record of her life. Occasionally, therefore, when she's writing without the letters at hand she misremembers a date, and I suspect this is one of those times. I doubt whether this episode occurred in 1981, because a letter included in *Beyond Innocence* describes her May 1981 visit to Gombe as "lousy" in terms of seeing chimps. She notes that she hasn't seen Fifi at all. In June 1982, on the other hand, a year later, she would write to Vanne about a particularly wonderful visit to Gombe, "absolutely perfect for following," which was so clearly a landmark in her recovery from grief that one wonders whether the particularly grand "follow" described above, and its quietly momentous aftermath, didn't take place during the same visit. She makes no reference in this letter to a mystical experience, but she does refer to a kind of awakening that is very much of a piece with the "outsight" she describes above.

June in West Africa is usually hot and humid, but in 1982 it was bright and sunny, with cool winds. Goodall was alone, and as she climbed the hills and relaxed into the familiar rhythms, she was surprised to realize that, "in a strange way I felt free as I have not felt free since Hugo arrived to film in 1963."[45]

How could this be? Well, at first, she remembers, "there was him," meaning Hugo himself, and then, of course, Grub, and the demands of writing and administration, and the necessity of training others to do the observing. Bryceson had loved the chimps, but she hadn't felt right following them when he was alive because he couldn't climb along with her. "I felt really guilty if I stayed out too long, when poor Derek was virtually a prisoner in the camp." Derek had by this time been dead nearly two years, but one suspects that until this very moment she'd been too grief-stricken to feel what she felt now, and quite suddenly "there was the incredible sense of freedom—wandering about and feeling 23 again."

How she had poured herself out—to family, to friends, to students and colleagues, to the Tanzanian staff she had worked so hard to train—and how devastating had been the losses. And yet it seemed that at the core of herself, she was oddly none the worse for wear.

She was free, and she was once again in touch with the ardent young pilgrim she'd been, stripped down for the journey, beholden to nobody.

We talk in the West about pivotal moments and turning points, but I wonder whether, once again, ancient India doesn't have a perspective on these things that can help us grasp more accurately what

---

[45] *Beyond Innocence*, 283.

actually happened to Jane Goodall in the summer of 1982. Traditional Hindus believe that life falls into four distinct stages or *ashramas*. We are students first, and answerable to our elders: teachers, parents, and spiritual mentors. These are the years when we absorb the basic precepts of our religious tradition even as we are learning a trade or a profession. As householders we try never to forget the vision of things we'd absorbed as young people, but we can expect to be almost consumed by family and professional obligations. This is the second stage. The third stage comes when our children are grown and we have discharged most of our responsibilities to family and community. We hand the business over to our children, we step back somewhat, but we draw energetically on everything we have learned and accumulated to serve and benefit others. At the very least, we help with the grandchildren. The fourth and final stage involves a more complete withdrawal so that we can focus once again, and uninter-ruptedly, on the great teachings of our spiritual legacy. For some, this stage might involve long pilgrimages or even relocation to a spiritu-ally charged city like Benares, home of Sri Krishna. (Assisi anyone? Chartres? Jerusalem?)

The real value of this model may be that it challenges our assump-tions about "the best years," when we are most fully engaged with work and family, and hints at the possibility that *if* we've laid the right kind of foundation, the last years really can be the best. India conveys this possibility in stories, like this one about a spiritual aspirant—celi-bate, as it happens—who thought himself impervious to the worldly attachments that encumber householders. The story is also a playful commentary on one of the most elusive concepts in the Indian spiri-tual tradition, *maya*, defined sometimes as the illusion of separateness and sometimes, too, as the wrongheaded notion that we can ever find happiness anywhere but in firsthand knowledge of the self within:

> Narada was a devoted disciple of Sri Krishna, and the two of them were walking one day when Narada asked Krishna to explain what *maya* is. Krishna was happy to oblige. "But you know," he said, "it's terribly hot. Let me sit here in the shade, and perhaps you wouldn't mind running on ahead into the village and getting me a drink of water."
>
> Narada is eager to oblige, he runs ahead, and as he runs he becomes almost unbearably thirsty. Dizzy with exertion and parched, he arrives at the village and knocks on the first door he sees. A beautiful young woman answers, and he is overcome with her loveliness. He hears himself stammer: "Will you marry me?"

The astrological charts are consulted and the pair are deemed a perfect match. They marry, and soon there are children, and Narada and his wife work from sunrise to sunset meeting their needs. In what seems no time at all, there are grandchildren, and a cluster of cottages to house them all.

What a happy life—what a full life! But then one night a tremendous storm rises. The wind levels the trees and all the crops in the field, and rain comes down in sheets, and the river overflows its banks. The cottages are swept away, the horses, the cows—and all of the children and grandchildren disappear, and so does Narada's beloved wife.

Devastated, Narada cries out "Krishna! Krishna! What am I to do? I cannot bear this grief!"

And close at hand, he hears a soft admonishing voice: "Narada, Narada! Where is my glass of water!"[46]

The story itself is, of course, Krishna's answer to Narada's question about *maya*—instruction and comeuppance in the same breath. Since nothing in the visible world is stable, worldly satisfactions cannot possibly make us permanently happy. Yet look at how easily every last one of us can be persuaded otherwise, including vowed renunciates like Narada himself. That's the power of *maya*, and indeed, says India, the word is cognate with magic.

It feels almost cruel, this cherished little tale, but it isn't saying anything the great teachers haven't always told us: *Everything passes; God alone is changeless.* All the loveliest things we experience are as ephemeral as if they were a dream.

Jane Goodall's work had never been merely a career to her at all. Her study of chimpanzees was as objective and clear eyed as it could have been, but it was always embedded as well in a larger, lifelong quest for meaning, truth, and connection. The practical realities of that life had absorbed her so completely for a time that she barely looked up. But even as she was raising Grub and observing the chimps and running the research center, she had been preparing herself, without knowing it, to move beyond that circle of intimate daily connection and resume a calling that was at its core religious.

"Jane! Jane! Where is that glass of water?"

---

[46] Traditional Indian story, adapted from Eknath Easwaran's recounting in *The Bhagavad Gita for Daily Living*, vol. 2 (Petaluma, CA: Nilgiri Press, 1979), 78–80.

While some of us collapse in times of grief and loss, others find their salvation in work. Goodall, who is a phenomenally hard worker, is clearly among those for whom the difficult is tonic. As it happened, an appropriately all-consuming piece of work was close at hand.

For two decades data had been piling up at Gombe, and it would have been gathered in vain if someone didn't pull it together into a book. Goodall was, of course, that someone. Living alone now at Derek's home by the sea at Dar es Salaam, her solitude punctuated by Grub's visits on holidays, she began work on a book she initially called *The Monograph,* probably because she couldn't bear to admit to herself, at the outset, what a huge undertaking it was actually going to be. Completed, it would run to more than 650 pages, and its abundance of maps, charts, graphs, tables, photographs, footnotes, and bibliography made it a nightmare to produce. It couldn't have helped that her typewriter was a beat-up old manual model and that, because Tanzania's economy was in a state of ongoing collapse, the only available paper was a particularly flimsy blue tissue. Even as she was assembling the record of twenty years' observation, she was also having to bring herself up to speed on the relevant science: new findings on the influence of hormones on aggression, for example, and current socio-biological theory.

One is often tempted to read Jane Goodall's life story as a heroic journey, and this is certainly one of those junctures. Repeated blows have brought her very low indeed. She is Odysseus fetched up on the shore of Ithaca, alone, broken, naked to the elements. She has always had this almost superhuman capacity for work, and now she deploys it entirely on the book but indirectly, too, on rebuilding herself toward whatever life has in store for her next.

"As thy days, so shall thy strength be" (Deut 33:25).

In October 1983, she exults in a letter to a friend that she has effectively "broken the back" of the book. In 1984, she writes friends that she has *finished* it. But that was only wishful thinking. At last, in 1986, her copy arrived and she held it and wrote to her publishers: "I gaze & gaze at the finished product. The dream that I believed would come true one day—that kept me going through the worst times."[47] Published by Harvard University Press to glowing reviews, *The Chimpanzees of Gombe* received the R. R. Hawkins Award for the Most Outstanding Technological, Scientific, or Medical Book of 1986.

---

[47] *Beyond Innocence,* 268.

Jane Goodall's worldwide popularity has very little to do with *The Chimpanzees of Gombe*. Had she never completed it, she would still be loved and respected on every continent. But its publication proved once and for all to her most distinguished colleagues that the whimsical spinner of tales was a dedicated, uncompromising scientist as well

The Chimpanzees of Gombe: Patterns of Behavior is magisterial, a seamless join of objective analysis and empirical, empathic observation. The book is massive, but it is organized so well, indexed so clearly, and punctuated by so many intriguing photographs and "word pictures" that it is actually quite accessible. The Gombe chimpanzees are, of course, the focal point, but they are not examined in a vacuum. At every salient point Goodall compares them with other chimps, observed both in the wild and in captivity. "The result? A whole that is even more fascinating, even more complex, than the sum of its parts."[48]

From this emerging composite picture, Goodall maintains, we see the full extent to which groups of chimpanzees, like groups of human beings, develop distinct cultures—coded gestures and facial expressions, for instance, and idiosyncratic ways of using tools—and pass these cultures on to their offspring, not genetically, but through the osmosis of daily life, pseudo-speciation in its benign aspect.

The Chimpanzees of Gombe is in a certain sense my favorite of Goodall's books. Freed for once from having to worry about the sensibilities of a general audience, she writes far less self-consciously than in her more popular books. If you really don't want to know all of the circumstances under which chimpanzees wipe their own bottoms and one another's with crumpled leaves, or learn about the rare occasions on which they have been seen eating their own dung, you may prefer to skip these sections. They're clearly marked. But don't expect her to exclude them, because from a field biologist's point of view these matters are of the essence!

And in fact, what a shame it would be to pass over the book's extensive treatment of the subject of bottom-wiping and thus never learn about the conscientious Melissa, one of Gombe's most effective mothers. Chimpanzees are, as a rule, quite fastidious in their dealings with excrement, using leaves, as mentioned above, to wipe themselves and one another clean. But Melissa went the extra mile. She had twins, and whenever either one of them defecated, she gave both bottoms a thorough once-over.

---

[48] *Chimpanzees of Gombe*, 591.

To celebrate the publication of Goodall's *magnum opus*, the Chicago Academy of Sciences hosted a four-day conference for "chimp people" from all over the world. The event would prove a crucial turning point for Goodall, not merely because it left her with a new understanding of her own authority as a scientist, but also because it thrust her directly into the next ferociously challenging engagement of her life.

Among the assembled experts, many of whom had never met, an alarming consensus had emerged almost at once: whether they were living in the wild or in captivity, chimpanzees were faring very badly indeed. The natural habitats of wild chimps were vanishing, and they were being hunted, either for meat or for the live captive trade. And the care of captive chimpanzees, whether they were living in zoos and labs, or as pets or "entertainers," was in many cases poor to deplorable and in some instances, diabolically cruel.

By her own admission, Goodall had been completely focused until now on the Gombe chimps. But from this point on, her relationship to them shifts. She sees, for example, that their days are probably numbered, for even within conservation-minded Tanzania, Gombe had become an island, surrounded on its three landward sides by desert.

When she left for the Chicago conference, Jane Goodall was a scientist who was eager to begin work on the second volume of her study of chimpanzees in the wild, a book that would focus on mother-infant relations, on child and adolescent development, and the structure(s) of chimpanzee families. But by the time the conference was over, she had committed herself to working full time on behalf of chimpanzees—not only the particular animals she had studied and grown to love, but all chimpanzees.

She calls it her "road to Damascus moment." Empathy had driven her investigation of chimpanzees all along. The more she knew about them, the more deeply she felt their distress as if it were her own, or Grub's, or Vanne's. There was no way in the world that she could turn away. So it was that the second phase of her life, defined primarily by personal and professional responsibilities, gave way now to a third. The passionate and far-reaching environmental activism that would characterize this third period arose directly out of her scientific expertise, but it would also require the substantial emotional and spiritual strengths she had acquired since she first arrived at Gombe.

Gandhi and other spiritual activists have attested to the swiftness with which a plan of action can open out before the individual who is prepared to act, and that certainly happened for Goodall. Right after the Chicago conference Goodall came to Bournemouth to spend Christmas with her family, and while she was there she received a videotape prepared by a group of animal rights activists who had, in Peterson's tactful phrase, "secretly eased themselves" into a biomedical research laboratory maintained by a company called SEMA, Inc., in Maryland, where hundreds of monkeys and chimpanzees were being kept for studies—in particular, for the experimental testing of vaccines. The images were devastating, but particularly so to anyone who was acquainted with chimps living in the wild.

Anguished at what the videotape revealed, Goodall sent copies to colleagues and anyone else she thought could be roused to act. She asked permission to visit herself, and SEMA officials agreed, believing, apparently, that their laboratories had been badly misrepresented. Goodall's friend and colleague Roger Fouts came along, because she wanted the eyes of someone who knew more about captive chimps than she did. They assumed that changes would have been made to counteract the videotape's damning impression—that the chimps would be in bigger cages, for example, and be given a few toys, or that they might be housed in pairs for company.

Eerily enough, though, the facility was exactly as the videotape had recorded. Squirrel monkeys were running in circles, other monkeys were banging their heads against the bars of their cages. "There were the pairs of infant chimpanzees, crammed into cages twenty-two inches by twenty-two inches, waiting to be separated, infected with HIV, and boxed in isolettes. There were the juvenile chimps, thirty-two of them, each one sealed in a stainless steel isolette that was twenty-six inches wide by thirty-two inches deep by forty inches high."[49]

There followed a meeting during which Goodall talked with all the tact she could muster about how chimpanzees live in the wild and proposed modest changes that would make their confinement more bearable. All of her suggestions were rebuffed, and she and Fouts left the facility wondering why they'd even been invited inside. They sat together in the backseat of a car driven by the National Institutes of Health official who had brought them there and who now said, casually, that he was sure Dr. Goodall would have no problem now writing a letter stating that the lab was up to USDA regulations. Fouts figures that the fellow couldn't see Jane in his rearview mirror—that if he had he'd have seen the tears rolling down her cheeks. She pulled herself together and answered him clearly and unequivocally: "By no means will I write you any such letter."[50]

---

[49] Fouts, *Next of Kin*, 317.
[50] Ibid., 320.

Instead, she wrote a searing article for the *New York Times Maga-zine* in which she described the SEMA chimpanzees as "prisoners of science" serving life sentences for crimes they'd never committed and under conditions "worse than those we accord to even the most evil human criminals," and she revealed that in the United States alone nearly two thousand chimpanzees were being held in this manner.

Even as Goodall was engaged with Roger Fouts and others in a struggle to get the National Institutes of Health to adopt and enforce even minimally humane standards for the treatment of chimpanzees used for scientific research, she had begun to work just as hard on behalf of chimps in the wild. At the end of the Chicago conference, thirty world experts on chimpanzees had formed an organization—the Committee for the Conservation and Care of Chimpanzees. The Jane Goodall Institute would fund its work, and Goodall would work closely with its members.

Worldwide, the greatest single threat to endangered species is loss of habitat. In Africa, nothing imperils wild chimpanzees more directly than the present rapid expansion of human populations into previously forested areas. The long-term prospects were grim. But that was surely all the more reason for identifying as soon as possible the areas it would be most important to preserve. African governments needed to develop conservation plans, and they would need international support to honor them. And it would be crucial that the United States government in particular be persuaded to give chimpanzees the protection as an endangered species that the Convention on International Trade in Endangered Species, or CITES, had already declared appropriate.

Committed to "conservation and captive welfare," Goodall would travel all over Africa now, taking her exhibit around African countries to encourage preservation of their habitats. When she discovered along the way how many chimps had been captured and mistreated, she began to visit existing sanctuaries and helped set up more. The affection she had once lavished on the Gombe chimps was extended now to all chimps, everywhere.

For more than four years, while she completed *The Chimpanzees of Gombe,* Jane Goodall had been relatively isolated at Dar es Salaam. Now she would be drawn into an ongoing cyclone of lectures, conferences, meetings, solicitations, fundraising galas, lobbying, arm twisting, and back scratching, which for all practical purposes continues today.

Her reference to Saint Paul's conversion on the road to Damascus is not isolated. She began to think of her work more and more now as a quasi-religious vocation. More than a year after the tour of the SEMA facility, she met her first adult chimpanzee in captivity. Jojo lived at the New York University's Laboratory for Experimental Medicine and Surgery in Primates—LEMSIP—in a cage that was five feet in length and width and seven feet high. The cage was hung from the ceiling, to make removal of feces easier, in a room without windows. JoJo had nothing in his cage but an old tire to sit on. His misery was so apparent, and his gentleness, that Goodall extended her rubber-gloved hand toward him. Immediately, he began to groom first the ridges of her fingernails and then, peeling back the glove, her wrist. When he saw that she was weeping, he reached out and touched her cheek, then sniffed his fingertips, looked at her again and continued to groom her wrist with audible "lipsmacking."

"I think Saint Francis stood beside us," she recalls, "and he too was weeping."[51]

Saint Francis wouldn't have stopped with weeping, and she didn't either. Goodall has never asked for a moratorium on the use of animals in biomedical research. She argues, rather, that we should be looking for alternatives and that, in the meantime, our gratitude should dictate that we treat laboratory animals humanely—with an informed understanding, that is, of how they live in the wild. When an NIH official said that the improvements she was asking for laboratory primates were too expensive (bigger cages, comfortable bedding, compassionate caregivers), she responded with the same white-hot indignation Saint Francis would have: "Look at your car. Look at your house. Look at your office, look at your administration building, look at the holidays you take."[52]

Look . . . and then try to convince yourself—let alone Jane Goodall—that you've done everything you reasonably could for captive animals that are entirely at your mercy. Her words carried all the weight they needed to, because her own life is simple to the point of austerity and entirely open for scrutiny. If there is a gene for materialism, she never got it.

Jane Goodall lives in a precarious equipoise, her constitutional optimism only just holding its own against what she knows about today's growing global environmental crisis. It is *because* of her growing sense of the nearly impossible scale of the challenges she and other envi-

---

[51] *Reason for Hope*, 217.
[52] Montgomery, *Walking with the Great Apes*, 208.

ronmental activists are up against that she is more and more inclined now to see her work as a religious calling. She writes in *Reason for Hope* that the most economically privileged human beings live in a "soft protective cocoon" of material well-being, and that nothing can reverse the present global environmental crisis if we can't figure out how to live outside that cocoon. One way to do this, she points out, would be for people to develop interior lives that are strong enough and nourishing enough to take the place of *all* ordinary comforts, which, she reminds us, is exactly what the saints and masters of the past did. They figured out how to tap into "the Spiritual Power we call God, or Allah, the Tao, Brahma, the Creator." They *lived* on this energy, she writes, and "breathed it into their lungs so that it ran in the blood, giving them strength."[53] Only, of course, she is describing herself, for she has certainly stepped way out of what constitutes the comfort zone of most human beings and, in the process, tapped into resources she hadn't imagined she possessed.

"We will have to evolve," she decides, and her tone is deceptively light and playful, "all of us, from ordinary, everyday human beings— into saints! . . . or at least mini-saints."[54]

Goodall believes that she has heard the voice of God, though she is quick to add that this isn't such a big deal, because the voice of God is nothing more than the "still, small voice" we call conscience. The real issue isn't the hearing the voice, but the willingness to heed it. When we do that, she believes, we take our evolution into our own hands.

Gombe itself is chief among the deep personal attachments that no longer fetter Goodall. Frodo, who grew up to be the one rogue male, was one factor. "He really has it in for me," she wrote in a 1992 letter. In his youth Frodo had dazzled observers, and sometimes set them running, with his skill at throwing good-sized rocks, and he only got better and more determined with time. In a letter written a couple of years later, she speaks of having had a fabulous visit to Gombe and not having seen Frodo once: "Of course I was heartbroken!"

This is all, of course, utterly casual. Frodo couldn't really spoil Gombe for her—nobody could. But she seems able now to experience in a number of different places the intense connection with the natural world that had been centered in Gombe. Asked today how she staves off exhaustion during her travels, she speaks of carefully planned "timeouts" that give her the spiritual sustenance she needs: a week spent with the Achua people in the dense Amazon rainforest,

---

[53] *Reason for Hope*, 199.
[54] Ibid., 200.

or a morning on the banks of the Platte River in Nebraska during the annual migration of the Sand Hill cranes, when the joyous cacophony of their calls to one another overwhelms and obliterates every other sound.

I think, too, that her attachment to Gombe and the Gombe chimps has to some extent given way over time to a deepening reliance on her human friends, for she has hundreds now, all over the world. She thoroughly enjoys seeing them and hearing from them, and as she moves into an increasingly activist mode, she relies on them as allies.

There is a particular moment, in fact, well before the Chicago conference, that marks a kind of epiphany, when she looks out across her new life and seems to see its bright possibilities for the first time. She is writing her family from a slow-moving, very nearly snowbound train in Switzerland, and her spirits are high. She is on her way back to Dar es Salaam by way of Zurich, where she's hoping to connect with her Harvard University Press editor, who's coming out to work through the final changes on *Chimpanzees of Gombe*. She's just spoken at a symposium on "auto-organization," and the lecture had been packed. She keeps interrupting herself to describe what she sees out the window. "We have now come to a complete stand-still in the middle of a cloud!" She's been invited to speak in Paris, Amsterdam, Spain, Basel, and Bern, and meanwhile she is nibbling on a fine chocolate from the box her hostess has sent along with big pieces of cake and apples.

"I am so well looked after."[55]

Another year would pass before she took up the cause of chimpanzees, but she was clearly beginning to realize already what kind of support she could count upon if she were to adopt the more activist stance that many of her colleagues had already taken up. Through her publications and appearances, and her tireless correspondence, she had called into being a vast web of caring individuals. They would be the most important resource the embattled animals had. Her modus operandi would continue to be exactly what it had always been—connect, and then work the connection. Six years later she would undertake an even grander project, and she would build it up in the same way.

For significant numbers of people to evolve into environmental "mini-saints," there needed to be a way for them to start early. This realization was the germ of Roots and Shoots, the environmental education program for youth that Goodall founded in Tanzania in 1991. Its members range in age from kindergarten through college, and they are encouraged to extend their care in three directions: to

---

[55] *Beyond Innocence*, 301.

the human community, to animals, and to the environment. Goodall believes that the three are so deeply intertwined that no problem can be solved within a single context. Today there are Roots and Shoots groups in 120 countries around the world. The success of the organization has everything to do with Goodall's genius for connecting, the "tend and befriend" vision of things she'd first tried to implement at Gombe in the early 1970s.

The foundational idea of Roots and Shoots is the principle that knowledge leads to compassion, which in turn inspires action, and that, of course, is exactly what had happened in Goodall's own experience. Because she has been so effective at winning allies, her ability to effect change is vastly disproportionate to the small, slender woman she actually is.

"Roots creep quietly," she loves to say, "everywhere, underground, making a firm foundation; shoots seem so new and fragile, but to reach the light they can move boulders, break concrete."[56]

Coming back, then, to the conundrum that gripped an eleven-year-old Valerie Jane Goodall: "How *could* people treat others so horribly?"

By the mid-1970s, as we've seen, she had a big and decidedly un-palatable piece of an answer. The Gombe wars, along with the chilling cannibalism of Passion and Pom, left little doubt that the ability to pseudo-speciate as a prelude to aggression is very much a part of our pre-human legacy.

But what can we do about it?

Has an in-group ever formed that did not at the same time create an out-group? Have people who lived next door to a vibrant, productive culture *ever* been able to look on and say, "Well, how nice for them, let's make one of our own," without deciding they'd have to annex the oil, coal, rubber plantations, fertile acreage, forests, or water rights of the other to do it?

Even as richness and diversity emerge, so, it seems, does a sense of difference that is keen enough to create anxiety and, even worse, abandonment issues, grievances on the perimeter, and a cycle of violence that perpetuates itself without end. This is true particularly when territory and resources are contested, as they almost invariably are.

For Goodall, though, recognizing the strong link between the formation of cultures, on the one hand, and the eruption of intergroup violence, on the other, doesn't mean that wanton aggression and war

---

[56] Ibid., 385.

are inevitable. We've inherited all *kinds* of abilities and impulses from our pre-human past, and in the meantime, she points out, we've developed these enormous brains as well. Intelligence is a wonderful thing; we can apply it to this as to any other problem.

We can apply it, in the first place, to the way we think about one another and teach our children and students to think about one another.

I've mentioned the intense delight with which Goodall recalls the discoveries she made during her first year at Gombe and how effectively they had *blurred the line* between human beings and chimpanzees. Blurring certain lines is one of her favorite strategies against "othering."

From her earliest conscious moments Goodall has seen continuities and connections where others insisted on seeing discontinuities and disconnections. She has determined over time that this way of looking at things is not merely emotionally and spiritually sustaining, it is phenomenally informative as well. "To the loving eye," Sara Ruddick, argues, "the lovable will be revealed,"[57] and one can just as aptly paraphrase: To the eye that marvels, the marvelous will be revealed.

Goodall came to see, over time, that the lines so many of her colleagues had been determined to draw and reinforce between chimps and humans weren't merely for the sake of classification at all. They'd become both pretext and rationale for keeping the whole animal kingdom at a critical distance from human beings and *beneath* them. If you could persuade yourself that chimpanzees don't have emotional lives similar to our own, it didn't matter very much how you treated them—easy to persuade yourself, as some have, that primates are legitimately seen as the servants of science.

Insofar as those lines were also both rehearsal and pretext for drawing similar lines *between* human groups, they have been phenomenally destructive. Identifying a class or group of people as animals or subhuman is almost invariably the first step toward subjugating and even annihilating them. Upon the lines that cultural speciation draws, walls are built and topped with broken glass.

But possession of these enormous brains of ours, Goodall reminds us, the one real edge we have over chimps, means that we can learn. So if we can be made to understand that chimpanzees aren't as far removed as we've pretended—that they are more like cousins than strangers—we will be more likely to treat them with compassion.

---

[57] Ruddick, *Maternal Thinking*, 119–20.

Goodall's partiality for blurred lines is of a piece with the way she experiences the natural world and its denizens, but there is nothing at all blurry about the scientific underpinnings of her cosmology. Her friend and colleague Roger Fouts offers a succinct description of the way contemporary scientists have come to view evolution. "Evolution is not a ladder of 'improvement' culminating in the human species. It is an ongoing process of adaptation for millions of related species, each on its own evolutionary pathway."[58]

This is a profound change in orientation whose implications are still being teased out. From a pinpoint, radiating out in every direction, life appears to explode out into nothingness, wriggling out into the most unlikely and yes, *extreme* niches we could imagine—deserts and glaciers, rocky escarpments, the floor of the sea. And wherever it goes, it takes form, and quickens: as cacti and lizards, walruses and waterfowl, hammerhead sharks and butterflies. As leopards, and chimpanzees and, of course, human beings, who, it turns out, share something like 98.7 percent of their DNA with chimpanzees and on the basis of that 1.3 percent difference presume to decide who will live in Manhattan, who will live on the Serengeti Plain, and who will be confined alone in small metal cages in experimental laboratories.

To imagine evolution in these terms—as inexhaustible life force exploding in every direction at once, adapting in every conceivable manner to every imaginable environment—is to render ridiculous the notion that any species is inherently superior to another or even radically apart from others. There are, rather, niches of all kinds, and there are life forms that have adapted in such a way as to inhabit them. To hold their own in the African rainforest, chimpanzees have never needed the much larger brain or vocal apparatus of the human being. If they had, they would probably have developed them by much the same long process human beings did.

Roger Fouts has realized that as a result of his many years working with chimpanzees, he finds himself disinclined to use the phrase *human beings* except in the context of "canine beings," "reptilian beings," and so on.[59] We are all in this "being" business together. Goodall herself describes the joy she took as a little girl in experiencing what she calls the "being-ness" of trees. Her own favorite, Beech, was as much a presence and refuge for her as the giant redwood Luna would be to Julia Butterfly Hill.

---

[58] Fouts, *Next of Kin*, 198.
[59] Ibid., 325.

If we take this orientation as seriously as Goodall appears to—if we see "being-ness" itself as the common denominator among all living things, and no less the miraculous for that fact—we must replace that "ladder of improvement" with another image: the "emanations" imagined by Neoplatonists, perhaps. Or maybe the sages of ancient India got it right when they argued that God did not, in fact, create the visible universe, God *became* the universe. Brother Sun, Sister Moon . . . we are all made of the same basic stuff, and the stuff is divine.

Certain of Jane Goodall's most deeply held religious views are coming to be substantiated by emerging scientific understanding. She leans more and more nowadays toward thinking that something very like religious conversion could be the only way things get straightened out. She isn't abandoning her commitment to science at all, or scientific principles, but she is on the lookout for laws that go still deeper.

For instance, the tendency to react aggressively to the unfamiliar "other" appears to be so very deeply threaded into our evolutionary background that human beings often find themselves acting on it quite without premeditation—unconsciously, and almost before they know they've acted. But what if we were able to become so profoundly *conscious*—so continuously wide awake—that unconscious impulses could no longer drive us? This is, of course, exactly what the great mystics are said to have done—the saints and "mini-saints" Goodall cites in *Reason for Hope*.

Jane Goodall is one of the most admired women of our time and probably the second-best-known scientist (Albert Einstein being first, and, interestingly, as comfortable with mystical perspectives as she). But she has never declared herself to be a feminist. I asked her biographer, Dale Peterson, what he thought about this, and he replied that he thinks of Goodall as "a natural feminist . . . tough, independent, who's always gone her own way." Peterson surmises that she has never identified herself as a feminist "because it's never occurred to her that she was doing anything different from what her family—matriarchal, as I note in the letters—taught her was possible and appropriate."[60]

A *natural* feminist, one is to understand, as opposed to a *nurtured* feminist, who may have been radicalized by life itself and/or a persuasive women's studies professor. It's not a distinction that will warm the hearts of many feminists, natural or nurtured, but there's a little

---

[60] Personal communication with Peterson.

history here, and before we rush to judgment, we need to know about it. There are two episodes in particular.

First, there were apparently several occasions during the early 1970s when Goodall was desperately juggling her multiple responsibilities as wife, mother, writer, researcher, and administrator, and women guests at Gombe remarked how fortunate she was to be able to combine her professional work and her parenting so easily. This rankled terribly, because Goodall felt that she had, in fact, made hard choices on Grub's behalf. She had given up the day-long follows that had been her heart's joy. Mornings were given over to administrative work, writing, and so on, but she spent every afternoon with her own small primate.

Goodall believed that, from what she could see, feminists were playing fast and loose with respect to the mother-child connection, which her work with the chimpanzees had convinced her was absolutely crucial to the emotional well-being and full development of the infant. She was particularly offput by feminist enthusiasm for universal child care. "I never, ever, *ever* put my career before my child," she told a *New York Times* reporter.[61] In fact, it has to be said, she did have excellent caretakers for Grub each morning and, later on, tutors whom she chose from among the Stanford students who'd come to study chimps. And when things got really problematic later, she was able to send him home to the incomparably supportive Vanne. (Let's hear it for the "granny advantage.")

Her work on chimpanzee aggression also brought her into indirect conflict with feminism, because it couldn't easily be squared with the theory that gender differences are primarily social constructs and therefore relatively amenable to change. Goodall didn't, to my knowledge, engage directly with these critics. She probably felt it would be a bit beneath her; after all, she had demonstrated beyond any doubt the marked differences between male and female chimpanzee behavior, and it was just ridiculous to pretend the research was irrelevant to understanding human behavior. On the other hand, the fact that she had documented the primate male's drive to dominate females and one another, and the female primate's preoccupation with children, hardly meant she advocated patriarchal familial structures.

The Chimpanzees of Gombe was written ten years after the Gombe wars and the ensuing controversy. Her initial anguish long gone, she notes coolly now that the whole catastrophe probably happened

---

[61] In Montgomery, *Walking with the Great Apes*, 38.

because there were four too many males: "It's hard for a dominant hierarchy to work with more than ten males."

Given that she could have begun this most important book of her scientific career in any way she'd wanted to, it is important, I think, to ask why she leads off with the "word picture" she does. The incident she describes is one she has written about often, but never in exactly this way. It's pure Gombe, but I strongly suspect it also refers obliquely to another occasion when she stumbled unaware into a territory patrolled by aggressive and hyper-vigilant males.

She had been at the Preserve for about eight months and hadn't been able to get within 100 meters of the chimps without frightening them away. On this particular day a morning of torrential rains had dwindled to a steady drizzle. Moving quietly along a forest path, Goodall suddenly realized she was within thirty feet of a chimpanzee who was hunkered down in the motionless "wake me when it's over" posture that Goodall herself would learn to strike during heavy rains. She hadn't seen him, and he certainly hadn't seen her. She went very still, and in the next few minutes became aware that she was surrounded by several chimpanzees, at least one of which was a large adult male in the tree above her.

"Above me the male uttered the eerie alarm call of the chimpanzee—a long, wailing *wraaaa*. He shook the vegetation more vigorously and I was showered with raindrops and falling twigs and leaves."[62]

She stayed low, kept her eyes down, acted as if she didn't notice them, and picked leaves and stems that she pretended to chew. Meanwhile the level of threat rose steadily. The end of a branch hit her head, and a male actually charged her, veering off at the last minute. "My instincts urged me to get up and leave; my scientific interest, my pride, and an intuitive feeling that the whole intimidating performance was merely bluff, kept me where I was."

In a few minutes the chimpanzees retreated into the forest. Over the next few months she had to endure several of these *faux* attacks, but at last the hazing stopped. The "white-skinned upright ape" had proven docile enough to be tolerated at increasingly close range. Looking back, she is understandably proud that she did not panic. Her intuition had proved correct. The hazing was real, it was inevitable, and at the same time, it was mostly bluff. These were just male chimps being male chimps, protecting the territory where the females and infants lived. Neither fight nor flight, Goodall's carefully crafted response had gotten her access to the social world of chimpanzees.

---

[62] Ibid., 1.

Whatever the story says about the courage it took for her to stand her ground when the chimps attacked, I've wondered whether it doesn't say just as much about Goodall's experience with the scientific establishment, beginning with her difficult days at Cambridge University as a young female "outsider-insider," but continuing even into the more recent past. Naturalist Sy Montgomery notes that Goodall doesn't like to talk about her early conflicts at Cambridge, because "things really have changed now." (That's partly code for the fact that she and her methodology won the day. She is a gracious victor.) Her adviser, Robert Hinde, who had pressed her to rely on numbers, not narrative, is a close friend now and an adviser to the Jane Goodall Institute. But in her 1991 book, *Walking with the Great Apes*, Montgomery draws a distinctly harsher picture of the opposition Goodall contended with than we get in Goodall's own writings, and she draws on interviews with Goodall herself to do it. She describes reminding Goodall that when Dian Fossey went to Cambridge to write *her* thesis she was told that Jane's thesis was considered the perfect example of what not to do. Montgomery got a distinct rise: "I didn't give two hoots for what they thought," Jane said, in a tone of voice that seemed just a little sharper and just a little louder. "They were wrong, and I was right. . . . And as I didn't care about the Ph.D., it didn't matter. I would listen, I just wouldn't do what they said. Then I would go back to what I was doing at Gombe."[63]

One could tell the story without reference to gender, and talk about different scientific methodologies, but as Goodall says, she was definitely "the wrong sex." Gender *was* part of the problem. She was dismissed in some quarters as "the blond bimbo," and one of Birute Galdikas's *female* professors at UCLA maintained that the only reason Goodall was so famous was that she had great legs that showed to advantage in short shorts. She mentioned this to Goodall years later, and Goodall said: "I don't let that sort of thing bother me. I just don't listen anymore."[64]

Goodall doesn't frame her objections to the then-prevailing view of science in terms of gender but rather in terms of a kind of arid, arrogant professionalism and obsession with mastery. "First of all, it's wonderful to be a scientist. Secondly, if you become a scientist, you become one of the elite, you wear a white coat, you're ranked with God, and what you say will be believed. Thirdly, if you're going to be

---

[63] In Montgomery, *Walking with the Great Apes*, 106.
[64] Ibid., 105.

a scientist you've got to be very objective; you mustn't get emotionally involved about those things."[65]

As an outsider-insider who has transformed her field, Goodall is in a position not unlike that of the women mystics in whose spiritual mother-line I've placed her. A close look at the stories of women like saints Teresa of Avila and Clare of Assisi, Mechthild of Magdeburg, and others reveals that they almost certainly could not have achieved what they did—managing, that is, not only to *have* their spiritual experiences but to write and speak about them with impunity—if they had not had the support of astute, appreciative, and well-placed males *and* if they hadn't taken scrupulous care to work *around* male church authorities. Jane Goodall's story, unfolding at the particular time it did, is no different, and I strongly suspect that the word picture with which she introduces her major scientific contribution to her field is a playful way of acknowledging this.

Stay low, gaze at the ground, pretend to be picking leaves and stems . . . and cultivate the David Greybeards at every opportunity.

The Chimpanzees of Gombe concludes with a dramatically different word picture. This one points toward a second volume she had intended to write that would have focused on the mother-child relationship among chimpanzees. It's a brief, lyrical description of a twilight scene in which little Getty dances up and down a tree before bedtime between the nests of his mother and his grandmother, apparently indecisive up to the last moment of light as to where he's going to settle in. It radiates tenderness, intimacy, and utter trust. The atmosphere couldn't be more different from that of the very first word picture with all of its swagger and incipient violence. Yet, by the time you've gotten to this point, you know that what "the boys" are doing out there on the perimeter is protecting the females and babies. It's their job.

Goodall is a devoted grandmother to Grub's three children. "The eldest is really very good with animals—he might follow in my footsteps. The little girl, she is much too beautiful for her own good. The youngest, he is a crazy little thug, filled with life." But she never lingers long at the strictly personal. She segues immediately to her abiding passion: "When I look at these little grandchildren and I think how we have harmed the planet since I was that age, I mean, it just makes me feel dreadful, desperate."[66]

---

[65] Ibid., 112.
[66] "Dame Jane Goodall: Lady and the Chimps," *The Telegraph,* December 16, 2008.

If that second volume ever appears, someone else will have to have written it, because Goodall's conservationist work is full time now, and then some. One regrets that she's had to set that work aside, because she has always been especially attuned to the relationships between mother and child chimpanzees.

The so-called granny advantage was identified in human cultures too recently to have found its way into Goodall's descriptions of chimpanzee family life, but her sensitivity to the value of strong mother-lines seems to have alerted her all along to something very like it among chimps. The granny advantage emerged soon after anthropologists began asking themselves why it is that, unlike other female mammals, women outlive their own reproductive years by a considerable period of time. What evolutionary advantage might there be in the survival of postmenopausal females? Some of the first clues emerged with the study of the Hadza, right there in Tanzania, and were augmented by studies of the skeletons of Australopithecus, found in the same general region.

It turns out (and yes, it does seem obvious once it's been stated) that maternal grandmothers who are still active but are not tied up with their own offspring provide supplementary food and/or babysitting services to their daughters and grandchildren. The granny advantage has been confirmed now in a number of different populations, including inner-city housing projects, and the findings keep pointing to the same scenario: When *maternal* grandmothers are in the household, their sons and daughters will have children sooner and more often, and their grandchildren are more likely to survive to adulthood.

I bring this up because I think it has bearing on the theme of mother-lines and also on Jane Goodall's somewhat complicated relationship to the women's movement. Because (think about it) if a woman could actually be in two places at once—at home with the kids *and* holding her own in the workplace—how much of a women's movement would we have needed? The granny advantage makes something very close to that possible, and Jane Goodall's story is living proof.

I don't believe that Goodall could very easily tell you where the line fell between her commitment to motherhood and the work she did as a scientist, and later, her environmental and peace activism. I strongly suspect that if pressed she would see that as another line well in need of "blurring," just as does Sara Ruddick.

Like the rest of us, Goodall has done the best she could all along, responding to the several and various claims on her heart. She has said repeatedly that she would have left her research in Africa to be with Grub in England had she not had the option of sending him to her mother. Considering that leaving Africa would also have meant leaving the love of her life, as well as her work, that would have been a devastating choice to make, and we are glad for her that, unlike a great many women under similar circumstances, she didn't have to make it.

What Jane Goodall had in her mother, and her mother's mother, was nothing more or less than what contemporary feminism wants for *all* women and girls: solid, reliable, loving backup. No merely political movement can achieve that. Over and over throughout Jane's life Vanne would step in and support her daughter's extraordinary trajectory. She, too, saw that Jane's commitment to Gombe was much, much more than just a career. Gombe—the place, the chimps, the research center, the young people who came and studied there—Gombe *as a whole*, with everything it meant—had a claim on Jane that was as strong as if it were another child. Vanne understood her vision and, it appears, shared it. And from what one gathers watching the movie *Jane's Journey*, Jane's younger sister, Judy, appears to have picked up right where Vanne left off.

Sara Ruddick's reflections on "maternal practice" and how it converges with the kind of religiousness that in turn inspires a politics of peace are very much to the point.

Dale Peterson's description of Jane as a "natural feminist" makes a deep, lovely kind of sense when we look back across her story and recognize that her stature, independence, and authority can be traced back to two sources that haven't always received the emphasis they could in feminist discourse. One is the mother-line—women connecting with younger and older women to whom they may or may not be connected "by blood," and supporting one another in the things they dream and undertake as scientists, artists, intellectuals, mothers, teachers, healers, and seers. One thinks of Julian of Norwich, describing her revelations and mentioning from time to time, as they unfold, that her mother was there beside her. The second under-reported wellspring of strength and authority for women may be the simple ability to "be thine own home and in thyself dwell"—the capacity, which can be fostered from earliest childhood, to be one's own best friend.[67]

In short, an interior life.

I've described the four-stage model of human existence outlined in India's earliest scriptures and suggested that it might still have a certain validity. The third stage is transitional; as you withdraw from

---

[67] From John Donne, "To Sir Henry Wotton."

the maelstrom of the householder years, you are able to engage more and more in selfless service and even resume spiritual practices that you may have cherished as a student and had to set aside during the childrearing and professional years. We've seen Jane Goodall's life opening out in just this manner from about the time of the Chicago conference in 1986.

The fourth stage is called in Sanskrit *sannyasin*, from a verb that means "to renounce," and it represents a more or less complete delinking from ordinary life. Meditation, pilgrimage, repetition of a holy name, and study of the scriptures take precedence now, and some will even leave their home and family altogether and move to the Himalayas or one of the great temple towns. This stage, too, is transitional; the individual becomes more and more absorbed in her religious ideals, and less and less *invested* in this world until the final change that, ideally, will be almost painless, the body falling away like wornout garments. And right up to that point there is a kind of gradual thinning out—we have one foot in this world, one in the next, and this one feels a little less real every day.

But there is a slightly different approach to the fourth stage that may be more in keeping with the dire state of today's world. Detachment from the personal is still in the picture, along with a growing conviction that all of life is one interconnected whole. Only the individual doesn't necessarily engage in religious practices in the ordinary sense.

Today, Jane Goodall grasps the interconnectedness of things so deeply that she can't help but be drawn into every urgent cause you could imagine: reduction of nuclear weapons, women's initiatives in developing countries, low-frequency sonar testing in the oceans by the US Navy, and more. The result is that she really does seem sometimes to be everywhere at once. Because she is so well known, she can accomplish more now with less active involvement than ever before in her life, effecting quiet but far-reaching changes in the world that are out of all proportion to what she actually has to get up every morning and *do*, though of course she continues to do a great deal. Around the time of her seventieth birthday she said over and over, "I certainly couldn't have done what I'm doing now when I was thirty. No way. I wouldn't have had the energy."

At this point her simple presence in a situation creates what economists call a multiplier effect, in part because she is such a magnet for likeminded souls. All she has to do is show up, embodying hope in spite of the odds. It doesn't hurt at all that her burning commitment to human and animal welfare is coupled with tremendous personal warmth and an indestructible gift for fun.

It may be that the difference between these two versions of the fourth stage amounts to no more than the difference between most people's ideas about God and Gandhi's, who said he never had visions but was sure he was looking into the eyes of God whenever he was in the presence of India's poor and disempowered. For people like Gandhi, or Goodall, God is not so much "up there," or "out there," or even "in there"; God is right in front of us, rather, in the unique "being-ness" of another creature. A child, a homeless war veteran, or, in Jane Goodall's case, a chimpanzee. Her love of the Gombe chimps was the hook, and once she'd swallowed it, she would be drawn into waters that have only gotten broader and deeper with time.

Tenzin Palmo

"Like a Wild Swan"

The Shambhala Meditation Center is on the sixth floor of a multi-use building on Manhattan's Lower West Side. The meditation hall is a large, high-ceilinged room that looks as if it had been a factory in some previous incarnation. The walls are white, and long yellow drapes cover the windows behind the dais. There is an altar at one end with representations of several Tibetan deities.

The room was full. Probably a hundred people were present, and I would guess the median age was forty, though there were much younger people and some quite a bit older. Most of us sat on the floor, on high, firm, red cushions. Everyone was chanting, and I assumed they were chanting in Tibetan until I looked at the handouts someone had left by each cushion and realized that no, the prayer was in English: the charged staccato rhythm only made the words *sound* foreign.

> I supplicate you, the Kagyu gurus. I hold your lineage
> Grant your blessings so that I will follow your example. . . .
> Devotion is the head of meditation, as is taught.
> The guru opens the gate to the treasure of oral instructions. To the meditator who continually supplicates him
> Grant your blessings so that genuine devotion is born in me.[1]

---

[1] The Mahamudra Lineage Supplication, or Dorje Chang Thungma, is used in Karma Kagyu centers at the start of a practice session. It is usually recited in Tibetan, but here is an English version by the Nalanda Translation Committee. (Tibetan-style chanting uses equal stress on each syllable.)

The venerable Tenzin Palmo came in now, wearing a gold sleeveless blouse and burgundy robes, and sat on a chair in front of the windows. She is thin, but she doesn't look at all fragile. Her eyes are a remarkably pale blue and ever so slightly hooded. Her face is serene and kindly, yet remote at the same time. I'd been told she'd been ill over the past couple of years, and I think I might have guessed as much, though I might have been reacting to the fact that her head was shaved. She looked to me rather like I imagine an aging Saint Clare of Assisi must have looked or, because she is every bit as English as Jane Goodall, Dame Julian of Norwich.

Only maybe Dame Julian as played by Vanessa Redgrave.

Had she not looked so very serious as she seated herself, the room probably wouldn't have exploded into laughter the way it did when her demeanor changed abruptly a couple of minutes later. The man who was introducing her was going on at some length about her having been one of the five first Westerners to have been ordained as Tibetan Buddhist religious, and he'd explained further that while one of the five had given back his robes and become a householder—this being Robert Thurman, distinguished professor of Buddhist Studies at Columbia University, and father of actress Uma Thurman—all three of the others, all of them women, had since died. Indeed, he said, pausing for effect, one of them, a Scottish debutante, had perished in a Himalayan avalanche.

Tenzin Palmo had been gazing almost blankly at a point high on the far wall, in the way speakers sometimes do when they're enduring their own introductions, but at the mention of the untimely end of the Scottish debutante and the implicit suggestion that the Himalayas may not want there to *be* Western Buddhists, or at least Western female Buddhists, her head swiveled around and her blue eyes opened wide in comic alarm. I doubt that the poor guy had meant to characterize her as a kind of latter day Ancient Mariner, but there it was. Vanessa Redgrave gave way to Buster Keaton, mugging now and playing shamelessly for laughs as she raised her bare, slender arms in a stylized victory gesture. Animated as a street mime, and just as silently, she'd managed to derail the formalities completely.

We had all relaxed now, and we were very much in her hands, so that when she grew silent again and sat very still, so did the rest of us, and the silence lasted longer by a full minute than one expected it to. Tacitly, she was inviting us to bring ourselves more fully into the moment, but she was also asking herself who we *were* and what kind of presentation would serve us best.

She would speak, she said at last, about the use of daily life for practice.

"Of course," she said, smiling slightly, "my daily life is very different from yours."

When Tenzin Palmo agrees to be interviewed these days, it's often with a caveat: "Please, let's not talk about the cave." To the extent she is known in this country, it is as "the British woman who became a Tibetan Buddhist nun and spent twelve years in a Himalayan cave." The twelve years in question ended, though, in 1988. Today, she would so much rather talk about the nunnery she's established in India for young girls from the Himalayan border regions of Tibet and India. Or the evolution of Buddhism in the West, and the growing prominence of women therein. Or even the weather!

But chances are she will continue having to field questions about her cave retreat for years to come, because the very thought of such an undertaking, particularly by someone from the West, and a woman, all but forces certain questions about traditional disciplines and contemporary seekers that barely arise when a friend pops off for a weekend or even a week-long retreat at a Zen center in upstate New York or Northern California.

We are fully prepared to recognize the therapeutic benefits of meditation. We can see how meditation might help a blocked artist jump start her creative processes or revive a burned-out political activist. Meditation as an adjunct to ordinary life, and an enhancement, yes. But Tenzin Palmo's twelve-year retreat in a Himalayan cave puts questions we raised almost playfully at the beginning of this book in a very different light. If we're going to ask ourselves what Teresa of Avila would be doing if she were alive today, we have to reckon with the possibility that she'd cut off her hair all over again, don full-length robes as blithely as she did the first time, and hole up incommunicado for years on end. In a cave? In a hole in the ground, if she thought she'd become more "recollected" there.

Teresa became a nun in order to withdraw her attention completely from the external world and redirect it inward, and so did Tenzin Palmo. When we try to imagine her sitting alone through long winters in her tiny, snowbound cave, the most helpful point of reference might actually *be* the analogy Saint Teresa offered: the soul as a castle "made entirely out of a diamond or of very clear crystal, in which there are many rooms."[2] Seven rooms, in fact, in the last of which, located "in the extreme interior" of herself, Teresa experienced complete and

---

[2] Teresa of Avila, *Interior Castle*, in *Collected Works*, vol. 2 (Washington, DC: Institute of Carmelite Studies, 1980), 283.

unutterable freedom and forgetfulness of self. Of the soul of one who lives in this state, she said simply, "Its life is now Christ."[3] Not "Christ's," note, but "Christ."

Tenzin Palmo did not enter her long retreat, in other words, to prove anything to anybody, least of all herself, but as a necessary phase in a rigorous and highly structured exploration of consciousness that she believes will culminate in essentially the same state of consciousness Teresa's did, and the same capacity to serve all of life. The traditional disciplines she had undertaken had brought her to the point where she needed long, *long* stretches of time with absolutely no interruption, and the cave provided these. During the first nine years she came down each summer for a few weeks to see her teacher and replenish her supplies, but during the last three years she didn't come down at all, and she remembers this period as the happiest in her life; there was simply nowhere on earth she would rather have been.

In London's East End in June 1943, Tenzin Palmo was born Diane Perry. Introspective and sensitive, she couldn't walk around her neighborhood in London without seeing the devastation wrought by repeated *Luftwaffe* assaults. She was well aware of the extent of "man's inhumanity to man," but her personal struggle to *understand* human cruelty ended while she was still a teenager. She was just eighteen when she found in the teachings of the Compassionate Buddha an analysis of the human condition that was so complete and so lucid that certain kinds of question would never arise for her again. This doesn't mean she ceased to grieve at what she saw people doing to one another, or that she has ever really turned her back on it, only that it didn't baffle her any longer, and that she identified as the only truly effective antidote a course of action that looks to most people like *in*action.

The problem, Tenzin Palmo had come to see, is the ego, which she links explicitly with the phenomenon of "othering," or "pseudo-speciation."

When Buddhists talk about ego, they aren't talking about the sturdy sense of self that is by any reasonable measure a healthy thing. They are referring, rather, to what Tenzin Palmo calls "this tight little sense of solidity in the center of our being which is 'me,' and which therefore makes everything else into 'non-me.'"[4] Ego isn't so much a *thing*, then,

---

[3] Ibid., 435.

[4] Tenzin Palmo, *Reflection on a Mountain Lake: Teachings on Practical Buddhism* (Ithaca, NY: Snow Lion Publications, 2002), 115. Subsequent references to this book will be made in the form of parenthesized page numbers.

as a condition: a narrowness and a paralysis and a grievous limitation. It's the tiny keyhole through which we normally experience life. When with deepening meditation the entire door swings open, and the dazzling truth of "things as they really are" pours in, belief in the solidity of that "me" takes a real beating. But so, of course, does the idea of a "not me"—of "the other," whether defined by ethnicity, age, size, species, class, or gender.

Etty Hillesum, who died in Auschwitz just a few months after Diane Perry was born, had come to believe that we are in error when we try to pin the blame for war on people like Hitler. Each of us moves things along in that direction, she observed, every time we fail in love. Tenzin Palmo would agree, but she would add that while love, in the ordinary sense, is always prone to failure, the compassion that arises in the deepest stages of meditation is far more resilient.

It works like this. . . .

The first objective of the Buddhist meditator is to become detached from the thinking process itself. We may be instructed to follow our own breath: thoughts arise, but we just keep bringing attention back to the incoming and outgoing breath until gradually the habit of involuntary discursive thought is broken. Like a pond that has always been turgid, the mind is clear now for the first time, and we are, in the language of Christian mystics like Teresa, *recollected,* and therefore fully present to our own experience.

To become established in this state is to attain *shamata* or "calm abiding." Prolonged experience of *shamata* is said in turn to render the mind supple and fluid. As thinking slows way, way down in *shamata,* there begin to be gaps between thoughts, and through them a new kind of awareness begins to gleam out at us. For fleeting moments we see life as it actually is, undistorted by the activities of the mind. This is *vipashyana,* or "penetrating insight," which turns in time into a prolonged interrogation of the mind itself. A self that recognizes itself as standing somewhat apart from the mind begins to ask questions like, What is a thought? and, Who is the thinker? or, as Tenzin Palmo herself wonders, "Who is this *I* like a spider at the center of the web?" (44).

Under the force of this relentless inquiry, the layers of ego fall away, one after another—all of one's false identities—and we arrive at the level of consciousness called *shunyata:* "the unconditioned" or "emptiness." Beyond thoughts, words, and concepts, emptiness is the deepest core of oneself, but it is also, paradoxically, the level at which there *is* no separate "I."

Only when we've experienced emptiness, the sages tell us, can our innate compassion arise. Once we have looked long and hard into the depths of our own pain and confusion, the result of our persistent misreading of reality, we come to a profoundly liberating realization: the bad behavior of other people arises, we now understand, out of the same kind of confusion.

"Everyone," as Tenzin Palmo puts it, "is in the same predicament. That's why people are so awful! They are awful because they are suffering, because they are confused" (110).

Emptiness, interestingly enough, is regarded as feminine; its very capaciousness is womblike, and out of that womb arises compassion or "skillful means," and these are regarded as masculine.

Tenzin Palmo's commitment to her Buddhist practice is absolute, yet she does not maintain that everyone else should adopt it or that it is the only way to become fully awakened. She says that what Buddhists call the unconditioned, the unborn, and the deathless is simply "a level of consciousness which is not ego-bound," and all true religions try to get access to it. "You can call it anything you like. You can call it *atman*. You can call it *anatman*. You can call it God. . . . Some people experience it through service, others through devotion. Some even think they can experience it through analysis and intellectual discipline" (96). Note that she can't bring herself to say that analysis and intellectual discipline actually work, only that some people think it can!

I had read Vicki Mackenzie's fine biography of Tenzin Palmo, *The Cave in the Snow,* and I'd read *Reflections in a Mountain Lake,* a collection of Tenzin Palmo's lectures. I had wanted very much to meet her in person, but it didn't seem at all likely that I would—certainly not in time to interview her for this book. She lives in India, and while she had come to this country several times in the past, most recently in 2002, there'd been no indication that she'd be coming again soon. Her health had deteriorated quite badly in 2003. The keepers of her website had asked friends to pray for her, and while they had announced her recovery in the summer of 2004, they'd said nothing about imminent travel plans.

The Quakers have a phrase they apply like balm to the wound of a desire that doesn't look as if it's ever going to be realized. "Way will open," they'll tell you, meaning that if your heartfelt wish is in line with what the universe wants, things can shift around in the most unexpected manner and suddenly there you are, walking in the door. And indeed, just about the time I'd concluded nothing was going to budge, my good friend Will Keepin came through town. It was Will who'd told me about her in the first place. He'd only known her through the books when we'd first talked about her, but since then he'd met her in India, heard her talk, and come to feel the same way about her I did.

And he had good news.

Tenzin Palmo would be taking part in a Global Women's Gathering in upstate New York, and she would be giving three lectures afterward in Manhattan. Will was acquainted with the woman she would be staying with in New York City. Would I like him to see if he could arrange for me to meet her?

Her arrival in New York was barely two weeks away, and her schedule was packed, but Will's phone call was well received. E-mails whipped halfway around the globe and back again, and I was told within a day or two that she could see me the morning after her second lecture.

Way, I decided somewhere over the Colorado Rockies, had opened. I used my flight time to review the story of how a British woman just a little older than I am had found her way from London's East End to India, her teacher, and a minuscule cave in the Himalayas thirteen thousand feet above sea level.

One knows, of course, about Indian *sadhus* who spend their whole adult lives moving blithely about the upper reaches of the Himalayas in loin cloth and sandals, meditating in caves and stoking mysterious inner fires when their toenails start to turn blue. They've been doing this kind of thing for probably five thousand years. Westerners haven't, and Western women most certainly haven't.

My imagination was balking, but at the same time, I had to recognize that most women I know would agree that there is something deeply appealing about the idea of just . . . heading out. Way off, way alone, and for more than a long weekend. Women spend so much of our time responding to people around us, accommodating children, partners, and parents with needs that are continually changing and never shrinking. We don't fight, we don't flee—tending and befriending, we stick around.

So many of us sit up straight and listen when we hear about a woman who found herself a proper cave with a view, got her friends to help her fit it out and lay in supplies, gave them all cups of tea when they were finished, and then quietly closed the door on them just as the autumn wind was turning chilly.

Tenzin Palmo is candid about her early life, but not wildly forth-coming. Her reticence is in keeping with the monastic traditions of India and Tibet, where it is considered bad form even to ask a monk or nun where he was born or where she went to school. Pressed, they will say, "That was another lifetime," and they mean it. The point, after all, is to be living fully in the present.

Here in the United States, curiosity tends to get the better of courtesy: Who *were* you? we want to know. What were your parents like? Did you have boyfriends before you shaved your head? Did you work? Did you go to college? What did you *do* in the cave? Did you get lonely? Were you afraid?

She would far rather talk about stilling the mind and opening the heart than her own past, but she knows, too, that curiosity isn't the only reason people ask her about herself.

When she tells her story—briefly, as she has done sometimes for students at her meditation workshops, or more fully, as she did over a couple of years for Vicki Mackenzie—she lingers over the ways in which the circumstances of her early life pointed toward the path she would take. She is positive, for that matter, that choices she made in past lives shaped the context into which she was born. While this certainty grows directly out of a lifelong belief in reincarnation, it is also very much in line with the teachings of her specific religious path.

Vajrayana Buddhism, to which Tenzin Palmo adheres, holds that at the core of our being, each of us is already fully aware of the unity of life. When we take up a spiritual practice, it is because our indwelling Buddha nature is stirring into wakefulness and beginning to rebuild us, from the inside out. Tenzin Palmo's description of her own spiritual development reflects her understanding that this is how the process works: She came into the world already aware of certain things, and throughout her early years she was gradually waking up and remembering them—becoming, once again, who she'd always been.

Diane Perry—I'll continue to call her that for the moment—was born in a country house well outside of London, but only be-cause the city was under such heavy bombardment that the maternity wards had been evacuated. In the flurry of things, someone must have miscalculated her mother's due date, because while labor was induced, Diane was born without hair or fingernails or eyelashes, and through the first year, her very survival was touch and go.

Her father was a fishmonger, and the family lived in an apartment above his shop in Bethnal Green, a neighborhood that was devastated by aerial bombing. Her mother was a former maid who took over the running of her husband's shop when he died in 1945. George Perry was decades older than his wife. He'd been gassed in World War I and suffered from chronic lung disease. His daughter was just two when he died at fifty-seven. "I'm told he was a very kind man," she recalls. But she doesn't regret having grown up without a father. "I noticed that we didn't have any conflict or tension in our house, whereas there often was in my friends' houses."

Diane Perry was raised by a decidedly independent single mother. Lee Perry was lively and open to new ideas, and she was quite comfortable with paranormal phenomena. They had seances in the apartment every Wednesday evening, "with tables flying around the room and that sort of thing."

A snapshot of Diane as a sixteen-year-old bridesmaid is of a fair and very pretty child, fragile in appearance, eyes cast down, with a high forehead and a wide, gentle smile. She has never been robust. She had meningitis twice before she was a year old and had to be hospitalized both times. In addition, she had been born with her spine twisted inward and bent to one side, so that her whole spinal column was off balance, a particularly grievous affliction for someone who would meditate long hours each day. Her shoulders became rounded and hunched in compensation, and the overall misalignment caused severe and chronic pain that extensive physical therapy treatments did nothing to relieve. Later on, as a schoolgirl, she was stricken with a recurring and mysterious illness that caused high fevers and terrible headaches.

"Because of these very high fevers," she recalls (and there is something so extraordinarily matter of fact about her that when she says things like this you don't even blink), "I used to have a lot of out-of-body experiences." She would travel around the neighborhood, floating above everything, but, she adds touchingly, "because I was a little girl I wouldn't go far from home, I didn't want to get lost."[5]

And she did feel rather lost, or at least, displaced, a lot of the time. She remembers vividly having had the sensation that she didn't belong in England—that it wasn't really her home. She was instinctively drawn to all things Asian. Much later she would decide that she had spent past lifetimes in India or perhaps Tibet, and that she had probably only been born in England because she had to be to get Lee Perry for a mother. "She was a wonderful mother," she recalls: intuitive, generous, and magnificently supportive.

---

[5] Vicki Mackenzie, *Cave in the Snow* (New York: Bloomsbury Publishing, 1998), 11.

She felt confused, too, by the fact she was a girl. She remembers now hearing adults say that when you're a teenager your body changes and thinking, "Oh, good. Now I'll get back to being a boy again." Today she's glad she's got a female body. "I think we females have a lot of work to do for other females."[6]

There is a practice dear to Tibetan Buddhists called *tonglen*— "sending and taking"—that allows one to receive the pain and suffering of another and send back compassion. Like a tree breathing in carbon dioxide and breathing out oxygen, the practitioner learns to breathe in grief and breathe out compassion. *Tonglen*, Tenzin Palmo maintains, is not for beginners. It takes great skill to be able to receive negativity and then release it "into emptiness" in such a way that it doesn't lodge within you. Yet she is certain that her mother performed *tonglen* for her when she was a little girl. She was playing in the apartment when the nylon dress she was wearing caught fire and she was suddenly engulfed in flames. Lee beat out the flames, smeared antibiotic cream over the burns, swathed the child in blankets, and took her to the hospital where, despite extensive burns that took weeks to heal, Diane experienced no pain. Years later her mother confided that throughout the experience, she was praying that the pain be taken from her daughter and given to her. Diane was indeed spared, but so, her mother insisted, was she. She felt no pain.

Diane had lots of friends, but she rarely brought them home, preferring to spend her time reading, sketching, *thinking*. She doesn't recall that the idea of God ever meant much more to her than "a sort of superior Santa Claus." What she does remember is wanting to be perfect: "As a child I believed that we are all innately perfect, that our original nature was perfection, and that we are here to discover who we really are" (9).

Well and good, but how does one do that? She asked teachers, vicars, a priest, her Jewish sister-in-law, and she even asked the spirit guides who turned up at the Wednesday evening seances, but none of them had anything particularly useful to say.

Meanwhile, she was growing up. The delicate child with long blond curly hair and expressive blue eyes had become a pretty, ebullient teenager who loved nice clothes, stiletto heels, and dancing. There were lots of boyfriends, most of them Asian (Elvis Presley was the

---

[6] Bethany Saltman, "Endless Lifetimes, Endless Benefits," *Buddhadharma: The Practitioner's Quarterly* (Summer, 2005), 59.

only Western man to whom she recalls feeling attracted), yet she knew, without knowing why, that she didn't want to marry.

Doctors had told Lee Perry all along that her daughter would be too frail for strenuous employment. If the money had been there, she'd certainly have gone to a university and studied English literature and philosophy. But it wasn't, and library work was the obvious place for someone with her seemingly limited vigor, the pleasure she took in quiet and solitude, and her passion for books.

She was eighteen, and deeply immersed in the works of Sartre and Camus (not bad choices for an incipient Buddhist), when she ran across a book called *The Mind Unshaken,* which introduced her to the teachings known collectively as the First Turning of the Dharma Wheel. Halfway through the book she said to her mother, "I'm a Buddhist!" Lee answered to the effect that this was very nice, dear, and to please tell her all about it when she'd finished the book. Six months later, she too declared herself a Buddhist.

The First Turning teachings, which the Compassionate Buddha divulged at the Deer Park in Benares, are also known as the Four Noble Truths. They are the basis of Theravada Buddhism, which took root in Sri Lanka, Burma, Laos, and Thailand. *Theravada* means "the elder way," connoting its rejection of teachings that emerged later.

The Four Noble Truths are as follows:

- Suffering is the essential truth of the human condition.
- Suffering arises out of selfish attachment or *drishna,* meaning "intense thirst."
- There is a way out of suffering.
- The way out of suffering consists in the Eightfold Path of Right View, Right Intention, Right Speech, Right Action, Right Livelihood, Right Effort, Right Mindfulness, and Right Concentration.

The path laid out in Theravada Buddhism culminates, our teenaged seeker learned, in the individual's liberation from suffering. Those who reach this state are called *arhats,* or "liberated ones."

Enthralled as she was with Buddhism, Diane didn't know a single Buddhist. She accepted the proposition that all sorrows arise from selfish desire. Elvis would have to go, and so would her high heels and the jazz clubs where she'd danced. "I gave away my clothing," she recalls, and fashioned a yellow tunic for herself, aiming for the look of saffron robes, which she wore with black tights and flat shoes.

She stopped wearing makeup and pulled her hair severely back from her face.

Within a couple of months she had found her way to the London Buddhist Society, whose members were for the most part Theravadins, and begun attending its meetings. Discovering that the other members all wore ordinary street clothes—high heels, even, and makeup—she came home kicking herself for having given her clothing away. Lee smiled, as mothers will, and pointed her toward the wardrobe, where she had carefully stashed everything away. "I gave away my clothing" appears to have meant, in fact, "I told my mother to give away my clothing." This was a very normal teenager indeed.

By the end of that year Diane had begun to feel the limitations of the only school of Buddhism she knew. Becoming an *arhat* was supposed to be the culmination of the path, but she couldn't warm to the concept. When she thought about the Buddha, on the other hand, she would cry tears of devotion. She *loved* the Buddha, and she wanted to be like him.

In effect, her personal religious development was recapitulating the historic evolution of Buddhism itself.

Theravada Buddhism is sometimes also known as Hinayana, which translates literally as "lesser vehicle." That is unfortunate, because Theravada's teachings are in fact foundational to all schools of Buddhism, but it does underscore the fact that Mahayana or "Greater Vehicle" Buddhists recognize, in addition to the Four Noble Truths, other teachings they believe to have been implicit in the Buddha's earliest discourses but that were only fully divulged in the Second and Third Turnings of the Dharma Wheel.

In Mahayana Buddhism, which took hold in China as ch'an and in Japan as Zen, the ideal of the *arhat* gave way to the ideal of the *bodhisattva*—the spiritual aspirant who refuses the ticket out of *samsara* and vows instead to return to human existence over and over and over, as many times as it takes, until all sentient beings are free. Attainment of perfect Buddhahood is understood to take three and a half incalculable aeons.

With the Second Turning of the Dharma Wheel, Mahayana Buddhists believe, the Compassionate Buddha revealed the truth of *shunyata*, or emptiness; substantial as the perceived world seems to be, it is devoid of objectifiable reality. Yet insight into emptiness, or the "unconditioned," is, as we've seen, the precondition for compassion, and because it is generative, emptiness is associated with the feminine. It is the matrix that births all of the Buddhas.

When she was just eighteen, and still a newcomer to Buddhism, Diane Perry had already begun to see life through Mahayana eyes. Working in the library, "there would be a sudden click," and she would find herself watching herself as if she were an outside witness. She saw, but she knew it was simply a matter of visual input being received and processed; she thought, but she knew that thoughts were simply coming up and down in the mind. And she knew, if only for a moment at a time, that the "I" she had assumed was doing all of that seeing and thinking was just a mental construct. Nobody was really home at all!

But it didn't stop there. When she was in that state, she recalls, she would look around and realize that nobody else in the room shared her perception of things. On the contrary, they were so involved with their ideas and emotions and sensations, and so wedded to the idea of "I," that there was no *space* at all. It was as if they were suffocating, which, she now saw, had been her own normal state as well. As soon as she realized this, she experienced a depth of love and compassion that she could scarcely bear. She grieved for the people moving in and out of her library, but she grieved for herself as well, for all beings.

She was already glimpsing one of the Buddha's most elusive and powerful teachings: that becoming detached from one's thoughts, emotions, sensations, does not make one cold or unfeeling at all. When there is spaciousness within, and when there is stillness, our innate compassion can rise. The heart can open.

With regard to the idea of emptiness, she never loses an opportunity to emphasize that when one actually experiences it, "it's not a cold emptiness, it's a warm spaciousness."[7] Buddhist scholar and teacher Reginald Ray agrees, adding that the "warmth and intelligence" that are now understood to fill the world continually arise "to correct one's balance."[8] This recognition is spelled out in the Third Turning teachings, which refine the doctrine of emptiness. In particular, they address the danger that some might interpret the doctrine of emptiness as justifying nihilism.

First, they caution, reality is not actually empty. On the contrary, reality is resplendent and glorious. What's empty is our limited *perception* of reality. There are levels, or degrees, of reality that reflect our own levels of development. In an ultimate sense, for example, my family and friends and the emotions they provoke in me are not real.

---

[7] Mackenzie, *Cave in the Snow*, 144.

[8] Reginald Ray, *Secret of the Vajra World: The Tantric Buddhism of the West*, vol. 2 in *World of Tibetan Buddhism* (Boston: Shambhala Publications, 2001), 177.

But in a hugely important provisional sense, corresponding to where I am in my own development, they are most decidedly real. They constitute, in effect, my karmic assignment. Until I learn how to negotiate my relationships "skillfully," I will remain locked down at a certain level so that I never do actually get to experience either the emptiness *or* the resplendence of what really is.

The second major Third Turning teaching maintains that despite all evidence to the contrary, "buddha-nature" exists within every human being. It may be covered over with all manner of negative qualities, yet every one of us is in full possession of *dharmakaya*—the body of reality, the enlightened mind, the "jewel in the lotus" that is in every one of us. As meditation deepens, buddha-nature stirs and begins to assist the process from within.

The *bodhisattva* ideal was far more suited to Diane Perry's temperament than the *arhat* model, but Mahayana Buddhism was not well represented in London during the 1960s. Only later, when she had found her way to *Vajrayana*, or *Tantric* Buddhism, did she learn about the Second and Third Turning teachings that are basic to both Vajrayana and Mahayana.

The word *vajra* means "diamond," and also "thunderbolt." *Vajrayana* is understood to convey indestructibility on the one hand and immediacy on the other. Vajrayana takes its "view" or philosophy from Mahayana Buddhism. It envisions no further turns of the Dharma Wheel—its special passion is for actualization of the contents of Mahayana. Called by some the "*yana* of skillful means," Vajrayana does not accept the proposition that we can only realize our buddhanature in the fullness of an impossibly long time. Since we already *are* enlightened, say the Vajrayana teachers, let's *cut through* ignorance and experience our buddha-nature here and now. They direct their students toward a broad and diverse array of means to do this, many of which are revealed in Indian scriptures known as *tantras*. (Buddhism had ripened in India for nearly twelve hundred years before coming to Tibet, and it had assimilated by that time a considerable number of traditional Indian practices and teachings.)

Diane Perry knew nothing about Vajrayana at first except that it was the form of Buddhism that prevailed in Tibet and had something to do with *tantra,* a word that for most London Buddhists of the time, Theravadins by and large, had only the darkest and most disreputable associations. Given the sensational associations that the word *tantra* carries, it may be helpful explore its meaning(s) for a moment. On one level, world religions scholar Huston Smith reminds us, one of the two roots of the word means, simply, "extension."[9] The *tantras* extended the range of earlier scriptures. But the word has a second meaning related to the craft of weaving and denoting "interpenetration," and this refers to the actual content of the *tantras*. They are texts, that is, that look at the interrelatedness of things. From the Tantric point of view, everything in life has its sacred dimension and uses, including, as Westerners are well aware, sexuality.

Tantric sexual practice is only one strand in the magnificently rich and complex tapestry of Vajrayana, and it is virtually incomprehensible outside the context of a much deeper exploration of Vajrayana than we can take up here. Since Tantric sexuality hasn't to my knowledge been part of Tenzin Palmo's spiritual path, we can pass over it here, except to say that just knowing it's there—knowing how differently human sexuality is regarded in Tibetan Buddhism—underscores the breathtaking inclusiveness of the tradition. *Nothing is left out.* Nothing is set aside. Nothing in human experience is classed as unclean or irrelevant or inappropriate.

Diane Perry knew none of this the day she picked up a book about Vajrayana Buddhism and learned of its four traditional schools: Nyingma, Kadam, Sakya, and Kagyu. But the last word leapt out at her.

"*I'm* a Kagyu." She knew this, as surely as she'd known she was a Buddhist. But what did that mean?

Well, to begin with, a Buddhist friend informed her, it meant that she should read the biography of Milarepa, because he had co-founded the Kagyu lineage and his riveting story would give her some idea of the "flavor" of Kagyu practice. She read his story, and immediately, "my mind went through a thousand somersaults" (12).

Unlike some of the other Vajrayana schools, which began in Indian monasteries, the Kagyu school originated from strictly Tantric roots and had been slow to take monastic form. Kagyu practitioners are unconventional, dedicated to meditation itself, and devoted to their teachers. A lineage of illumined teachers connects the student back through time to the founder, and ultimately, all the way back to the Compassionate Buddha himself. The importance of this relationship is conveyed in an arresting metaphor. A ritual called *abhishekha* recognizes that the seeker is connected with his or her lineage as if by an

---

[9] Huston Smith and Philip Novak, *Buddhism: A Concise Introduction* (San Francisco: Harper San Francisco, 2003), 106.

umbilical cord. The teacher *is* that channel or cord. One must keep the cord wet and pliant by regularly revitalizing that sacred relationship.

Eager, now, to go to India as soon as she could and find her own teacher, Diane Perry learned that there was in fact a Kagyu nunnery in Dalhousie, a hill station in the Western Himalayas that was headed up by a British woman, Freda Bedi, who had married an Indian she'd met at Oxford thirty years earlier. A veteran of India's Freedom Movement, Freda Bedi was working today for the Indian government in the resettlement in India of Tibetan refugee lamas and nuns. Diane wrote immediately: Could she come and work? She couldn't offer much in the way of skills, but . . .

"Please come, come. Don't worry, just come!" came the reply, and within weeks, barely twenty years old, Diane had managed to get a job at London's School of Oriental and African Studies that not only paid enough so that she could save toward her passage, but it also gave her free access to lessons in Tibetan. Her rudimentary grasp of Tibetan would prove invaluable, because when she did find her teacher, he did not speak English.

In February 1964, then, still only twenty, she boarded a banana boat at Marseilles called *Le Vietnam* that was headed for India. She traveled with a couple of girlfriends and, lest we think asceticism had claimed her entirely, a young Japanese man she'd just met and with whom she was much taken. Before the end of the voyage he had proposed marriage and even playfully tricked her into accepting. She extricated herself with real difficulty—the relationship was quite delightful to her—and made her way to Dalhousie, fending off two more would-be suitors on the way.

Dalhousie itself was all but overrun with Tibetan refugees when she arrived—more than five thousand, who lived, for the most part, in tents made of flour sacks. Her own accommodations were comparable; the roof leaked so badly she had to sleep under the bed. Rats were everywhere, jumping on her throughout the night. And the spiders, she remembers, were even worse.

She divided her time between carrying out secretarial duties for Freda Bedi and giving English lessons to the young "incarnate lamas," or *tulkus*. These were little boys believed to have been spiritual heavyweights in former lives. Their group photo is of ten radiantly happy little goofballs doing all they can not to fall over laughing, but we are not to be fooled. "When you see these genuine incarnations when they're tiny children, and see how much they already know, you really have to believe in this whole tulku system. . . . If you see young tulkus when they're with other young monks, it's like in a Broadway show where the main character is spotlighted and the others kind of fade into the background."[10]

In those days a Westerner with a genuine interest in the Dharma was still a rarity, and Tenzin Palmo feels now that doors were open to her then that might not be today. In June of 1964, wearing the traditional, elegant Tibetan costume called a *chuba*, she was presented to the Dalai Lama. Baffling their interpreter, he addressed her as "Ani-la," which is the honorific title used to nuns, and he greeted her in a phrase that is ordinarily used only when two hermits meet.

She was working in Freda Bedi's office not long afterward when a letter came across the desk from the head of a particular community of Tibetan monks. When she saw the signature, and read the name, Khamtrul Rinpoche, she again felt one of those jolts of recognition: "Faith spontaneously arose."

Who was he? A high Kagyu lama, Freda Bedi answered, but of the Drukpa order as opposed to the Karma Kagyu order to which her own nunnery belonged. And he would be coming soon to Dalhousie.

Instantly, Tenzin Palmo knew that the eighth Khamtrul Rinpoche was the teacher she had come to India to meet: he was her *lama,* a word that means, literally, "high mother." He arrived on her twenty-first birthday, a full-moon night, the 30th of June.

"As I looked at him, it seemed as though two things were happening simultaneously. There was a sense of recognition, like meeting an old friend you haven't seen for a long time. At the same time it was as if the very deepest thing inside me had suddenly taken an external form" (14).

And Khamtrul Rinpoche recognized her. They had been very close to one another, he would tell her, for many lifetimes. She had been a monk, or perhaps a yogi, but definitely part of his community. She told him that she wanted to become a nun, and he agreed to ordain her.

For most Westerners the idea of becoming a nun is associated with limitation—enclosure, renunciation, loss of freedom. But in a traditional Tibetan culture, where women spent their entire lives taking care of their families—as wife and mother if they wed, as daughter and auntie if they did not—being a nun represented a degree of physical and emotional freedom unattainable under any other circumstances: freedom, it is understood, to devote themselves entirely to the Dharma.

---

[10] Saltman, "Endless Lifetimes, Endless Benefits," 60.

"The Indians used to compare being ordained to a wild swan leaving lake after lake behind without any impediment," Tenzin Palmo has explained. "And ideally, that is how it should be."[11] In fact, institutional support for nuns is and for a long time has been so poor that many of these "swans" end up staying with their families and doing housework and childcare to pay their keep, while still others work in monastery kitchens serving the monks. Their spiritual practices are typically confined to repetition of mantras and certain simple rituals. And if they do find their way to spiritual attainments, their lack of education makes it all but impossible to pass on what they know.

Tenzin Palmo's experience would not be notably better. Three weeks after meeting her teacher, her head newly shaved, wearing the maroon robes and gold blouse of a Tibetan Buddhist nun, she took ordination from him and received the name Drugbyu Tenzin Palmo, "Glorious Lady Who Upholds the Doctrine of the Practice Succession."

And that was about as good as things would get, for a long time to come.

There was no Drukpa Kagyu nunnery for her to join. There were only the monks, and because she was a woman, she could not live with them. Nor could she study with them, eat with them, speak with them; she couldn't learn the rituals they did, or the dances. . . . They might as well have lived on the other side of a thick pane of glass.

And, on the other hand, now that she had been ordained, she was no longer part of the lay community, either. She worked in the daytime as Rinpoche's secretary in the monastery office, and that was thoroughly enjoyable. But each evening she walked alone down into the town to a cramped little room barely big enough to hold a bed, a table, a standing pipe for (cold) baths, and a bucket for a toilet, and there she cried herself to sleep night after night.

Interestingly, the monks themselves seem to have known that she was one of them. A cloth painting had come with them from their monastery in Tibet that depicted a mysterious individual with piercing blue eyes and a long, pointed nose like hers. Believing that this was she, and that he/she had mysteriously rejoined them, they treated her from the first with the deference they would have given a recognized tulku. But they were well trained in traditional disciplines that forbade a monk to have anything to do with a woman. Khamtrul

---

[11] Ray, *Secret of the Vajra World*, 444.

Rinpoche himself was terribly busy trying to set his community on a sound economic footing, and he, too, was constrained by tradition: "Previously I was always able to keep you close by me," he told her. "But in this lifetime, you took form as a female, so I'm doing the best I can, but I cannot keep you close forever because it's very difficult" (14). So near, and so unspeakably far, she couldn't have been much more miserable, and she continued in this state for six years.

Tenzin Palmo's story spins along nicely up to this point, from one serendipitous plot point to the next. She treats even the very real hardships of the first few months in India so lightly that they come off more comical than grim. But now the narrative seems to hit a wall.

Read against the background of similar stories, though, the hiatus makes perfect sense, because right up to the moment of ordination, her trials have all been external. She'd had to survive her childhood, acquire work skills, make her way through distracting pleasures of London in the early 1960s, find her way to Buddhism, and earn her passage to India—and she'd come through splendidly. But from here on out the significant events would be internal, and so subtle they were invisible to anyone but her and, of course, her teacher.

No student of spiritual biography would hesitate to say of this first six years that Tenzin Palmo was undergoing the first round of a series of tests. *Test* isn't really the right word, because no one was sitting there with a stopwatch or gauge. *Tempering* is probably the better term. A blacksmith forging a blade doesn't plunge it into the fire and then water to see whether it breaks, but to strengthen it so that it *won't* break under pressure of use. Seekers withstand loneliness, deprivation, hunger sometimes, and thirst, as a way of strengthening themselves for the considerably more arduous mental disciplines that lie ahead.

Or maybe *test* is all right as long as we understand that what is being tested is the depth and singleness of our own desire, and that we ourselves are doing the assessment.

Among the best known traditional accounts of this sort of tempering is the story of Milarepa, co-founder with Marpa the Translator of the Kagyupa lineage. When Milarepa first came to Marpa and asked to take refuge with him, Marpa knew that he had accumulated a considerable fund of bad karma. So while other students came and took instruction, he kept putting Milarepa off, ordering him instead to build a stone structure high on a ridge. When it was completed, Marpa rejected it, saying it was all wrong and needed to be taken apart and rebuilt on a completely different ridge. Three times this took place, and finally he was told to build a considerably more elaborate structure on yet a fourth ridge. This went on for years, but never did Milarepa lose faith that he would one day receive the teachings.

Tenzin Palmo's trials were of a very different nature, but no less real. There was, for one thing, the return of her erstwhile fiance, the Japanese youth, who looked right past the shorn head and the voluminous robes and saw, still, the woman of his dreams. Dalhousie was a sea of mud with no running water, and he had a lovely home in Japan. Wouldn't she reconsider? Come for just a visit? And though she knew, as she'd always known, that marriage was absolutely not for her, she didn't turn his offer down right away. He was so lovely, they got along so well. She still couldn't see herself married, but maybe they could just live together for a while until the relationship cooled.

But there, she couldn't do it. She'd come too far to pretend there was any turning back. Even as she wept at what she was losing, she prayed to her teacher to help her. She felt her whole body fill with a golden light, and her teacher's voice saying she should come back to India immediately. After that, she insists, she was perfectly happy.

One group of monks within Khamtrul Rinpoche's community who did not keep her at arm's length were the men known as *togdens,* who represent the yogic wing of Tibetan Buddhism. They wear their hair in matted dreadlocks, like the Indian yogis who live near the Ganges, and in place of robes they wear white skirts. They specialize in meditation, she explains; they are the "professionals," who undergo rigorous training in secret practices. They don't concern themselves with monastic goings-on; in fact, before they'd had to leave Tibet, they had lived in caves. The *togdens* hold a large body of teachings received ultimately from Milarepa himself.

For a year Tenzin Palmo had her own room in the *togden* compound, where she was made to feel completely at home. She came to hold these gentle men in awe—all the more so when one of them told her she shouldn't assume that their "secret" had to do with esoteric teachings: "There is nothing I am doing that you have not been taught. The only difference is that I am doing it and you aren't!"[12]

Within the *togden* tradition, she learned, there is a body of teachings just for women, and back in Tibet there had been women, the *togden-mas,* who were adept in those teachings. None had made it

---

[12] Mackenzie, *Cave in the Snow,* 62.

out of Tibet, but there were *togdens* who held the teachings, and it wasn't inconceivable the lineage could be revived.

Halfway through this extremely difficult period, she came into a small windfall and used the money to pay a visit to Sikkim, where the head of the Kagyu lineage resided. He was in a position to give her a somewhat fuller ordination than Khamtrul Rinpoche had, and he did, but not before he had spoken very seriously to her. She was the first Western nun he had ordained. She was young; she'd never married or had children. She would be dealing with temptations that would not be nearly as troublesome to an older woman. Many more Western women would be ordained in the future, but because she was the first, much depended on her keeping her vows.

Others have addressed the complicated question of misogyny in the Buddhist tradition: I won't take it up here except to note that Tenzin Palmo herself distinguishes between out-and-out misogyny and a monastic prejudice against women's bodies that she traces to negative imagery the Buddha himself had originally applied to *all* bodies. By way of encouraging detachment from the physical realm, he appears to have invoked the same kind of images we find in Western monasticism, calling the body a sack of blood, spittle, and excrement, and describing in grizzly detail the decomposition of a corpse. At some point, she thinks, those teachings were co-opted and focused solely on women's bodies, probably as a way to encourage monastic abstinence.

Suffice it to say that in 1967, when Tenzin Palmo was all but begging to receive instruction in the esoteric teachings and sacred rituals of the Kagyupa tradition, the almost unanimous opinion of the monks themselves was that women aren't worthy of such knowledge because they aren't capable of attaining enlightenment. A woman might strive for lifetimes to realize her buddha-nature, but she wouldn't succeed unless, at the last minute, she doffed her female form and took a male body. While nuns were working in their parents' homes or monastery kitchens, they were presumably praying for this boon.

At one point Tenzin Palmo asked a very high lama what it was about a penis that is so essential for becoming Enlightened. Could he think of *any* advantage there might be in having female form? He wanted to think about it, he told her, and when he saw her the next day he said, no, he had decided there were no advantages. She differed: "I thought, one advantage is that we don't have a male ego."[13]

---

[13] Ibid., 55.

Surely, given what she'd seen of male egos, getting rid of a female ego couldn't be inherently *more* difficult!

Years later she would say of the monks' unrelenting refusal to share the lineage teachings with women that it "lacerated my heart" (79). I think it's important to bear this in mind when she distances herself explicitly on occasion from "those angry feminists."[14] I doubt whether there are many issues feminists hold dear that Tenzin Palmo doesn't also embrace to some extent, and she is perfectly willing to use terms like *male chauvinism*. What she will not buy into, though, is the notion that anger is "a clear and forceful emotion" that it is correct to use as fuel in the struggle against oppressive institutions or individuals. Whenever we act or speak out of anger, she maintains, we are guaranteed an angry response. "Hatred does not cease by hatred at any time," the Compassionate Buddha had said. "Hatred ceases by love."

For Tenzin Palmo, anger is an unskillful emotion. Period.

But this does not mean that she advocated silent acceptance of things as they are.

While she was still at the Tashi Jong monastery, she amplified her commitment to the *bodhisattva* ideal. In a moment of deep frustration, when she had been rebuffed yet again because she was female, she made "a heartfelt pledge" that she also calls "a strong prayer." (She seems to be fighting shy of the word *vow,* and I would guess that it's out of a certain modesty): "I'm going to continue to take female form and achieve Enlightenment! . . . Even if I can't do that much in this lifetime, in the future, may this stream of consciousness go forward and take on the transitory form of a female rather than a male."[15]

If we were to look at this event from the point of view of reincarnation, and accept the proposition that Tenzin Palmo had indeed been a Kagyu monk in the past, how fascinating it is to speculate that *he* had chosen to come back this time as a woman because *he* saw that barring women from the Dharma was a crime against the Dharma. And if that was indeed what had happened, how prescient of him to have chosen to come back as a Western woman as well and a child of the 1960s, whose background had steeled her not to take no from much of anybody.

But there is another rather thrilling dimension to Tenzin Palmo's "heartfelt pledge" that would be recognized by anyone familiar with Tibetan Buddhism. I learned about it from my friend China Gal-

[14] Mackenzie, *Cave in the Snow,* 199.
[15] Ibid., 58.

land, author of *Longing for Darkness: Tara and the Black Madonna*.
China had been studying in the Soto Zen tradition and meditating
regularly with other Zen students for a couple of years before she
ran headlong into the teaching—dismissed, to be sure, by her Western
teachers—that you have to have a man's body to become illumined.
Her distress was acute, but her spirits began to lift when she heard
that Tibetan Buddhists honor Tara not only as a deity, but as a female
Buddha—a woman, originally, who had vowed to be enlightened only
in a woman's body.

China's journey towards Tara would take her halfway around the
world—initially to India, where she met with the Dalai Lama, who
assured her that women could of course be fully enlightened. Eventually she got the whole story, of a woman named Yeshe Dawa, which
means "Wisdom Moon," and how she had become Tara, the Savior-
ess. China loves the story for several reasons, not least because, as she
puts it, "How Buddhist is this? Tara relied completely upon her own
experience, against all the received tradition that said she needed to
have a man's body to be enlightened."[16]

When Tenzin Palmo made her "heartfelt pledge," then, she was
locating herself squarely in Tara's mother-line, and I suspect that this
is why she avoided the word *vow*. It probably felt presumptuous. I
don't believe that her decision to become a Tibetan Buddhist had
anything to do with Tara or that she even knew about her at first.
But once she got to India she would certainly have learned not only
that the beloved deity Tara had once been a woman, but that she has
twenty-one traditional forms, all of which emanate from Green Tara,
who dwells in a forest where tigers and antelope play together.

In other words, just as the women mystics of the Middle Ages were
able to find the spiritual resources they needed within the very religious tradition that had silenced and marginalized them, women like
Tenzin Palmo have been able to ground their spiritual endeavors, and
in particular their resistance to monastic misogyny, in a longstanding
lineage of female strength and awareness.

There were bright patches during this first six years in India. Not
long after Tenzin Palmo took her second ordination, her mother
came to visit. Was her world-renouncing daughter at risk of getting
out of touch? She brought along audio tapes of Bob Dylan as an
antidote.

---

[16] China Galland, "The Goddesses Save the World," *Inquiring Mind: A Semian-
nual Journal of the Vipassana Community* 22, no. 2 (Fall 2005): 15.

Lee Perry loved India. She stayed on for ten months and took refuge with Khamtrul Rinpoche. On the very morning of the ceremony, before she'd even gotten out of bed, she had a vision of Green Tara. She'd have liked to stay, but the food and general discomfort were too much for her. She returned to London, where Tenzin Palmo would visit her for a few months in 1984. Lee died not long afterward, and it was painful for her daughter not to have been there at the time, but knowing that Lee had taken refuge—that she had "entered the stream," as Buddhists say—lightened her grief considerably.

Tenzin Palmo had done everything she could, but six years out, she was stuck. She was still being denied the teachings that would allow her to seek the Dharma through meditation. An impossibly wrenching choice seemed to be forcing itself on her, and in 1970, she chose. She packed her bags and told her teacher that she was leaving.

But what was this? She couldn't leave! Where would she go?

He would always be her lama, she told him, but it seemed that she was going to have to go somewhere else to get the essential teachings.

"Otherwise I could die and still not have received any Dharma."

Suddenly, and inexplicably, everything turned around. Khamtrul Rinpoche promised her that she would not die before receiving the teachings she needed, and he set her up immediately to study with one of the *togdens*. And no sooner had she received the basic teachings (not the advanced *togden-ma* instructions) than he told her she would need to go away now so that she could practice them in real earnest. She suggested Nepal, but he countered with Lahoul, a remote mountainous region bordering on Tibet and, for all intents and purposes, Tibetan.

His behavior sounds distressingly capricious, but read in the context of spiritual biography as a genre, it makes perfect sense. Before she could have access to teachings that would demand every ounce of her will and devotion, she had to want them more than anything else in the world—more, even, than day-to-day contact with her teacher. Indeed, the whole point of that kind of intimate daily association is that eventually the student begins to hear the teacher's voice from within herself and to know that in fact nothing *could* really separate her from him. That Tenzin Palmo was able to even think about leaving Khamtrul Rinpoche suggests that their relationship was entering this stage.

It should be added, too, that as someone who had taken the *bodhisattva* vow, Tenzin Palmo had more than merely personal motivation to push ahead now at whatever the cost.

In Lahoul, which is about six thousand feet higher than Tashi Jong, Tenzin Palmo was part of a community of some twenty monks and nuns, each of whom had a small stone and mud cottage on a hillside behind a handsome temple. It was quite a social scene, and during the summer and fall she allowed herself to enjoy it to some extent, but during the long winter months she embraced the opportunity for full retreat. She had her instructions, and she gave herself over joyously now to following them. She studied Buddhist texts, and she carried out what are called Preliminary Practices: full-body prostrations to be performed at least a hundred thousand times, repetitions of various mantras, and mandala offerings, in which the practitioner constructs a symbolic universe in her mind and offers it up—this ritual, too, to be carried out thousands and thousands of time. On the face of things, it sounds numbing, but the effect is to soften the mind and make it pliable for the extreme demands of advanced meditative practice.

She would spend six tranquil years in this way, traveling back to Tashi Jong each summer to check in with Khamtrul Rinpoche. By 1976, though, she had determined that she really couldn't stay where she was any longer. Her meditation was deepening, and she needed real privacy now, and long stretches of uninterrupted silence. Her neighbors were dear, but far too noisy—they would shout to one another from the rooftops of their cottages and have loud, jolly dinner parties. The final straw was when a young monk moved into the room above her. He might as well have been a wild yak.

Once again, it is almost as if circumstances were pushing her along, on the one hand, and clearing the way ahead, on the other. Circumstances, or the dakinis. Because she gives them considerable credit for what happened next.

The Tibetan name for Lahoul is Karsha Khandro Ling, which means Lahoul, Land of the Dakinis. Tenzin Palmo had been assured by more than one lama that the region was indeed populated by these wild, glorious, naked women: sky dancers, handmaidens of the goddess Tara, staunch allies of the dedicated meditator.

Among the Tantric practices and perspectives that Vajrayana Buddhism had incorporated into itself before coming to India was a deep veneration for *shakti* in all of its various forms. Shakti, consort to Shiva, embodies resilience in nature and, within human beings, the coiled evolutionary energy that is believed to lie dormant at the base of the spine until it is awakened through deep meditation. The rich, complex, multivalent wealth of material associated with *shakti* in India coalesced in Tibet around the figure of the dakini.

The dakini has myriad forms and identities and ultimately *no* form and *no* identity. She can manifest in dreams, in visions, and in meditation experiences. Sometimes she turns up as a rheumy-eyed old hag (and woe betide the inattentive practitioner who fails to recognize her), sometimes as an alluring maiden. She has antecedents in the seductive dancers called in Indian tradition *apsaras*, some of whom tested the strength of the Buddha's enlightenment, but she is also related to the terrifying handmaidens of the goddess Kali, who live in cremation grounds and decorate themselves with the bones of the dead. They carry special knives designed to strip flesh from bones, and she does too, only she uses it to strip the "flesh" of worldly illusion from the "bones" of spiritual wisdom.

Confused by the sheer number of manifestations in which they encounter the dakini, Western scholars have often tried to interpret her through the lens of feminist or Jungian theory. In her brilliant study *The Dakini's Warm Breath: The Feminine Principle in Tibetan Buddhism* Tibetan Buddhist scholar and *acharya* Judith Simmer-Brown demonstrates the inadequacy of these approaches and offers instead a reading that draws on her extensive knowledge of the Tibetan tradition as well as on interviews with living lamas. She cautions us, for example, not to think of the dakini as a mother goddess, but rather as a mother *principle*, whose full meaning is much more than the sum of her manifestations. Ultimately, and most important, she is the feminine principle at the heart of Varjrayana Buddhism: the awakening into emptiness that in turn gives rise to wisdom and compassion. She soars, as Sky Dancer, because in emptiness there is no reference point and no ground.[17]

> She is an emissary of awakening. She represents the lineages of awakening traced all the way back to the Buddha, but at the same time she represents personal awakening in the present moment.[18]

Yet the old stories cling, reminding us that she is never, ever to be trifled with.

After living for six years on the backstairs of an exclusive men's club, Tenzin Palmo had found her way to a place her biographer describes as "a vortex of female energy." And her teacher certainly

---

[17] Judith Simmer-Brown, *The Dakini's Warm Breath: The Feminine Principle in Tibetan Buddhism* (Boston: Shambhala, 2001), 51.

[18] Ibid., 286.

knew this when he sent her there. Indeed, it is said that the dakini is literally right in the middle of the relationship between teacher and student, because the teacher's warm breath *is* the dakini's warm breath. With six years of serious discipline under her belt, she was qualified to seek the dakinis' help directly.

So it was that she petitioned them. If they would help her find a place for retreat, she promised, she, for her part, would practice very, very hard. In short order, another Lahouli nun suddenly remembered that a much older nun had told her there was a cave up the hill from their community with a spring nearby. . . .

They found the old nun ("old nun" is one of the dakinis' favorite aliases), and she sprinted up the mountain ahead of them to something that could only euphemistically be called a cave, for it was really no more than a ledge with an overhang, exposed on three sides. The total floor space was about ten feet by six feet.

But the view.

And the silence.

And the air: like liquid crystal.

Her Lahouli friends helped her brick up the three sides, wall off part of the space for storage, level the ledge to form a terrace, put in a door and a window and even a tiny garden. It was an arduous undertaking, as, of course, all the materials had to be carried straight up the slippery, pathless, rock-strewn mountain. But by the autumn of 1976, as the weather was beginning to turn, Tenzin Palmo moved into her new home.

The cave was almost absurdly small now, contracted by its alterations to about six feet by six feet. There was certainly no room for a bed, but that didn't matter, as she would meditate and sleep in a square "prayer box," two and a half feet on a side. There was a tiny wood-burning stove that vented outside that she fired up just once a day to prepare her midday meal. An indentation in one wall held her books, and she set up an altar with sacred implements and a few pictures of deities. A small chest held her clothing, and that was about it, except for a pressure cooker: at an elevation of 13,200 feet, it would have taken next to forever to cook the rice and lentils that were the staples of her diet. There was just room enough next to the box to do hatha yoga.

Among the things that were *not* in the cave, and that most of us can barely imagine doing without for more than a weekend, were telephone, radio, television, magazines, secular reading of any kind, space heaters, a bathtub or toilet . . . except for the pressure cooker, she could have been making this retreat a thousand years ago.

Her day was structured around four three-hour meditation periods. During an afternoon break she would sometimes copy Tibetan manuscripts, for she had developed a fine hand as a calligrapher, or she might paint watercolors of deities like Green Tara. She studied Buddhist scriptures, but she read widely, too, in other religious traditions.

There were adventures. A blizzard blocked her door and window so completely one winter that she decided she was going to die. Even as she was composing herself for death—unaware that, in fact, snow "breathes"—she heard the voice of her teacher commanding her: "Dig yourself out!" And of course she did, not once, but repeatedly.

In the spring as the snows thawed, the cave would flood and everything would have to be set out on the ledge during the day to dry. Wolves passed by often, and on one occasion she found the track of a snow leopard.

But of course the real events were interior, and she only speaks about these in the broadest and most impersonal terms. Kagyupa Buddhists are strict on this point.

Was there bliss? Well, yes, she says, of course one experiences bliss. "Bliss is the fuel of retreat. . . . You can't do any long-term practice seriously unless there is inner joy, because the joy and enthusiasm is what carries you along."[19]

But bliss is not what you're really after.

What, then, *were* the real benefits of her long retreat?

Her answers are circumspect. Her tradition discourages talk of one's spiritual experiences, but so do her own predilections; she observes that some people like to talk about their sexual experiences, too, while most of us don't. Spiritual experiences are at least that intimate.

She does always speak, in absolutely prosaic terms, of the strides she made in the cave toward ordinary self-sufficiency. There was no choice, really. When you're completely alone, you have to figure out for yourself how to keep mice out of the food stocks and not let yourself run out of firewood. But she's talking about the mind as well. Twelve years in a cave had taught her how the mind *works*. In the absence of television, for example, she found that the mind is quite good at putting on its own shows, replaying emotional events of the past, stirring up anxieties and fears—and she learned to step back from the show and let it go on without her.

And when she speaks of having realized the nature of the mind, much more is implied than is obvious. Because as we learned at the

---

[19] Mackenzie, *Cave in the Snow*, 113.

very beginning of this chapter, once one has passed through calm abiding and become established in penetrating insight, the nature of the mind is experienced as unconditioned, or empty. Through Penetrating Insight, sustained over long periods of time, one arrives at "the state of Knowing without the Knower." Momentous as this experience is, she insists at the same time that it is not cataclysmic; it is simply waking up, after a lifetime of dreaming. (The Sanskrit verb *bodhi*, which is the etymological root of the word *Buddha,* means "to wake up." The Compassionate Buddha is the Awakened One.)

Was she lonely? Never. Which, she agrees, is interesting, because back at Tashi Jong, affiliated with the monastery, she had been terribly lonely.

Bored? Not once. Miserable? Well, in fact she does remember feeling, in the middle of one of those spring thaws, thoroughly unhappy. The walls were dripping with water, everything was wet, and she was sick. The dampness regularly induced chills and high fevers. But just as her misery back at Tashi Jong had dissolved almost overnight once she looked deeply into it and saw "clinging mind," so now as soon as she became fully aware that she was feeling oppressed, the first of the Buddha's Four Noble Truths came to her in a flash: *suffering is inherent in existence.*

Of course. What had she been thinking? The physical universe is in continuous flux: it can never support human happiness. "I thought 'Why are you still looking for happiness in *samsara?*' and my mind just changed around. . . . *Since then I have never really cared about external circumstances.*"[20]

In 1981, Tenzin Palmo had left her cave to come down for her annual visit to meet Khamtrul when word reached her that he had died quite suddenly of diabetes. The shock was ferocious. She felt as if she were in a huge desert and had just lost her guide. She remembers crying and crying—"I never realized I could cry so much."

But it had become such an ingrained habit for her to step back from her own thought processes, and make the nature of mind her study, that she allowed her grief to become the object of her meditation, and as she gazed down into it, its fundamental unreality revealed itself: "I looked into the pain in my heart, and as I looked it was like layer after layer peeled away until in the end I reached this level of great

---

[20] Ibid., 114.

peace and calm, almost bliss, and I realized that of course the Lama is always in your heart."[21]

There is a lingering suspicion, I think, on the part of some, that detachment is consonant with coldness, or apathy. It's hard to imagine that this prejudice could survive a close reading of Mackenzie's fine portrait of Tenzin Palmo. The celibate religious life works beautifully for her, but not because she is anti-social or has difficulty relating to people. Ten minutes in her presence quickly squelches the notion. In fact, with respect to her long retreats in solitude, it's interesting to learn that she didn't believe herself to be alone up there at all. She determined that her lama was in her heart even after his death, but that wasn't the half of it. Long retreats are central to Vajrayana practice, and they are always undertaken in the *bodhisattva* spirit; one goes into retreat to cultivate wisdom and compassion in order to be of the greatest possible benefit to sentient beings, and those sentient beings are understood to be right there *with* you. For Tenzin Palmo, this is true of every period of meditation. In a talk she gave several years ago to a group of Zen Buddhists, she reminded them that when we sit in *zazen* we aren't just sitting for ourselves. We're sitting for all beings and in fact *"all beings are sitting here with us."* We are not alone when we meditate, "We are supported by all the Buddhas and *bodhisattvas* who are likewise here only to benefit other beings" (33). She can't seem to say it emphatically enough. They are "right here and now, right in front of us, right with us. . . . They are here and now because they are none other than the essential nature of the mind. . . . Once we plug into all that energy, we no longer feel alone."

Clearly she had experienced this level of companionship in her cave. But it is important to emphasize that the reason she is so keenly aware of all that energy and presence is that she has been bringing it to life within herself all along.

In another context she gives us an idea as to how that sense of presence came about. Asked about fear, and in particular about the fear that can arise when meditation deepens and the ego begins to anticipate its own demise, she replied that fear is the last barrier of the ego. This, she explains, is why Buddhists sometimes begin their meditation by taking refuge in the "three jewels"—the Buddha, the Dharma, and the enlightened Community or *Sangham*—and *then* take the *Bodhisattva* Vow, and finally perform a "Guru Yoga," in which they visualize the entire lineage of their teachers going all the way back to the all of the Compassionate Buddha. "We absorb that into

---

[21] Ray, *Secret of the Vajra World*, 174.

ourselves. This gives us protection. It is like being held in the palms
of the Buddha's hands. Nothing can hurt us. With that kind of inner
assurance, we gain the courage to jump" (151).

Tradition required her to remain in complete seclusion for the last
three years, three months, and three days of her retreat, and she
almost did. But near the very end of the third year her meditation was
interrupted by a loud banging on her door, and when she answered it
there was a police chief telling her she had just ten days to quit India.
She hadn't been evading the law, she'd simply had one of those very
Indian informal understandings with the old police chief: He had
renewed her visa for her so that she wouldn't have to keep coming
down to do it herself. But he was gone now, the law had changed,
and she would have to go.

It must have been agony to be ripped out of retreat so close to
the end, but the damage had been done and there was nothing for it.
Samsara in spades.

"Of course," she said, smiling slightly, "My daily life is very different from yours."

Her New York City audience could take her words quite literally,
because obviously her life is not like theirs. It was a perfectly innocuous remark, intended, one would assume, to make everyone feel
comfortable.

Only I had done my homework pretty carefully for this evening,
and I thought I knew a pointed reference when I heard it. In fact,
I would recognize a number of pointed references that evening. In
a very down-to-earth and unassuming Dharma talk, Tenzin Palmo
would manage to weigh in on several of American Buddhism's most
vexed issues.

In Asia the overwhelming majority of Buddhist practitioners are
monks and nuns; they are the professionals, the specialists. The role
of the devout householder is, typically, to support the monasteries
and draw religious guidance from the monks, much as European
Catholics did before the Gregorian Reforms. But in the United States
most practitioners are lay people, with careers, families, cultural and
community involvements. Their desire for the Dharma is very real,
everyone agrees, yet they have little time for long retreats or anything
like the extensive daily observances that are basic to traditional Tibetan Buddhist practice. And while they do send money to Buddhist
communities in Asia, they've done little to support monastic orders
here in the West.

It's a very complicated issue. Are Americans being quintessentially American in their desire to "have it all"—a stellar and rewarding career, a rich and equally rewarding family life, and a meditative practice as deep and all-absorbing as the Dalai Lama's?

Tenzin Palmo is so concerned about the plight of Buddhist monastics in the West that she has spoken directly to the Dalai Lama about them. She is just as unhappy, though, about the misplaced zeal many American Buddhists have for advanced practices when they haven't even begun to absorb and live out the basic precepts. Only a few minutes into her lecture, she found a quietly devastating way to express her misgivings.

She was speaking about compassion, and the need to realize that "each of us holds himself most dear," which is why Buddhists vow not to harm any sentient being. Even the smallest organism holds itself most dear. Nobody wants to be hurt, or shamed, or ignored. And of course everybody in the room knew that.

We knew, at least, the theory. But we were about to be reminded how ignorant we are of the practice. She paused, and then said: "I have met kids who grew up resenting Buddhism because their parents seemed to love the Dharma more than they did their children. They felt as if they were in the way of their parents' practice. So we must ask ourselves: Do the people closest to us see themselves as obstacles to our Dharma practice?"

Did the room grow as abruptly silent as I remember? Or was it just me, pierced by certain memories that are still hot to the touch, of the look in my own son's eyes more than once as I was bolting out the door to a retreat?

She wanted to revisit a question someone had asked after the talk she'd given two nights earlier, because she wasn't happy with the answer she'd given then. She'd been talking about the need to replace negative thoughts with positive ones and someone had asked whether we don't need to be open to dark as well as light experiences.

Yes, she said now, of course we do. It is certainly not good practice to censor experience itself. But there is a difference between acknowledging to oneself that a negative thought has arisen and actively encouraging it to stay. Anger, for example is not a *skillful* thought, so once we've watched it arise, we should do our best to replace it.

The problem with negative or "unskillful" thoughts, she further clarified, naming anger, fear, and greed as examples, is not only the harm they do immediately, but the fact that they can so easily overcome us.

We would be coming back again and again to the issue of anger—along with "Do I need a teacher?" it's the topic she's asked about most frequently—but for now her focus was on the six *paramitas* or "perfections," whose mastery is required for Attainment of Buddhahood. The six are giving, ethics, patience, effort, meditation, and wisdom. The first three, she reminds us, actually cannot be practiced in a relational vacuum. Turn your back on family, friends, and co-workers, and you have sacrificed precious opportunities for going beyond ego.

I was reminded suddenly of the opening of Teresa of Avila's *Way of Perfection*, which she wrote specifically for her own nuns, who'd been forbidden by church authorities to read Teresa's *Autobiography*. She'd promised them that in this book she would give them the instructions in contemplative prayer they'd been begging her for, and eventually she did, but she played with their expectations, too, spending the first half of the book telling them that their meditation would never ever deepen unless they cultivated deep love for one another, detachment from all created things, and humility.

Of the first perfection, generosity, or *danna*, Tenzin Palmo said that open hands really do seem to make for open hearts. In America, a country where everybody has so much, it should be easy to give. But curiously, she reflects, one sees much more generosity in other parts of the world, where "you have to be careful not to say you like something, because they strip it off and hand it to you."

Of ethics, or *shila*, sometimes translated as "good conduct," she remarked that lamas these days almost never give lectures on ethics. They talk, rather—she tucked her chin way in now and uttered the words from deep in her chest—about *dzogchen*, the "formless practices" associated with the highest levels of realization.

"We just don't *get* it," she said. "The precepts are the *foundation*. Everything else flows from them." And of course that had been Saint Teresa's point, too. If the mind is being jerked around all the time by grudges, cravings, or an injured sense of honor, one will never be at peace, no matter how many hours one spends in meditation.

Patience, Tenzin Palmo continued, means "open spaciousness." When you are patient, she added, the mind isn't *tight*, and by way of illustration she described the harrowing background of the monks who'd poured out of Tibet in 1959, and how amazingly cheerful they were in spite of what they'd suffered. Out of every hundred trying to escape into India, only a couple actually made it, and then they had to contend with a tremendously different climate. They were refugees now, many of them working on road gangs. "Some of them had been aristocrats, high lamas, and now they were living in tents made of flour bags. When you went to see them, they were laughing, smiling, cheerful, they'd run out and buy biscuits for tea . . . as they broke up the rocks for the road bed, they'd be singing their mantras . . . so *alive*. They had such faith in the Dharma. No-one could take that from them."

Leaning forward, now, closed fist on her chest, she said emphatically, "The Dharma has to be *here* . . . in the heart. . . . Every lama I know continues to practice." And again, after a pause, with great force:
   "For everything that happens there is a Dharma solution."
   Another pause.
   "Please believe me."
   And another.
   "Do you understand?"
   I don't know for sure whether she covered all six *paramitas*, because I stopped taking notes for a while and simply sat there enjoying what Indians would call her *darshan*—her simple presence, and everything that was flowing from it.

After about an hour, although it seemed much less than that, she ended her talk and invited questions, and sure enough, the first one was about anger and how to transform it. She sat quietly for a moment before she answered.
   "I could give you what the scriptures say," she said a little wryly, "but it won't work." By which she did not mean that the scriptures are wrong, or that the people in the room were thickheaded, but that the scriptures are useless to us if they're just parroted or applied in a literal, ham-handed fashion. Vajrayana Buddhism is a living tradition, whose students are not expected to absorb the teachings by study alone. The teachings descend, rather, from teacher to student in what is sometimes called "the whispered lineage." In fact, during monastic training one is not even permitted to study a particular text without having first received it in a ceremony of transmission from a teacher who *carries that lineage* and can, as it were, introduce one personally.
   Indeed, this is another context in which the dakini turns up. For when teachings are transmitted directly, Simmer-Brown tells us, and they haven't been tarnished by intellectualization or controversy, they carry with them *the warm breath of the mother dakinis*.[22] It was

---

[22] Simmer-Brown, *The Dakini's Warm Breath.*

Tenzin Palmo's job, then, to meet the student halfway and draw upon her own experience to make Vajrayana teachings on anger immediate and real.

In the first place, she said that before one can transform anger, she must *understand* that anger is a self-defeating emotion. The problem isn't that angry thoughts arise, but that we allow them to stay around. They accumulate, and gain force, and sweep us away. So the more mindful one could become, and the better able to relax the mind, the better able one would be to transform those thoughts.

"So everything really depends on being conscious of what is happening. One trick, therefore, is to look back after an episode and identify the moment when you blew it. Replay the scene and try to imagine what you could have done and said differently. Keep replaying it until you've got it right.

"Do you see how much more skillful this is?"

She was silent for a moment, and then added, gazing directly at the person who'd asked the question, that often when we are angry we're angry at ourselves—afflicted by a sense of low self worth: "The Buddha himself said we must begin by sending loving thoughts toward ourselves."

On anger again: A man, this time, who was still not comfortable with the idea of replacing anger with positive thoughts. Couldn't one just "relax into the great expanse" of the unconditioned?

"This other approach feels like another of those dualistic spiritual battles," he said. "You know, the *white-knuckled bodhisattva*!" He smiled engagingly, and sympathetic laughter rippled around the room, particularly when he added that he was especially wary of that modality, "because I'm German."

But Tenzin Palmo wasn't buying it, and she didn't join in the laughter. Ever so gently, but without the trace of a smile, she told him, "We are slaves to our emotions."

The room got very quiet again.

"I'm sorry," she added, almost tenderly, "but we are. If you can 're-lax into that great expanse,' fine. But most people who say that are just kidding themselves. They talk about the expanse, and then they turn around and get addicted, or they get angry. . . . At the root of all our suffering are the three poisoned arrows of greed, anger, and stupidity."

"Our minds should be as spacious as the sky," she would say a few minutes later, "but our conduct as carefully sifted as barley flour. Guru Rinpoche."[23]

---

[23] Padmasambhava, who brought Buddhism to Tibet.

Without saying so, she had addressed the problem of anger by drawing upon one of the fundamental teachings of Mahayana (and therefore Vajrayana as well). Buddhism. Because what the "white-knuckled *bodhisattva*" had asked was, in effect, this: If you've accepted the basic Buddhist perspective on emotions—that along with everything else, they have no ultimate reality—then what sense does it make to sift them into good emotions you'll accept and bad emotions that have to go? Isn't that like saying they're real after all?

On the face of things, it would seem to have been a reasonable question. One guesses it was just such a question that had prompted the Buddha to issue the second of his Third Turning teachings, in which we learn that reality reveals itself by stages.

Because as Tenzin Palmo explained, holding the *idea* of emptiness as an intellectual principle can be an interesting exercise, but is not even remotely the same thing as awakening into emptiness by stilling the mind and going beyond ego. You may "know" that your anger is merely an emotion, and that emotions are ephemeral, but when rage has consumed you and is pushing you into actions destructive to others and to yourself, that *knowledge* is nowhere within reach. Your anger is far more real to you at that moment than the emptiness of all forms that you have only heard about, and you absolutely must deal with it.

Of *course* we are trying to break through to the unconditioned, Tenzin Palmo has said in a similar conversation, "but we start with *these* minds, *these* problems, *these* weaknesses, *these* strengths" (96).

After the talk, members of the audience were invited to form a line and come speak to her personally if they wished. The line didn't seem terribly long at first, but after a while I realized that the room was barely emptying because people just remained sitting until the line shortened and then joined up. It was almost an hour before I reached her. She looked both worn and fiercely, warmly attentive; calm abiding and penetrating insight had fused into one countenance. I thanked her for the evening and told her how grateful I was that she had set time aside for me the next morning.

Occasions like the one I just described are opportunities, of course, for Tenzin Palmo to teach the Dharma, and she takes them very seriously as such. She certainly does warm to whatever audience she is addressing. But she has no desire to set herself up as a teacher, initiate students, or establish centers in the West.

In fact, there was an awkward moment at the end of this particular lecture when one of the organizers of the event rose, thanked her on everyone's behalf for coming, and asked whether she could please not wait another two years for her next visit. Could she be persuaded to come again in a year? Everyone applauded, but Tenzin Palmo appeared not to have known that this was coming, and as soon as she got the drift her hands flew up in front of her in the universal gesture of "Stop! Stop!" Clearly, another trip to New York was not in her immediate plans.

"I'll be traveling in Asia next year," she explained, and the speaker recovered: "Well, then, I guess we'll just have to be patient for two more years."

But again Tenzin Palmo's hands flew up and she shook her head vigorously. No promises. Not now. Not this far in advance, certainly.

Teaching, she has said, gives her no joy. It's hard to take this in when you have watched her hold a crowd spellbound, and do it with no gimmicks, no party tricks whatsoever, just solid, lucid, inspired Dharma discourse. But she means it. Sometimes, she says, when she *is* teaching she can almost hear a voice asking "What are you doing?" And she never once heard that voice while she was in her cave.

"I would like to gain very deep realizations," she told Vicki Mackenzie. "And all my teachers, including the Dalai Lama, have told me that retreat is the most important thing for me to do in this lifetime. When I am in retreat I know at a very deep level that I am in the right place doing the right thing."[24]

She had come to New York for a reason, and she would be traveling in Asia next year for the same reason, and it had nothing to do with solidifying her reputation as a Buddhist teacher.

When she first left the cave in 1988, Tenzin Palmo had no concrete plans. In fact, she moved for the time being into a kind of controlled free-fall. A vowed renunciate, she was, of course, penniless, but more than that, she cultivated what the Christian monastic tradition calls poverty of the spirit; whatever she was going to do with the rest of her life, she wanted it not to be her own decision. She had placed her life in the hands of the Buddha, the Dharma, and the Sangha. She wished only to live and work on behalf of all beings. "Besides," she discloses, "I've discovered that if I try to push things the way I think they should be done everything goes wrong."[25]

She'd been in India for twenty-four years when the long retreat ended, and it felt imperative to reconnect now with the West. I would

---

[24] Mackenzie, *Cave in the Snow,* 206.

[25] Ibid., 202.

ask her about this when we met the morning after the lecture, and she spoke pointedly about the perils of reaching outside your own culture for spiritual sustenance—and the discoveries you make when you do.

"You know," she said, "when you come across a spiritual path or even a culture that has the simplicity your own culture lacks, you want to *become that*, and the point is to realize that you can't. You *can* take elements from it that fit your own path, and your own life, but you can't turn yourself into an Indian or a Native American or an Eskimo because you're *not*. . . . It's no good masquerading and pretending that because we change our name for example, it's going to change your personality. . . . In my own case, I'm not a Tibetan. I don't want to be a Tibetan. You have to be true to yourself."

Before she could be altogether true to herself as a *Western* seeker and teacher, then, she needed to know much more about Western culture itself—in particular, the places in the culture where spirituality had emerged decisively enough to shape art, music, architecture, and literature.

When they heard that she had come out, friends from all over the world wrote and invited her to visit. But when an invitation came from Assisi, she knew right away that was where she would go. Italy felt wonderfully like India: "the bureaucracy, the postal system, the general nothing-quite-works environment" (20). Living in Europe allowed her to begin filling in the considerable gaps in her education. She soaked up the legacy of Italian religious art, and she discovered Mozart, of whom she says, with Tibetan vividness, "I completely fell in love with him. . . . It was very moisturizing. I think I had become extremely dry, somewhere."[26]

She read extensively now in the literature of Western mysticism and was stunned at the wealth she found there. Nothing was missing in the Christian mystical tradition, she decided, except a living lineage with which one might connect.

A merely intellectual knowledge of Buddhism would not have served her in this regard, but because she had direct experience of the realities in question, she was equipped to see through the apparent differences between the Buddhist and Christian paths and grasp their underlying harmony. She was invited to teach meditation to groups of Catholic religious and was taken aback to find that there was little interest in dredging up methods of meditation that may once have been used by Christians but been forgotten since. These nuns and

---

[26] Ibid., 148.

priests were quite ready to adopt Buddhist techniques and saw no reason they couldn't be incorporated into their practice as Catholics.

Tenzin Palmo became an increasingly popular interlocutor for Tibetan Buddhism. She was one of the few Westerners who could explicate the tradition on the basis of her own experience as well as solid learning. She was invited to give several retreats, and she gave lectures in Umbria and other parts of Italy, in Devon, and in Poland. While she was in Poland, she visited Auschwitz, as Jane Goodall had, looked long and hard at photographs of people who had died there, and took the images deep into herself.

"So many of them were bright-eyed and beautiful. Some were even smiling. I found that incredibly painful."[27]

As she came to know other Western women Buddhists, Tenzin Palmo came to see that her experience as the lone and deeply lonely woman at Khamtrul Rinpoche's monastery had not been unique at all. Almost nowhere were Buddhist women getting the support they deserved. Ordained Buddhist women from and in the West were struggling not only against the misogyny that had worked its way into the tradition, but against Western prejudice against monasticism as well. She took all of this in, but she didn't act on it right away.

Her host in Assisi had obtained permission from the Chinese government to visit Mount Kailash, the spiritual epicenter of Tantric Buddhism, located in Tibet. Would she like to accompany him? She leapt at the chance; she'd never imagined she'd have the opportunity. The trip was arduous in the extreme. Driving a Land Rover packed with tents and sleeping bags, she and her companion had to cross the eighteen-thousand-foot-high Dolma Pass in a snowstorm. Exhausted and disoriented, they would probably have perished had a black dog not appeared out of nowhere and guided them down. They spent two and a half joyous days circumambulating the mountain, swimming afterward in the icy waters of nearby Lake Manasarova, the "lake of the mind" and a holy place in its own right. She was nearly fifty years old now, and it's hard to believe this is the same woman who had been told as a teenager that she must not undertake a strenuous occupation. Sky Dancer and then some!

She would spend several years with her friends in Assisi, and she even began to build a small cottage on their property, thinking she would resume her long retreat in the region sanctified by saints Francis

---

[27] Ibid., 150.

and Clare. But she hadn't reckoned with zoning laws; once again, she would be set adrift, waiting for guidance.

Her movements during this period were tentative and spontaneous, utterly different from the extremely focused and inward-turning quality of the long retreat. Gradually, though, a plan began to take shape. She seems almost to have tiptoed around it for a time, waiting for some sort of signal that would persuade her this was the direction she was to take.

Her lama, Khamtrul Rinpoche, had suggested on a number of occasions before his death in 1980 that she build a nunnery on the same property where his own monastery had been rebuilt. She'd dragged her heels at the time—wasn't sure he'd really meant it, and doubted whether she was equal to the task anyway—but the idea seems gradually now to have become more and more attractive. She consulted with many people, including the Dalai Lama, and they all seemed to concur. It was a good plan, they told her, though even the Dalai Lama urged her to dispatch it in short order so that she could get back into retreat as soon as possible.

She was becoming increasingly aware, meanwhile, that Buddhist women in both the East and West were struggling badly. In 1993, she helped organize a pivotal conference in Bodhgaya for Western Buddhist women, and she joined a group of women who were committed to securing full ordination for women—something she herself had had to travel to Taiwan to receive.

Building a nunnery had begun to seem a very good idea indeed. Still, it didn't seem the sort of project one should undertake without close guidance. Her lama had reincarnated, but he'd only been in his present body for three years. She'd been putting off going to meet him: she was afraid she might look very odd to him, that he'd cry, and she would be upset. But she went at last, and he took one look while she was prostrating before him and shouted to his attendant, "It's my nun! It's my nun!"

"He was jumping up and down and laughing and so happy. I burst into tears! *I* was the one who started crying, and then he became worried because I was crying, so tears started running down his cheeks. The two of us were just a riot."[28] They spent the rest of the morning running around together and playing, and it was quite wonderful, but no help at all where her future plans were concerned.

---

[28] Bethany Saltman, "Endless Lifetimes, Endless Benefits," *Buddhadharma* (Summer 2005), 60.

Watching her edge up on this undertaking, I am reminded once again of Saint Teresa of Avila—in this case of the point in her life when after twenty years of struggle and vacillation she'd at last been able to move into what she called "the light without a night." For a while she simply lived a day at a time, with no particular plan of action. But before long young women started coming to her. Couldn't they form a strictly cloistered community and live with her and practice contemplative prayer under her guidance? She really couldn't say no—she'd been just such a girl herself, and no one had helped her. Over the next twenty years, her health badly compromised, La Santa Madre would travel all over Spain establishing reformed Carmelite convents. Repeatedly, her younger companion in reform, Saint John of the Cross, would beg her to come in off the road and give herself over to completely to prayer. But there was always one more town, one more cluster of young women. . . .

And I wonder whether finally, for Tenzin Palmo, too, the scales might not have been tipped by the bright faces of young women she met in the Himalayan region—the kind of young women who would embrace this life with all the joy she had. "I really regard these girls as having been sent by Tara," she would say much later. "They're just so good!"[29] As for the guidance she'd at first thought she would need, she would laugh later, when the project was well under way, and say she believed she has, in fact, been receiving guidance all along—from the dakinis.

The lamas of Tenzin Palmo's order have been fully and vocally supportive of the nunnery all along. As early as 1992, she recalls, they spoke out in support of Khamtrul Rinpoche's suggestion and urged her to set things in motion. This is a tradition, after all, with a healthy respect for "the feminine." On the other hand, acting in what she calls a "very Tibetan" fashion, the monastery officials also insisted they be paid for the land where the nunnery would be built—even though that land had been a gift to them in the first place when they'd arrived in India as refugees.

If the nunnery were to be established, someone would have to raise hundreds of thousands of dollars to purchase the land and building materials. The eventual cost, to cover an International Retreat Center

---

[29] Hilary Hart, *The Unknown She: Eight Faces of an Emerging Consciousness* (Inverness, CA: Golden Sufi Center, 2003), 225.

for Buddhist lay women as well, will be somewhere around one and a quarter million dollars.

So it was that in 1994 Tenzin Palmo set out on her first lecture tour, accepting whatever donations were offered, and so it was that in the fall of 2004 she had come to New York.

I was terribly curious about what my impressions of Tenzin Palmo would be, because several of the people who've interviewed her have made roughly the same observation. Hilary Hart compares her eyes to "ponds of frozen light," and says that "often while we talk she moves instantly from coldness to warmth, as though something completely unrelenting gives way to sudden softness and generosity."[30] Vicki Mackenzie remarks that Tenzin Palmo's most outstanding characteristic is "her overt and spontaneous sociability," and that "her circle of friends is immense, and once anyone has entered into her domain they are never forgotten." Yet just a few lines later she adds, "Yet you know in your heart that if she never saw you again she really would not miss you."[31]

I believed I had caught glimpses of what they were talking about the night before—moments when she would be leaning toward someone she was talking to, warmth almost pouring out of her eyes, and others when she looked so remote she seemed almost to have left her own body behind.

As my elevator glided up to the twelfth floor of a heavily secured apartment building just off the United Nations Plaza, I smiled at the incongruity of having come here to meet a woman who had spent the twelve happiest years of her life in a tiny mouse-ridden cave that flooded every spring when the snow melted.

For here were stunning floor-to-ceiling views of the East River; here were couches upholstered in pastel brocade, and thick, soft carpets, and jewel-tone Tibetan wall hangings; On the other hand, here was a small altar, too, with sacred images, and a meditation cushion that had seen considerable use.

Comfort aside, this twelfth-story island of serenity was in fact a perfect setting for Tenzin Palmo, for we were so high above the streets that the racket of Manhattan traffic was inaudible, and the view out the window was mostly sky—sky above and sky below, reflected in the broad sunlit expanse of the river.

"I don't think I've ever been in a place like this," I blurted.

---

[30] Ibid., 200.
[31] Mackenzie, *Cave in the Snow*, 204.

"Nor have we," she said, smiling, with a bemused glance around the room. The "we" including her traveling companion, Tenzin Dolmo, a British woman as well, dressed just as she was in maroon robes worn over a gold sleeveless blouse.

I fiddled briefly with my tape recorder, said I hoped she didn't mind my recording our talk, but that I hadn't wanted to risk misquoting her. She nodded with a slight smile that suggested she was no stranger to being misquoted.

One of Tenzin Palmo's hostesses had told me on the phone that she had had a good deal to say about the conference she'd just attended, the Global Women's Gathering, which had brought activists like Gloria Steinem, Wilma Mankiller, and Alice Walker into conversation with indigenous women from different parts of the world—grandmothers, for the most part and leaders within their own communities.

In fact, when I mentioned the conference, she looked absolutely blank for an instant and I realized that this was a woman who lives entirely in the moment. What on earth was I talking about? But she got her bearings and began by recalling that throughout what had been a very cold weekend indeed, the only men present were those responsible for keeping a big ceremonial fire burning the whole time. They'd worked really hard, and that made it all the more awful, she said, that at the end of this whole weekend celebrating grandmothers—and grandmothers of grandmothers!—someone realized that nobody had said a word about grandfathers!

"I *loved* my grandfather! I remember very much sitting on his lap and—my grandmother was very stern, but—well, actually, my mother remembered that he was an awful father, but by the time I came along he'd mellowed—anyway, I remember he used to do this thing, let's see . . . (she paused, wrinkled her brow, tried to remember how it had worked) we'd be out in the garden, and he would say, 'Oh, look!' as a plane went across, and I would look up and somehow he would get hold of a coin and toss it up so that he could say, 'See! They're dropping money for you!'

"And I could never catch him at it. . . . So yes, I remember my grandfather with great affection. . . . He was an important part of my life, where my grandmother was always a figure of don't do this and don't do that."

She poured us tea, and invited me to admire the pot itself, Cambodian she thought, and wasn't it lovely?

Her feelings about to the conference?

"Well, you know, these things can be very New Age-y, but the grandmothers were not at all. There were twelve of them, and they were very dignified, very grounded—healers, working with herbal medicines—one of them was a medium. . . .

"What was interesting, though at first I found it irritating, was the emphasis on seven generations: looking seven generations back toward ancestors from whom they'd received knowledge, and feeling the commitment and responsibility of handing it on to seven succeeding generations. So the emphasis was not only do you receive, you use it and you handed it on, and therefore you had a responsibility for everything you did, and for the environment, all your decisions, because of the effect they would have on future generations."

We talked for a bit about the dilemma that indigenous people are up against worldwide: That while women like the ones she was describing do want to hand everything they know on to the next generation, they often can't. "They told us that it's very difficult because of drugs and alcohol—kids lying in hospital not even knowing who they are. They really don't know what the future's going to hold."

I told her a little about the Pomo Indians near where I live and in particular the extremely sophisticated basketry traditions of Pomo women. Handed down from mother to daughter for thousands of years, these skills have all but disappeared. There are a number of white women who really do grasp the beauty and value of the indigenous traditions and who would love to step in and take the place of the missing daughters. But in fact, that rarely works out. The poignancy is all the greater because so few of these women feel they have a meaningful mother-line of their own.

She nodded in agreement, remembering that someone had pointed out during the weekend that when the first white people arrived in America, they had left their grandmothers behind. "And that is in a way very profound, because it means that that whole lineage was cut off."

But she agreed, too, that wishing you had a mother-line of your own doesn't automatically qualify you to carry on someone else's. It was at this point that she made the remarks I cited earlier about how you really can't adopt someone else's tradition as your own.

Could we talk about the nunnery? Absolutely. We moved to a table near the window where the light was better, and she brought out a great stack of photos taken just before she'd left India—of buildings in various stages of construction, amazing views of the mountains that surround the plateau where the nunnery stands, and wonderful candid pictures of the nuns themselves as they worked, studied, and played. Sturdy, attractive young women in their late teens and early twenties, robed and with their heads shaved, they all seemed to have beautiful teeth. Like children on a playground, they leaned into each other, hands on one another's shoulders, smiling, laughing.

And here they are looking both delicate and ferocious as they enact elaborately choreographed traditional debates punctuated with ritualized shouts, gestures, and stamping of feet. These have been a staple of monastery life for thousands of years, but nuns have rarely been permitted to take part until now.

"This is Elizabeth, who manages our office, meeting the Dalai Lama when he came to visit. He caught her nose between two fingers like this, you know, and tweaked it as if she were a little girl, and she swore she would never wash her face again!"

And here was Tenzin Palmo photographed in the midst of a crowd of girls, her face absolutely glowing.

"Yes," she murmured, "it's just a joy to teach them, and they are very affectionate. When I was ill they would just come in quietly and stand around and gaze at me without a word but with so much tenderness."

The nunnery is called Dongyu Gatsal Ling, which means Delightful Grove of the True Lineage. Located on seven acres near the Khampagar Monastery in Himachal Pradesh, it opened in 2000 with twenty-five postulants. The first were from Ladakh, and soon others arrived from Nepal, Tibet, and Indian Himalayan regions like Spiti and Kinnaur.

In shaping the nunnery's daily routine, Tenzin Palmo has drawn heavily on the Benedictine Rule with its emphasis on a healthy balance among work, study, and prayer. The day begins with Tara Puja (*puja* is the Sanskrit word for ritual worship). Afterward they meditate every day with Ani-la. The nuns receive daily teachings in Buddhist logic and debate, the Tibetan language, English, and, currently, classes in accounting and budgeting so that they will be able to run the place themselves in years to come.

I had read that there had been plans to teach the nuns traditional crafts, which would be sold to support the nunnery, but I was told now that the idea had been discarded. The young women had much too much to do without painting *tangkas* in addition.

Among the chief prerequisites for joining the nunnery was the completion of a certain level of secular education. The candidate didn't

have to be learned, but she had to have demonstrated the capacity
to learn.

"We're emphasizing both the practice and the intellectual side,
because traditionally, nuns weren't given educations. It's not
that they didn't become realized practitioners, they did practice.
In fact that was the only avenue left for them, and often they
became great yogis, but because they had no education, not only
were they not known, but also they didn't have much ability to
pass on what they knew to others. So therefore they relied on
lamas and male practitioners to carry on.

"So what we're trying to do is give the nuns the chance to
develop their own potential. They *love* studying. We don't have
to push them in the least bit, we almost have to restrain them.
They love feeling that their minds are expanding and that they
are finally understanding the Dharma."

A detectable measure of indignation had slipped into her voice.

"I mean, the whole idea that women didn't want to study! Of
course it's been the same in the West. My grandmother wouldn't
have dreamed of going to college, and even my mother's generation, so, you know, so it's not just in 'backward Asia.' . . .

"Studying the Dharma is vital because it gives the nuns inner
confidence, and belief in themselves, and self-respect . . . and the
ability therefore to impart what they know to others. This is very
important because in the future teachers have to be females, not
always males. Why do we always have to rely on male teachers?
However wonderful they may be, they don't understand our
problems. There are a lot of things that you just can't bring to
male teachers because they're males—they don't *know*."

Her companion was hovering meaningfully in the doorway, and I
realized that my hour was up. I began to thank her and reached
for my recorder, but she waved me down again with real warmth—she
knew I'd come from California just for this and seemed to want me to
get everything I could from our time together. Tenzin Dolmo smiled
slightly, shrugged, and vanished again.

I think, too, that she wanted to say a bit more about nuns and
monks.

"The problem has always been that it's very easy for men to take ordination . . . almost anybody can. Traditionally, in Tibet, you were placed in a monastery at a very early age, and your studies and your monastic training were your training. So then once you had mastered that, and memorized what needed to be memorized, it was a fairly easy life. You were given food and clothing and shelter and respect from the lay people, and so as an option it was pretty good, which attracted people to it who probably would have been better off doing something else. "

"So now, His Holiness the Dalai Lama says that out of every hundred monks, no more than ten *should* be, and I think he's quite right. There are some absolutely wonderful monks, and there are some who bring shame to the robes. A lot of them are drones, basically, who'd really be better off doing something else.

"For the nuns it's different. The nuns are much more devout, they take it much more seriously. It's the same, I think, with Catholic nuns—the women have it in their *heart.*

"His Holiness has said to me, 'You know, sometimes I think the future of the Dharma is in the hands of the women.' Because if you look around, in Dharma centers, it's almost all women! And if you look at the difference between the monks and the nuns, for the nuns, it's their whole life. They *believe* in it. And so they practice so hard. Every year the nuns do a two-month retreat, and they have to do it together because we don't have enough rooms for them to be alone (and anyway at this point they *want* to be together) and they have to keep silence. These are girls in their late teens, early twenties, and even though there are seven of them to a room, they are silent from early, early morning when they get up at three, until night. And they are *so* devoted and they try so hard."

She showed me photographs of the almost completed dormitory where the nuns would be moving shortly; they'd been living in the building that would now house the nunnery offices. Interviews would begin in the spring for twenty or more new postulants. Eventually, she told me, there would be room for eighty. But a tremendous amount of work still lies ahead, and a great deal of money still has to be raised.

Ani Tenzin Palmo is clearly the nunnery's guiding light—the nuns obviously regard her as their spiritual mother. But she has never wanted to be its permanent abbess. It is her intention, as soon as the place is established, to go back into long retreat.

As we pored over the photos together—maybe it was the rock piles or half-framed classrooms—I suddenly remembered the story of Milarepa, founder of the Kagyu lineage, and the stone structure his teacher kept ordering him to build, tear apart, and rebuild. Knowing that she was desperately eager to get back into retreat, I had to wonder how it felt to be supervising a project that had originally been seen as something she would quickly set in place on her way back into seclusion but was so obviously not going to be that at all.

How much longer did she think it would take? She rolled her eyes and said that the temple hadn't been begun yet—the money wasn't even there for it—that once it was built, there would be statues to find and purchase, and other decorations. It would be at least four or five more years.

Did she ever feel as if there was something a bit Milarepa-ish about all this?

She shook her head gently, smiled a little, and said only: "The important thing is that the nuns are lovely. They are really developing well: you couldn't wish for better. Eventually we hope that some of them will become very learned, and some will carry on the *togden-ma* tradition."

In fact, there were at least two she strongly suspects will be up to the mark.

I brought up last night's discussion of anger, and told her that what she'd said about compassion rising when we see into our own confusion had rung particularly true for me in terms of the anger I'd had to deal with in my most intensely feminist years. Once I'd begun to see how much negativity I had internalized, I had to accept too that the men I was dealing with had also internalized negativity. I couldn't do much about theirs, but if I could start dismantling mine, our interactions would be that much healthier—a bit like the instructions they give you on the airplane: put on your own oxygen mask before you try to help anybody else with theirs—the upshot being that I really had no choice but to meditate more diligently.

"Absolutely," she said, and asked me about my own practice. We talked a while longer, and I asked a broad question about Buddhism in the United States and what she thought was emerging. She answered me at first from the perspective of a teacher who is herself a monastic walking into the American Buddhist context and trying to figure out how to address their needs most directly.

"Nowadays, the challenge we have to face is that people who are seeking Buddhadharma here today aren't monastics, and they don't live in isolation, but they want to practice. They want to become enlightened, or at least more liberated than they are, they need to be able to figure out how to use what they've got at hand as their spiritual path. It's no good dreaming, 'Oh, I'm going to go off and live in silence with just the waves and the sky,' because that's not the reality of their lives. If we don't use what we've got what'll we use? People will just end up feeling resentful, and angry, and resentful of their family."

We talked more about the challenges of adapting traditional Eastern teachings to the contemporary West, and the struggles, and the fears some of us have that babies might sometimes be flying out with the bath water.

She said at last:

"But look, these are early years. In Tibet, too, there were a lot of vexed problems about what was valid and what wasn't. So many translators had been coming into Tibet, and you never knew who their teachers had been, and a lot of resistance came up from certain quarters: 'Hey, wait, we're Tibetans. Why do we need all of this stuff from India?' and so on. It wasn't until the fourteenth century that they actually compiled their equivalent of a canon and decided what was Buddhism and what was not. Now, from a distance, it looks all lovely and harmonious, but at the time it wasn't."

Suddenly Tenzin Dolmo was back, and this time it was real; they were scheduled to meet in just half an hour with Khandro Rinpoche. Tenzin Palmo was clearly thrilled at the prospect. Born in 1967, Khandro Rinpoche was recognized immediately as the current "emanation" of a renowned abbess whose lineage goes back ultimately to Tara herself and whose own students insisted that this young woman be educated and enthroned as a Rinpoche. Khandro Rinpoche is a highly regarded teacher who has established a nunnery and retreat center in India called Samten Tse for Asian and Western women monastics.[32]

Goodbyes were hurried but tender. Are you supposed to kiss a Venerable on the cheek? It felt so natural I forgot to wonder until afterward.

Buddhist teacher and scholar Reginald Ray has said of self-realized men or women that because they simply have no agenda at all

---

[32] Simmer-Brown, *The Dakini's Warm Breath*, 185.

and no "self" they are trying to put forward, being with them is extraordinary, because it's as though there were a huge vacuum in the room—one can feel a little giddy at the sensation of all that space. I think he's right.

Of the more remote, austere side of Tenzin Palmo I hadn't seen much that morning. Yet I know it exists. Writer and Sufi practitioner Hilary Hart spent a couple of weeks at the nunnery in India and interviewed her repeatedly, and over the course of time she drew "Ani-la" into a far-reaching conversation that included frank and occasionally *salty* discussions of the present state of Buddhism in the West:

- Of American enthusiasts, for example, who plunged into Buddhist monasteries in the 1960s only to bounce back out long before they should have because they confused experiences with realizations.
- Of aspiring Western Buddhists who "get it" in the head almost immediately, but not in the heart.
- Of our unbridled individualism and consequent incapacity to benefit from the *sangham.*

Tenzin Palmo is by temperament and vocation a monastic, as surely as Teresa of Avila was. Like Teresa, she is both far more comfortable in solitude than most people and, at the same time, far, far more sociable as well. The term *capaciousness,* beloved of Tibetan Buddhists, probably applies: The more deeply inward such an individual travels, the more deeply aware she seems to become of the human beings around her. It's the affective equivalent of someone who can sing whole octaves higher than most of us, but whole octaves lower as well.

Hilary Hart shares Tenzin Palmo's affinity for the monastic path, and at the same time, she retains some of the skepticism of a contemporary Westerner. She asked one day, almost bluntly, whether time spent in deep meditation actually can affect one's outer life. The answer was startling— and uncharacteristically extravagant.

You do dissolve into emptiness, said Tenzin Palmo. "But when you come out you appear as a deity, you see all beings as deities in a mandala, all sounds are *mantras,* the whole environment is a pure land. All experiences are included, nothing is left out, everything partakes. All of reality is transformed!"[33]

Her language couldn't be more remote from the postmodern minimalist "cool" that we tend to ascribe to Buddhism. It's an ecstatic state

---

[33] Hart, *The Unknown She,* 219.

she's describing, and I think it brings us around again to what Teresa of Avila said about that final chamber—the room at the very center of the Interior Castle that is the soul and where the life of the soul is Christ. One who has dissolved into emptiness, it appears, *is Buddha*—is completely awake, and sees reality whole.

Does such an awakening really benefit anybody else? Because I think this question is implied in Hart's. Suppose one does see everything with new eyes, see life as an unbroken whole, and realizes once and for all the folly of grasping at transient pleasures: will that in itself begin to relieve the suffering of others?

Mahatma Gandhi thought so, and he said as much in language that reflects the concept of *shunyata*, or emptiness. "There comes a time when an individual becomes irresistible and his action becomes all-pervasive in its effects. This comes when he reduces himself to zero."[34] The individual who has absolutely no personal agendas can become not just a transparency, in other words, but a conduit. For what? For truth—for that vision of reality as it actually is—but for compassion as well. The actions that are now irresistible might be nothing more initially than a refusal to hate, or to exploit the earth, or to support the lie that one gender is not as fully human as the other, but they don't stop there.

One has to wonder whether in her unsought role as abbess of the nunnery Tenzin Palmo hasn't consulted with the consummate abbess, because when Teresa of Avila elaborates on what goes on in that seventh chamber, she says that at this point the soul becomes both Mary and Martha: True it may be that Mary "has the better part," but when we are occupied in prayer it must not be for the sake of our own enjoyment, but to gain the strength to serve. Just so Tenzin Palmo tells Hilary Hart: "The perfection is to have a Mary/Martha—to be Mary in Martha's part and to be Martha in Mary's part. To integrate the two." Hart asks why, then, Mary is said to have the better part, and Tenzin Palmo replies, "Because . . . it's very hard to be a Mary/Martha until you have really sat and practiced one-pointedly."[35]

I've only barely begun to understand what's going on with Tibetan Buddhism, but through Tenzin Palmo I've started to absorb some of its distinctive teachings gratefully into my own religious vocabulary. I'd like to return to just a few these before we end this chapter.

---

[34] Mahatma Gandhi, as quoted in Eknath Easwaran, *Gandhi the Man: The Story of His Tranformation*, 3rd ed. (Tomales, CA: The Blue Mountain Center of Meditation/Nilgiri Press, 1997).

[35] Hart, *The Unknown She*, 216.

The first is *tonglen,* or "taking and giving." Because women sit traditionally and everywhere at the intersections between being and non-being, it is often our lot to witness extreme suffering—difficult birthings, injury, illness, and the onset of death. As sisters, mothers, lovers, wives, healers, and friends, we have learned that among the ways we can alleviate the pain of others, there are some that are frankly mysterious. Love sometimes allows us to work small miracles, and if pressed to explain how we'd performed them, we wouldn't know what to say.

The challenge in performing *tonglen* is to open oneself to another's suffering without absorbing it so deeply and permanently that we fall into illness or despair ourselves. From Tenzin Palmo and her tradition, I've come to believe that if there is a "trick" to *tonglen* it lies in being able to let go. Only if we are able to let go of pleasure—to "kiss it as it flies," in William Blake's formulation—will we be able to let go of pain when we wish to. And that in turn has to do with living entirely in the present. It is in our receiving and letting go that we become one link in a universe of circulating grace and kindness, which is also, inevitably, a cycle of sacrifice and letting go.

In Tibetan or Vajrayana Buddhism, the reader will recall, the basic teachings are indistinguishable from those of Mahayana Buddhism, but the preoccupation is to achieve realization in this life and by as direct a route as possible. When an individual is successful in cutting through illusion, the particular method or discipline or orientation that worked for him or her will be reverently preserved and handed down to lineage holders who preserve it for succeeding generations. A lineage holder typically has to do a tremendous amount of memorizing, and it's my impression that this act in itself facilitates the clearing out of inauthentic selves that is part of becoming fully awake.

I'd thought from time to time in the past about what it would be like for Western women to have the benefit of strong, continuous mother-lines, but it was only after I'd come to see how definitive the idea of lineage is for Tibetan Buddhism, and how it literally holds everything and everybody together in a structure that is far more complex and weblike than an ordinary hierarchical model, that the possibilities really started to open up.

Mother-lines have a funny way of getting broken up in patriarchal cultures and institutions, and it may be that "repair and maintenance" is one of the primary responsibilities of women who shake free, regardless of what else they decide to do with their lives. Honor the foremothers, reach out to the daughters. But here's a thought: It may be that just as a Tibetan Buddhist can only receive the teachings of a lineage when he or she has mastered the preliminary disciplines, we women can only be lineage holders for other women when we have done the preliminary work of stripping away our own internalized misogyny.

Could we ever say enough about what it would mean to have the dakinis operative within one's religious imagination? Exposure to figures like Shakti, Kali, and the dakinis has taught Western women how to discern manifestations of the sacred feminine in their own traditions: in Hildegard of Bingen, for example, and Julian of Norwich, or a personal favorite of mine, the fourteenth-century German mystic Mechthild of Magdeburg, who created in her extraordinary cycle of poems called *The Flowing Light of the Divine Godhead* a persona who in many ways resembles the dakinis. Insatiable for the "unmixed wine" of religious ecstasy, defiant of public or ecclesiastical opinion, brutally frank, she portrays herself as naked in token of her abandonment of all proprieties and all disguises.

When we honor the dakinis we pay homage to something women everywhere know even if we haven't put it into words: in order for civilization to move along the very linear, hierarchical, materialistic and aggressive pathways that it has, a tremendous quantity of a very different kind of psychic energy has been checked. Figures like the dakinis or their great-grandmother Kali are apt symbols of that potentially explosive thing called *shakti*.

To describe the evolution of a religious tradition as rounds in a continuously widening spiral is to recognize that only a living religious tradition will serve living human beings, for life *is* change. Living organisms survive by evolving—by responding creatively to the stresses of continuous environmental change. So do communities of organisms: bacteria, penguins, Lutherans, and multi-national corporations. There may be no more Turnings of the Dharma Wheel in the largest sense, but an American Buddhism is certainly emerging that will have its own unique flavor. (So, for that matter, is American Catholicism!) How intriguing, then, to apply the model of Turnings to women's movement. Enough with the waves. Perhaps, instead, we are women at the Fourth Turning; without discrediting or abandoning anything we experienced at the First or Second or Third Turning, we move now into a fourth and wider ring that holds and reveres what's come before but opens out now to include what we are coming to know as spiritual seekers.

Just a few weeks after I met with Tenzin Palmo in New York, my friend Will traveled to India. He'd been invited to address a group of Catholic religious who wanted to know more about mysticism and meditative practices than they'd been able to receive from their own tradition. After the workshop he traveled north to the Himalayan region and was able to talk again with Tenzin Palmo. When she heard what he was doing, she got very animated. She took hold of his arm and said, "Here is what you need to do!" She described a practice for them that was an adaptation of a Green Tara visualization. They were to imagine the Virgin Mary—get very clear, very centered, and then picture her—her radiance, her compassion, her purity. Once the image was complete, they were to allow her to approach them, and merge into them, and feel themselves united with her.

"But these are people who won't have done the *ngoro* practices first," I said, referring to the thousands of prostrations and other disciplines that I understood were to precede any visualization practice.

"I asked her about that," Will said, "and she said they wouldn't have to have done the *ngoro* practices first to get empowerment. She was emphatic: This would work for them."

Wait. This would work because she *said* it would? My hunch is, rather, that she meant Never *mind* that it wouldn't work in exactly the same way it would if undertaken by an experienced Buddhist meditator who'd done all the *ngoro* practices beforehand. It would certainly have an effect!

I remembered something else: it was undoubtedly not just any old Madonna she was thinking about. Among the Renaissance paintings she'd come to love in Italy, there was one in particular that she has declared her favorite. Piero della Francesca was the painter, and he'd portrayed Mary standing, with a cloak that extended away from her body and gave shelter to multitudes of people. The image is above all else spacious. It embodies the breadth of compassion that comes with having swept all counterfeit identities out of the way so that, in the words of the Taoist seer, "within herself there is room for everything."

"She looks straight out at the viewer," says Tenzin Palmo. "She's strong, confident. . . . There is love there, compassion, and *gravitas*. She is a very powerful lady."[36]

A Sky Dancer, one might almost say, is Mary.

Will brought back a welcome piece of news. I had been feeling wistful on Tenzin Palmo's behalf, knowing how much she longs to be back in retreat, and now I learned that a small hermitage has been

---

[36] Ibid., 200.

built just for her that is set well apart from the other buildings at the nunnery. It has a turnstile so that food can be brought there without her having to see anyone.

You can imagine the coaxing: "See, you don't have to go anywhere. You can be right here close enough that we'll know you're safe, and we promise not to disturb you!"

I mentioned the Saraswati River in the Introduction, but there is a contemporary sequel to the story of her disappearance. In 1972, satellite photos revealed what is incontrovertibly the outline of a long, wide river bed running roughly parallel to the Indus. Scientists believe now that sometime in the fourth millennium BCE a seismic event occurred that disrupted the river's connection with the Himalayan glacier where it originated, and the river dried up, and the consensus is solid that the river in question was Saraswati—a river and a goddess at once, embodiment of wisdom, intuition, artistry, music, poetry, and flow itself.

Today, the river only flows in India's religious imagination, but it provides a perfect metaphor for Tenzin Palmo's decision to build a nunnery for young women who are as truly the daughters of the Himalayas as the rivers Ganga, Jamuna, and Saraswati. With the restoration of the *togden-ma* lineage, a stream of India's feminine sacred tradition begins to flow again, and surely that event is of a piece with the resistance India's eco-feminists are putting up to the damming of the Narada and the deforestation of the slopes of the Himalayas.

Saraswati is back, the dakinis are present, Green Tara smiles from her forest dwelling. . . .

Sister Helen Prejean

"It Opened Like a Rose"

It's a mild Sunday evening late in January, and Sister Helen Prejean is about to speak at an event sponsored jointly by Berkeley's independent radio station KPFA and the Catholic social justice group Pace e Bene. We've gathered at the Martin Luther King, Jr., Middle School; bright murals celebrate the Reverend King, Cesar Chavez, Rosa Parks, and other champions of the powerless and dispossessed. It's a quintessentially Berkeley crowd, vocal and animated as they greet one another, longtime veterans of resistance actions against war, racism, poverty, and injustice. Right in front of us sit two of the town's legendary Little Old Ladies of the Left. Their white heads barely clear the tops of the seatbacks, and I'm sure they're closing in on ninety, but I know they got here on their own steam because an equally venerable pal in a "Free Mumia Abu-Jamal" t-shirt has just come by and secured a lift home.

Quite a few of the people here tonight kept vigil for most of last week outside of San Quentin, where a man named Donald Beardslee was to die by lethal injection. It had taken Beardlee's executioners a full fifteen minutes to find a vein and set up an intravenous feed for the chemicals that would end his life.

Undertaking this exploration of Sister Helen Prejean and her battle for America's soul has been a somewhat wrenching experience for me. Obliged now to follow closely the kind of news story that I've studiously ignored for years, I'm feeling the strain. I go online every day, for example, to follow a desperate courtroom drama unfolding in Hartford, Connecticut, where a confessed serial murderer is asking the court to *let* him be executed. And because Sister Helen asks that anybody who is working on behalf of people facing the death penalty be concerned with the families of their victims as well, I have read my way through the descriptions of the eight young women that man destroyed. I have read statements from their families too. It's almost inconceivable that one individual could wreak so much havoc.

Sister Helen is on tour right now to promote her second book, *The Death of Innocents*, and her itinerary is packed, but she has already had to reschedule a number of appearances because of executions that require her presence. I'm only following her vicariously as she travels from New Orleans to Saint Louis to Los Angeles to Sydney, Australia, back to Chicago, and then to Japan, but I'm experiencing something very like battle fatigue on her behalf, and I can't imagine how she herself must be feeling.

Tonight's event happens to be taking place during the same week when dignitaries from all over the world have come together in Poland to observe the sixtieth anniversary of the day when Allied troops opened the death camps at Auschwitz and Birkenau. Even as participants are outdoing one another in the delivery of "Never again" speeches, they are also well aware of the growing presence throughout Europe of an ugly neo-Nazi movement. And even as official recognition is being paid there to the special contributions American troops made to winning that war—for democracy, freedom, and human rights—a panel of US senators is investigating the abuse of prisoners by American military and civilian personnel in Iraq, a probe that will later extend to Afghanistan and the Guantanamo Bay prison in Cuba.

Most Americans would like to believe that these atrocities are aberrations—the work of a few bad apples, nothing systemic, surely, because these are, after all, our daughters and sons. But even our closest world allies appear to think otherwise. To many of them, these crimes against humanity are regrettably but undeniably consistent with Americans' unwillingness to leave the company of countries like Syria, Iran, and Libya by abandoning the death penalty.

Sister Helen Prejean agrees. When we ask ourselves how human beings can behave like this toward other human beings, we can't confine our curiosity to Auschwitz, or Cambodia, or Rwanda. We can't even stop with prisoner abuse at Abu Ghraib. We have to ask about San Quentin, too, where 640 men sit on Death Row. The question has everything to do with us, as a nation, and the ideals we supposedly cherish.

It has to do with the prosecuting attorneys in Louisiana that Sister Helen has told us about who give out plaques to one another when one of them wins a capital punishment trial. Called the Louisiana Prick Award, the plaques carry representations of a pelican, the Louisiana state bird, carrying a hypodermic as it flies.

Sister Helen had talked about all of this on Saturday night at Copperfield's Bookstore in Petaluma, noting that the cells at Abu Ghraib are actually a foot *longer* than those at San Quentin. The death penalty is torture, she'd said flatly. Her own experience convinces her Amnesty International's description is exactly right: "an extreme mental or physical assault on someone who has been rendered defenseless."[1]

With consummate storytelling skill she had drawn her audience along with her on two journeys with men who had been executed, and for seconds at a time I think we were able to grasp some measure of the anguish she had experienced on their behalf. And yet, weirdly enough, as I recalled the evening now, I found myself smiling. Because she invites her audiences to find in her accounts of Southern jurisprudence and the bizarre rituals that accompany an execution not only the horrific but the darkly and preposterously funny as well. I hadn't laughed so hard in weeks, and I'm sure that's just what she wanted, because the right kind of laughter has a way of shaking loose habitual patterns of thinking, and until a great deal of that kind of shaking has happened, the death penalty will abide.

Larry Bensky has come to center stage now to introduce Sister Helen, and, once again, I smile. I've listened to this man on KPFA for decades, and I'd always pictured him as small and wiry, but look at him! He must be six foot three, and he's having to bend way over to speak into a microphone that's set up for someone barely five foot two. Sister Helen had been his guest that morning on his Sunday Salon program, and their mutual appreciation couldn't have been more evident.

Bensky had begun with a confession: People in the media have an open invitation to witness executions, but he'd never accepted the offer. Was it cowardly of him to have stayed away? She had set him straight immediately. He'd been right to stay away, because if he had come merely as a journalist, he would have been acting in complicity with the state. She herself was only there for the men being executed. They talked for a bit, and Bensky summed up what was for him the fundamental flaw in a judicial system that invokes the death penalty: "Human beings and human justice are fallible, but the death penalty is irrevocable."

---

[1] Sister Helen Prejean, *The Death of Innocents* (New York: Random House, 2004), 108. Subsequent references to this book will be made in the form of parenthesized *DI* plus page numbers.

"You've got it, Larry," she answered, sounding for all the world like a high school English teacher congratulating her brightest student for having figured out what the handkerchief meant in the structure of *Othello*. She did teach junior and senior high school English and religious education for eleven years before receiving what she's called a "vocation within a vocation," and she still describes herself as, fundamentally, an educator.

"Well," Bensky laughed, "I hope I've got it, because I've been campaigning against the death penalty for more than fifty years."

Bensky had just gotten back from Washington, DC, where he'd been covering Senate confirmation hearings of a public official he described, audibly exasperated, as "a very cold and calculating and rigid person."

Sister Prejean didn't disagree outright, but she offered another interpretation. "There are people who go through life living in a bubble," she said. "It's as if they wore five pair of gloves, layer after layer, so they've never felt a human tear, never really touched a human cheek."

In every talk she gives, it should be said, she portrays *herself* as having lived inside just such a bubble—sometimes she calls it a terrarium, a shell, or a membrane—until she was forty-two years old. If there is a secret to her success as a communicator, it is that she doesn't set herself apart from anyone on earth. When she tells her story, she always leaves in the parts that convey how tentative and faltering her journey has sometimes been. She has been at every step in the way, she emphasizes, "the new kid on the block," and, much of the time, frightened half to death.

"I knew *nothing*," she insists. "But by admitting that I give my readers permission to learn along with me."

She loves a good metaphor.

"There's a new edge to the discourse now," she'd told Bensky, "Back in 1993, you put the plow in the ground, and man, you were goin' through *rock*." But now crowds turn out wherever she goes. In Petaluma, she exulted, Copperfield's Bookstore had been so full of people that "they were spilling right up onto the shelves." The signal difference between 1993 and 2005 is, of course, the fact that in 1996 *Dead Man Walking* had been made into a major feature film, and Susan Sarandon, who played Sister Helen, won an Oscar for her performance.

Last night Helen had worn a navy blue "Saint Mary's Church" sweatshirt over black slacks and a white blouse with an openwork collar, an ensemble that backed up a running joke she and Sarandon share to the effect that while they do resemble each other uncannily, Helen has her own distinct fashion sense.

Tonight, she looks every bit the Berkeley academic—a tenured professor from the Graduate Theological Union, maybe. She's in black slacks again, but they're worn now with a burgundy turtleneck, a gray blazer, and a crucifix. As she reaches the podium, she shoves her hands into her pockets and rocks back on her heels just a little, beaming out across a packed house that is on its feet now, cheering.

And she was at least as happy to see them. Watching her that evening I was surprised when the word *androgyny* came to me. Not because anyone would ever be confused about her gender, but because like her friend Susan Sarandon, Sister Helen is in full possession of her whole self—convictions, confidence, faith, tenderness, wit, and honed intellect. She is skilled at gauging her audience and what they can handle, but when she speaks, nothing is held back, and no strength is checked because it might be deemed unfeminine. She is by turn forceful, tender, incisive, lyrical, and implacable. Her voice is low and throaty, and she uses it like a musical instrument. I remember that she plays saxophone to blow off steam.

I know that her ease before audiences didn't come easily. She's described how hard it was at first to summon the authority she felt she needed to give a talk on the death penalty. But now she looks completely at home. When she cracks a joke and her audience laughs, she chuckles along with them. The jokes are still fresh for her because they aren't actually even jokes—more typically they are literal descriptions of the surreal terrain she has traveled this past twenty-some years.

Surreal, she tells us, is the word that Sarandon used over and over as they were making the movie, and yes, she says, *surreal* is exactly right.

"Did you know, that before the executioner gives someone the lethal injection, a nurse swabs his arm with alcohol first?"

"To prevent infection?"

And did we know that when someone's been executed and the coroner is filling in the death certificate, he enters "homicide" as the cause of death?

In this morning's radio interview it had seemed to me that Helen might have consciously reined in the more explicitly religious language she sometimes uses. But tonight, looking down at the crowd of Pace e Bene folks who hold down the first couple of rows, among them three of the five people who'd been arrested at the San Quentin demonstrations and spent several nights in jail, there was no way that she was going to censor herself. References to Jesus slipped in within the first couple of minutes.

If she plays as well with the Berkeley Left as she does with the Catholic social justice crowd, I think it's because for her the very idea of democracy is holy—the political equivalent of the belief that no one on earth should be cut out from the web of life. Over the course of her talk she built toward an impassioned exhortation to cherish and protect the Constitution, and along the way there she would keep coming back to the argument that the death penalty violates our basic rights to equal treatment under the law. Death sentences are capricious and arbitrary, just as the Supreme Court had ruled in 1972, and they should be abandoned on those grounds alone.

She also thinks that American acceptance of the death penalty has desensitized us toward life as a whole: "We've put a death penalty on the earth, just as we've done to human beings here. Every twenty minutes another species is lost from the planet. We have to learn to live in a way that is mutually enhancing, and we have to learn that the answer to our problems is not to throw away and destroy."

In conclusion, she described a very small oak table that some friends of hers had shown her. It had come from a parish in Montgomery, and it was the table where the Reverend Martin Luther King, Jr., had sat with a couple of deacons the day they'd heard one of their parishioners, Rosa Parks, had been arrested. She described how small the table was in proportion to what happened in the civil rights movement, and she reminded us of Dr. King's own words to the effect that when an idea is true and a cause is just, and noble, and right, the people awaken and demand change. "And then we have a working democracy: when we care enough to change the things that are wrong."

Larry Bensky had asked her that morning how she was holding up under the rigors of her book tour, and she came back strong: "No, I don't get drained. This is *democracy*. The energy comes back to you when your boat is on the waves and you are doing what you are supposed to be doing."

The Reverend Jim Wallis, editor of *Sojourners* magazine, likes to say of Dr. King that he carried a bible in one hand and the Constitution in the other. The description applies equally well to Helen Prejean.

Hovering right behind the compelling narrative Sister Helen spins out in her two books, and making a special kind of sense of it, is another dramatic story that is badly in need of telling. That is the story of American women religious over the past fifty years and the far-reaching renewal of religious life they undertook well before Vatican II and continue even today.

The word *renewal* connotes a stripping away of accretions and a return to the original alive-ness of the religious tradition in question. Buddhism, at its outset, was a Hindu renewal movement, and Tibetan or Vajrayana Buddhism was a Buddhist renewal movement. Just so, Christianity started out as a Jewish renewal movement, and I've wondered whether the renewal of religious life undertaken by the Catholic women's orders in the late 1950s and accelerated with Vatican II might not turn out to be almost as momentous.

I can't begin to do justice here to the full history of this movement, but I want to at least touch on its broad outlines, because of the many ways in which it illuminates Sister Helen's story. I strongly suspect she may share my thinking. Throughout the late 1990s she referred often in public talks to a book she was writing called *Hand on the Tiller, Face to the Wind: Travel Notes of a Believer.* She intended it to be a spiritual memoir—an account of her "vocation within a vocation"— interlaced with the stories of other Catholic women whom she had already begun to interview. The tenor of her remarks suggests that the book may have had some sizzle. "The book I'm writing now is about the Catholic Church's discrimination against women, which is upheld by the religious principle that only men can represent Christ. Well, I want to explore that. . . . If only men can represent Christ at the altar, does that connect with why women are beaten in the home and kept down in education? Because that's a sacrament, as if God wants this. How does it affect everything else?"[2]

Hand on the Tiller was put on hold for a time. I talked at one point to her assistant, who told me that her publisher advised her to stay with her passion, but she has since resumed work on the book. Sister Helen did not write her two books to tell her life story. She wrote them to end the death penalty, and most of the glimpses she does give us of her own life are provided as a kind of foil, meant to help us understand how almost inconceivably different the life circumstances have been of the men and women who end up on Death Row.

Unlike the other three women we've considered so far, whose lives were all affected directly by World War II, our one American enjoyed an enviably untroubled childhood thousands of miles from the havoc. But by her own ready admission, it was only when she had learned of the profound desolation in which men like Patrick Sonnier and Robert

---

[2] Quoted in Judy Pennington, *Progressive* 60, no. 1 (January 1996): 33.

Lee Willie had spent their formative years that she had begun to see how privileged her own upbringing had been.

Robert Lee Willie, the second man she accompanied, had barely even known his father, a man who'd spent half of his own life at Angola. Sister Prejean tells us this, but she doesn't belabor the point; almost parenthetically, though, she recalls right afterward how she used to feel standing next to her own father, too shy to look up, conscious only of his big, polished black shoes and the special tone in his voice when he introduced his "pretty little girl"—his scholar, his public speaker.

"A kid can sail to the moon with that feeling of security from a father."

She follows that observation up immediately with the disclosure that she had looked up Robert Willie's record once and read in his lengthy juvenile record that after one arrest he'd asked whether he couldn't stay in jail; he had no place else to go. Born in 1939, the second of three children, Helen Prejean grew up in a spacious, two-story home in Baton Rouge, Louisiana. Her father was a lawyer, her mother a nurse: to the one she traces her love of books and a good argument; to the other, her compassion. Her parents were devout Catholics. Each of them had weighed the possibility of a religious vocation before they married. *Dead Man Walking* is dedicated "To my mother, Gusta Mae, and my father, Louis, who loved me into life." The tenderness of that wording could slip right past us, but in case it does we also have her word that "I was loved more than the law allows," and even, "They *hosed us down* with love."

The mind lurches, as perhaps it is supposed to, over that last image—a subliminal reminder of the tensions that were gathering throughout the South and that would explode in 1963 in Birmingham, Alabama, where police chief Bull Connor set upon civil rights demonstrators with firehoses and dogs. Helen Prejean was, by her own account, entirely oblivious to these tensions. The only black people she knew were the family servants, who ate in the kitchen and lived in a cottage out back.

She is utterly forthcoming about her childhood insensitivity. She doesn't *have* to tell us about riding the segregated bus downtown with her girlfriends and running to the back on a dare to sit for a few seconds among the black people, giggling wildly the whole time. . . . She doesn't have to tell us, but she does. Or about the day she and her girlfriend were leaving the bus and the driver suddenly shouted an obscenity and kicked a young black woman off his bus—literally kicked her. Moments like this could have penetrated the walls of Helen's bubble existence, but they didn't. In acknowledging that they didn't she is once again extending her hand toward her readers, expressing that we're all asleep, insensitivity is the human lot, it's never too late to wake up.

Catholicism, she likes to say, was in her family's DNA, and the 1950s were a fine time to be a Catholic. Between 1950 and 1963, the number of Catholics in the United States rose from fewer than twenty-eight million to more than forty-three million. The television broadcasts Bishop Fulton J. Sheen made between 1951 and 1957 reached an estimated thirty million viewers a week. *The Nun's Story*, starring Audrey Hepburn, was released in 1959, and while it failed to win any of the eight Oscars for which it was nominated, it was Warner Brothers' most successful film to date. Thomas Merton's *Seven Storey Mountain* was a national bestseller in the late 1950s.

Religious vocations were also increasing during this period. The number of women leaving orders had, in fact, begun to rise—an early hint of what was to come—but the number entering was so great that between 1950 and 1965 the number of women religious rose from 147,000 to 179,974 ("Way too many nuns," Sister Helen says today, laughing. "There were *herds* of nuns.")

Helen Prejean's family was very much part of that confident Catholic world. Her family prayed the Rosary together daily, priests were in and out of the big, comfortable house, and Helen's mother and father hoped aloud that one of the children would be called to the religious life. Meanwhile there were family trips every summer around the United States, to Canada, and to Europe. Helen was the scribe, assigned by her father to keep a record of their travels. Long hours in the car honed everyone's storytelling skills.

Her teachers were Sisters of Saint Joseph of Medaille. The sisters were smart, but they were funny, too. They were warm, human, and loving. Helen wanted to be just like them. She can't remember ever not believing in God. She loved the mystery of the mass itself: the music, the stained-glass windows, the silence, and the music. "It gave me a sense of this invisible presence—that God was somehow with me and the most important thing was to do God's will, to hear that voice and follow it."[3]

Helen grew up in a house where there was without question a man at the head of the table—a man, though, who encouraged

---

[3] Ibid., 32.

his daughter to excel in her studies and her ability to debate, who told her all the time that she was pretty and that he was proud of her. There are young women who grow up determined to find a man and have the terrific family their own parents failed to provide, but Helen wasn't one of them. How could she improve on what she'd been blessed with? She wanted something bigger.

"I didn't want to marry just one little husband and have one little family and this tight little circle," she recalls. "I wanted to go *wide*."[4]

And yet, of course, it has to be said. She was so young. Just eighteen years old. A "child bride of Christ," as she would call herself later.

In 1957, the year that Louisiana's public transportation was integrated, Helen Prejean left her family home to enter the convent of the Sisters of Saint Joseph of Medaille. There she stood, she remembers, in her Baton Rouge kitchen, her trunk packed with black and white clothes and a pair of "old lady shoes." Her composure was intact and so was her commitment, until her mother happened to ask if she had fed Billy Boy, the parakeet she had taught to recite half of the Hail Mary.

"I leaned over and began to sob. I cried all the way to New Orleans. It was the parakeet that did me in."[5]

Convent life had not altered significantly for hundreds of years. As far as she knew, she was embarking on a life of seclusion, forbidden to visit her childhood home ever again. More than forty years later, a seventeen-year-old writer interviewed Sister Helen for *New Moon* magazine, which is staffed entirely by girls under eighteen. Did she have advice for young women considering a religious vocation? She certainly did. "Don't make the decision too young. Make sure to have a lot of experience and maturity. Then go check out a community of sisters and work alongside them to really get to know them before joining them. You need to have experienced the lives of sisters so you know that their spirit is your spirit and that your gifts will be respected in the group."[6]

The Sisters of Saint Joseph is one of the larger Catholic religious communities in the world. It numbers around sixteen thousand members worldwide, and half of them live in the United States. Theirs is an apostolic order, which is to say that unlike cloistered

---

[4] Debra Pickett, "Sunday Lunch with the 'Dead Man Walking' Nun," *Chicago Sun Times*, June 8, 2003.

[5] *U.S. News and World Report*, February 5, 1996.

[6] Anna Schifsky, interviewer, *New Moon—The Magazine for Girls and Their Dreams* (May 1998), 16.

nuns, they work in the world. The order was founded in LePuy-en-Velay, France, in 1650. Standard Catholic reference books name a Jesuit, Jean-Pierre Medaille, as the founder, but if you ask a Saint Joseph sister, she'll tell you that's nonsense, the founders were actually four (or six) women, lace-makers by profession, who needed, as Catholic women religious did in those days, a male sponsor. The first members of the order dressed like widows because their initial mission was to take care of homeless children, and widows were the only women who could move through the streets unaccompanied. More than three hundred years later, the Saint Joseph sisters were still dressed like seventeenth-century widows, a fact that nearly got a young Sister Helen Prejean killed when her habit caught fire from an advent wreath.

The Saint Joseph Sisters do enjoy a longstanding, warm connection with the Jesuits, whose motto is "to be a person for others." The Ignatian *Exercises,* developed by Jesuit founder Saint Ignatius of Loyola, have long been part of the sisters' own spiritual framework, but the connection today has just as much to do with shared dedication to social justice. Sister Helen reviewed a book in 2001 by Jesuit George Anderson called *With Christ in Prison: Jesuits in Jail from St. Ignatius to the Present.* "I *know* these guys," she writes of two close friends, Dan Berrigan and John Dear. "I go out with them when I'm in New York to eat sushi. I've sat with them in Dan's apartment and told Cajun jokes. And here they are, *voluntarily* going to prison in consequence of protests against the U.S. military establishment."[7]

The charism of the Sisters of Saint Joseph is broad. It has to do with bringing people into connection with one another and with God. "Inevitably," says Sister Helen, "as part of this process, we come face to face with all kinds of human wounds, all the painful experiences that separate people from one another and from God."[8] In keeping with their mission, and so that they never forget it, they identify everyone with whom they come in contact as "the dear neighbor."

While the Sisters of Saint Joseph are not cloistered, their external work is carried out from a strong prayer foundation. Their work is "gospel driven," Sister Helen notes, but she cites in addition two maxims that are especially beloved. "The first is 'Never leap ahead of grace, but wait for grace and quietly follow with the gentleness of the spirit of God.'" One doesn't have to get cerebral, she explains, or lay

---

[7] *America* (July 2–9, 2001).
[8] Margaret Wolff, *In Sweet Company* (San Diego, CA: Margaret Wolff, Unlimited, 2004), 4.

out master plans. "I simply wait and watch for grace to unfold like the petals of a flower." The second maxim is "to be a congregation of the great love of God, to be a group of women who love." This translates, she explains, "into the ability to work for people's good, to be present to those who are suffering."[9]

Change was already in the air when Sister Helen first entered her order. In 1962, Pope John XXIII opened a series of momentous councils, known popularly as Vatican II, that were intended both to revitalize the Catholic Church and bring it into the twentieth century. Roughly twenty-five hundred men—cardinals, bishops, theologians, and canon lawyers—met in Rome four times between 1962 and 1965. Fifteen Catholic women attended, *but only as auditors*. Leaders of religious orders, male and female alike, were told after Vatican II to consult with members and discuss changes that would bring about a far-reaching *aggiornamento* ("coming into the present").

In fact, though, women religious had embarked on their own *aggiornamento* more than ten years earlier, under instruction from the very top. Alarmed by the decrease in both membership and religious vocations in post-war Europe, Pope Pius XII had called an international meeting in 1950 of heads of congregations of men and of women. In an unprecedented convocation they gathered in Rome to undertake a far-reaching renewal of religious life. The pope was particularly concerned about upgrading the professional credentials of those who were teaching and the theological training of all religious. He was also eager to eliminate customs and clothing that had become outdated lest they alienate young people around the world.

By the time Vatican II came along, then, the leaders of women's religious orders were already engaged in the mandated discussions. In response to the earlier impetus, far more sisters had already begun to be sent to college than in the past, so sizeable numbers of well-educated women religious were ready to take leadership roles immediately in the changing environment.

The timing of this attempt to revitalize Catholicism was either inspired or disastrous, depending on your point of view. As prominent Catholic thinker Peter Steinfels explains, "The Catholicism of the radical sixties left a permanent mark on the church's presence in the public square. It melded the imperatives of the Council with the civil rights movement's techniques of civil disobedience and nonviolent direct action and with the antiwar movement's nearly apocalyptic

---

[9] Ibid., 4–5.

mood of urgency. Added was the influence of Latin American liberation theology."[10]

Among the several changes that flowed from Vatican II, the one to which American women religious responded most wholeheartedly was the enunciation of "the preferential option for the poor." Rooted in the Gospels, concern for the poor had been underscored by Pope Leo XIII in 1891 in his encyclical *Rerum Novarum,* but it took on new life now as a mandate for *all* Catholics to address the needs of the poor—not only the homeless people in their own towns, but the dispossessed of the whole world—not only through charitable acts but by identifying the root causes of poverty and working to end them.

This was a call that resonated powerfully across a culture already in the grips of the civil rights movement, a vehement antiwar movement, and a nascent women's movement, and American sisters heard it clearly. Answering what they understood to be a gospel call for global social justice, many of them simplified their lifestyles and left jobs in relatively comfortable settings to relocate themselves among the poor. They looked long and hard at the social, economic, and political structures in the United States and the developing world that were keeping the poor poor, and before long they began to see that nearly identical structures were keeping women silent and disempowered within the church itself.

As part of the mandatory revitalization of religious life they'd embarked upon, sisters had been told to rewrite their constitutions, and they did so now, moving swiftly away from the old hierarchic, authoritarian models toward more egalitarian and participatory patterns. They adapted and even discarded habits designed three hundred years ago and revised the *horarium,* the cycle of daily prayers that had evolved within the cloister but that was no longer compatible with the sisters' working life.

Even the traditional vows, of poverty, chastity, and obedience came under scrutiny.

"After the Nuremberg trials," Sister Anonymous asked me recently, "what kind of sense can we make of vowed obedience to another individual? And how many of us are truly poor, compared to the people we work with? Chastity? That's just conscious loving, and everybody should be doing *that*." (And yes, the keenly intelligent, resourceful, and charismatic woman I've called Sister Anonymous did interrupt herself

---

[10] Peter Steinfels, *A People Adrift: The Crisis of the Roman Catholic Church in America* (New York: Scribners and Co., 2003), 75.

to ask that I not use her name *"because the bottom line is, they can still come after us."*)

Over time, for many sisters, the very idea of a consecrated life would begin to seem dubious, for did not the word *consecrated* imply *separated*? And hadn't Jesus Christ's own life been spent in intimate proximity to those he'd come to serve?

The diminished importance that many contemporary sisters attach to their entrance vows might seem breathtakingly bold until we remember the Beguines, prodigious travelers of inner space, who more than five hundred years ago determined that permanent vows were irrelevant to the lives of prayer and service they were undertaking.

Consensus formed swiftly around certain recognitions. One was that traditional authority structures that assumed unquestioning obedience really aren't compatible with the model of self-scrutiny and openness to life experience that emerged from the new directives. Instead of simply accepting work assignments from a mother superior, individuals began to try to discern for themselves what kind of "calling within a calling" they might be hearing. For help in that discernment process, and support afterward, they drew more and more frequently now on the sisterhood itself rather than on a "superior." Sisters moved out of convents into apartments closer to their work—in twos and threes, and sometimes even by themselves.

All parameters for nuns were widening swiftly, and now that they were educated well enough to make a living if they did leave their order, the question rose with real force: What is keeping you here? For thousands of nuns the answer turned out to be, Not a whole lot. A friend who entered in 1969 jokes that "so many women were coming out that I could barely squeeze past them to get in!"

Sister Helen Prejean was fine with the elimination of the habit, and she enjoyed being able to go out for pizzas and talk with men. In fact, the young woman who had entered the convent at eighteen probably had some unfinished business to deal with, and the overall disequilibrium of the late 1960s allowed her to wrap some of it up. While she was a graduate student at the Divine Word Centre in London, Ontario, she told an interviewer in 2003, she was involved romantically with a priest. The relationship did not contravene her vows, but it did continue for several years during the late 1960s and early 1970s. "It took some sorting out. . . . People were asking, 'What's happening with Helen? Is she going to be the next one to leave?'"[11]

---

[11] *Chicago Sun Times*, June 8, 2003.

What finally ended the liaison was her realization that "he depended on me for his happiness."

In effect, though, she rode out the turbulence of religious revitalization from the sidelines, managing to keep herself well clear of what many women religious were regarding as a collective conversion. She kept to a quiet routine, teaching by day and hurrying home in the evening to what was still a consciously cloistered way of life. She was not drawn to the cause of social justice. "The way I saw it, there were activist sisters and spiritual sisters, and I was a spiritual sister. . . . 'We are *nuns*,' I used to argue at retreats, 'not social workers!'" She put her own spin on the Beatitudes, maintaining that there are plenty of different ways to be poor. She knew that the comfortable homes of her suburban New Orleans students weren't always the safe, supportive places they appeared to be and that the work she was doing there mattered. She laughs today at the naivete of one of her few "activist" gestures. "You remember those 'Dominique-nique-nique nuns'? I was one of those." With a couple of sisters she would visit a local jail and play and sing requests. They were singing "If I Had a Hammer" one day, and the inmates sang along with unprecedented enthusiasm. It took her a few minutes to realize they were improvising: "If I had a switchblade . . . If I had a shotgun, etc."

But in June 1980, at an annual chapter retreat in Terre Haute, Indiana, her world broke open.

> "I was not thrilled when I heard that Sister Marie Augusta Neal was going to be there—and for three days! I got through the first day unscathed—she gave us a lot of statistics about the poor in the world, and yeah, yeah, I knew there were bad things happening. . . .
>
> "The next day she talked about Jesus, and when she got to the part about how Jesus preached good news to the poor, I thought I knew what came next . . . but instead of talking about how they would be with God in Heaven she said *'and integral to the good news was that they would be poor no longer.'*
>
> "And I got it. She cracked me open."[12]

Conversion stories are a genre unto themselves. Typically they give the impression that lightning has struck, but in fact one can always

---

[12] Sister Helen Prejean, opening address, Envision an Engaged Cosmology Institute, July 7, 2007, Holy Names University, Oakland, CA, transcription.

trace back across the convert's life and find that a slowly unfolding revolution has been under way for some time. Sister Helen had been holding out against the likes of Sister Mary Augusta for more than fifteen years. It has to have been a war of attrition, though, because some of her sisters had moved to the New Orleans Projects as early as 1969. In June 1981, she packed her belongings into a brown Toyota pickup truck and drove from the manicured lakefront neighborhood where she'd been living to her new home in the noisy, chaotic Saint Thomas Housing Project. She traveled less than five miles, "but it was galaxies away."

Carefully, lest random gunfire from the street bring her new life to a swift end, she set up her bed so that it was below the windowsill. She went to work at an adult learning center. And even as she was teaching others to read, she herself began to read as if for the first time: "I was reading the lives of the saints now—I was *ready* for the lives of the saints now: Gandhi and Martin Luther King, Jr., and Dorothy Day." Saints, and some Alice Walker on the side.

Sister Prejean has said of this period that it marked the beginning of "her physical journey with Christ," and she makes her meaning clearer when she cites, as she does often, words from the first chapter of the Gospel According to John: "*What we have seen and heard and watched and touched with our own hands, this is the gospel we proclaim.*"

Before she stepped out of the bubble of privilege, everything she had seen, heard, and touched had been filtered and censored. She'd been like someone half asleep. She *sees* now, and hears, and touches what she hadn't dreamed existed: adults who had graduated from the city's public high schools unable to read at a third-grade level; fourteen-year-old girls clutching infants and saying how happy they were that for the first time they had something of their own; women catatonic with grief because they hadn't been able to keep their sons out of the hands of drug dealers, brutal cops, or both.

"The dear neighbor" had never been so real to her, or so dear.

I had read both of Sister Prejean's books and dozens of published articles and interviews before I finally paused over the name "Sister Marie Augusta Neal" and realized it was time to find out a little more about her. Close call: if I hadn't, the epic dimensions of what has gone on among American women religious this past fifty years would still be lost on me, and the part of Sister Helen's story that is also the story of "the sisterhood" would have slipped right by me.

Sister Marie Augusta Neal had played a key role in the revitalization of American women religious from its very inception. A Sister of
Notre Dame de Namur, she had received her doctorate in sociology
from Harvard in 1963. Two years later, when the Conference of Major
Superiors of Women Religious decided to sponsor a survey of their
membership to determine their readiness to take part in renewal, she
was asked to design the research instrument.

The survey hypothesized that ideas about God and God's action
in the world would be a key variable in determining the choices that
specific religious congregations would make in response to the newly
issued mandates to change. Completed in 1967 by almost 140,000
sisters, the survey did indeed find a clear divide between sisters who
still embraced pre–Vatican II beliefs about God and those who welcomed post–Vatican II beliefs. Those of the first group saw themselves
as called *out of the world* and into the cloister, where their role was to
pray that God would bring about the conversion of the world. God,
for them, was transcendent. Those of the second group experienced
God as calling them to share a transformation process with him. For
these nuns, God was immanent, guiding them in prayer and the performance of acts of charity, but teaching them, too, to be agents of social
change. Readers will recognize Sister Helen as someone who moved
over time, as would many other sisters, from the first to the second
group. The survey predicted with striking accuracy the direction various congregations would take, as it would when it was administered
again in 1980 and once more in 1989–90.

The Conference of Major Superiors of Women Religious became the
Leadership Council of Women Religious, and its new name reflected a
growing interest in fostering leadership capacities among the membership. Sister Mary Augusta Neal was a key figure the evolution of the
LCWR, which today represents more than 90 percent of American
sisters. She was among the most ardent and effective exponents of
what she called "the expanding vocation" of women religious and
their transformation from "nuns" into "sisters."

She had her critics. Some still regard the survey as a "push poll,"
comparable to those used today by politicians who want to nudge
voters in a particular direction and pretend they're being objective.[13]
Others were indignant at her persistent and surely mischievous use of
the terms *pre-Vatican* and *post-Vatican* when she presumably meant

---

[13] John J. Fialka, *Sisters: Catholic Nuns and the Making of America* (New
York: St. Martin's Press, 2003), 204.

pre–Vatican II and *post–Vatican II*. But among women religious, her admirers far outweigh her detractors.

"Elegant, soft-spoken, and radical," as one of her students recalls, Sister Marie Augusta Neal would have a distinguished career as a college teacher. She headed the sociology department at Boston's Emmanuel College, which her order ran, and she would teach at a number of other institutions, including Harvard Divinity School and U.C. Berkeley, as a visiting professor. She continued to publish books and articles into the 1990s. She died at eighty-two in 2004. Three generations of Catholic activist women credit her with awakening them to work for social justice. Dominican sister Kaye Ashe, author of *The Feminization of the Church,* knew her as "a consummate scholar . . . exquisitely sensitive to global inequities and to the plight of the poor."[14] Relentlessly she would reel off the numbers that reflected the unconscionable gap between the rich and the poor. And even as her students were confronting the full extent of their own privilege for the first time, she held out an antidote—a new theology.

All over Latin America during the 1970s advocates of "liberation theology"—Jesuit priests for the most part—were sitting down with the poor and explaining to them, at the same time as they were teaching them to read and write, that their poverty was not the will of God. They had the right to organize so as to claim their share of the world's goods and services.

But if liberation theology was to be the new rallying point for the poor, asked Sister Marie Augusta Neal, what was the equivalent theology for the non-poor? In 1977, she offered an answer in a book called *A Socio-Theology of Letting Go: The Role of a First World Church Facing Third World Peoples.* One can assume that when she addressed Sister Helen and her sisters in Terre Haute, Indiana, just three years later, the challenge to *let go* of privilege would have been substantive to her remarks. And Sister Helen, as she says, *got it.*

Watching the little boys playing near her new home in the Projects, Sister Helen saw more than one she thought could have been the next Martin Luther King, Jr. She watched the older boys, too, and their mamas' losing battles to keep them away from the drug dealers, and she saw the change in them when they began to swagger and wear gold chains anyway. So slight were the odds that they would ever get out except, as their mothers put it, "in a

---

[14] In Jane Redmont, "Maria Augusta Neal, Teacher, Author, Researcher, Dead at 82," *National Catholic Reporter* (April 16, 2004).

police wagon or a hearse" that it was as if they'd been born onto a greased track.

But in fact, she had set foot on a greased track of her own the day she'd moved here. She had relinquished a measure of comfort and safety, but above all else, she had relinquished the option of averting her eyes from other people's suffering. Living with the poor, she believes, is a spiritual discipline that is as important as going to mass. "Being with them is to be in the presence of love, which then leads you to do what love requires, so praying and action begin to be one."[15]

So when someone from the Louisiana Coalition on Jails and Prisons asked her one evening in January 1982 whether she'd be willing to be a pen pal to someone on Death Row, she said yes—initially, one suspects, because saying yes was becoming a habit, but also because she already knew that if you were on Death Row in Louisiana, you were poor, and she was here to serve the poor. Doing "what love required," she wrote to Patrick Sonnier. "And everything would have been fine. Except that he wrote back."

Sonnier was hugely surprised to be getting a letter—from anyone— and grateful. He made no demands—not for money, or her phone number, or a visit. But "the sheer weight of his loneliness" began to draw her—that and "some sheer and essential humanness." She asked if he would like a visit, and when he said that he most surely would, she began to make the arrangements.

In the meantime she went back to the coalition and asked to see the files on his case. It was time she knew what he'd done. It was late in the afternoon, and she remembers that a warm sun slanted through the window. She opened up the first folder and looked into the faces of two beautiful teenagers killed in the autumn of 1977.

Loretta Bourque had been eighteen and David LeBlanc seventeen the night they were murdered in a sugar-cane field after a Friday-night homecoming game. Loretta had been raped. The two had been left in the field, face-down in the dirt, shot in the back of the head. Years later, when Sister Helen became close to David's father, she would learn that he still couldn't bear to sit behind teenagers in church because he couldn't look at the back of their heads.

All of the details were there, and as she took them in, grief and rage overwhelmed her on behalf of everyone affected: the young victims, but their families, too, who would live out their years under a death sentence of their own, never able to forget what had happened

---

[15] "Opposing the Death Penalty: An Interview with Helen Prejean," *America* (November 9, 1996), 9.

to their loved sons, daughters, and grandchildren. The man she was going to visit had been convicted, with his younger brother Eddie, of the kidnap and murder of Loretta and David. He'd been on Death Row at Angola for five years.

Sister Helen had no sooner stepped out of her "bubble" than she entered what she herself would call a crucible. She is entirely serious about the metaphor and the terrible, transformative heat that it implies. To do what love required all the way to the end of Patrick Sonnier's life would change her forever, and this execution was only the first of six that she has witnessed to date. As she accompanied both Death Row victims and the families of those who had been murdered, she would encounter the core elements of her religious faith as if for the first time—at a depth, in any case, that she simply never had before.

In *The Death of Innocents* she would write, "On this path I have learned that love, far from being passive in the face of injustice, is a vibrant force that resists and takes bold action to 'build a new society within the shell of the old,' as Dorothy Day used to say" (*DI,* 121). It is every bit as accurate to say that Sister Helen and thousands of likeminded souls have been quietly building a new *church* within the shell of the old. Only they wouldn't call it old at all, but rather a recovery of what had been supposed to be all along: primitive Christianity? Maybe, or maybe, with a nod to Sister Mary Augusta Neal, pre–Vatican Christianity. They are doing what Professor Jacob Needleman says religious reformers have always done: "Almost without exception, the great reformers within every spiritual tradition have sought *to restore its original vision* by re-establishing the internal, psychological meaning of the ideals and symbols that define the teaching."[16]

Sister Helen Prejean has been carrying out that restorative work for the past twenty-some years, and at the risk of passing too lightly over the "death penalty narrative," which I must hope readers will fill in for themselves by reading Sister Helen's own books, I want to focus our attention on that work—the religious subtext, if you will, and the particular ways in which each of those "ideals and symbols" has opened out for her in the course of her work: pilgrimage, last rites, holy communion, the crucifixion, the parables, sainthood, and even the very idea of *church.*

---

[16] Jacob Needleman, *American Soul* (New York: J. P. Tarcher/Putnam, 2002), 26.

But it is hugely important to understand first that she has done none of this in a vacuum. Her work has been absolutely continuous with the far-reaching religious renewal that American women religious undertook nearly fifty years ago. I know a considerable number of nuns whose stories run parallel to hers. Sister Helen probably knows hundreds. Her discourse has its own inimitable savor, but everything she says and writes takes on still richer meaning when we read it in the context of that larger story.

American nuns have been at the center of so much controversy since Vatican II that it comes as a surprise to many people to learn that prior to Vatican II, women religious of the United States were the fair-haired daughters of the Roman Catholic Church. For over a hundred years they had ministered heroically and resourcefully to the needs of wave after wave of Catholic immigrants, founding schools, hospitals, orphanages, and colleges under conditions that were often just barely believable, and operating them afterward at extraordinary personal cost. American Catholic nuns were the straight-A students and the volunteers of the year. "I wanted to be the best," Sister Helen remembers of herself. "I wanted to be like Saint Teresa of Avila."

The sisters took the idea of religious renewal deeply to heart, as they did the announcement of the preferential option for the poor. In fact, they responded to the two calls almost as if they were one. Many of them took up active roles in the civil rights movement and the sanctuary movement; they protested the war in Vietnam, they established shelters for the homeless or for battered women; they provided legal counsel for the poor both in and out of prison; and they became ardent environmentalists. And as their commitment to social justice deepened, bringing them into increasingly intimate contact with "the dear neighbor," these women began to experience in that very connection, and in the most unexpected ways, something they had been brought up to think is only accessible in the context of a sacrament: grace-full moments when it really did feel as if Christ was present in the shelter, the prison cell, the soup kitchen. There was nothing remotely hysterical in this discovery, but it was pronounced and exhilarating and contagious.

When you decide to renovate an old house, you have to be prepared for anything—dry rot, water damage, infestation—and American sisters have carried out their mandated religious renewal in exactly this spirit. Once they've determined *by consensus* that something feels inauthentic and obstructive, they simply let it go. If the process takes them all the way down to the foundation, that's fine, because they know the foundation is indestructible. Their touchstone has not been theology, though there are theologies that fully support what they've been doing, but rather the Gospels and their own lived experience—everything that they have encountered within themselves and the world as they sought to configure their lives to Christ's. Very few Catholics who grew up before Vatican II read or studied the Bible, but today's sisters read the scriptures attentively, and they've determined from doing so that Jesus lived in full solidarity with the poor, not behind institutional walls or in costly dwellings. They take at face value verses like those that rebuke his supposed followers: "I was . . . naked and you did not give me clothing, sick and in prison and you did not visit me."

Sister Marie Augusta Neal would see this gradual shift as an ongoing collective conversion, and one wonders—well, conversion to *what*? American women religious have been reluctant to make definitive statements about their spirituality.

But right around the time that Helen Prejean was beginning her work as a full-time anti–death penalty advocate, the term *incarnational spirituality* was gaining wide currency among the membership of the LCWR. Sandra M. Schneiders, IHM, professor of New Testament and spirituality at the Jesuit School of Theology in Berkeley, described their reflective process as "inductive rather than deductive, and widely collaborative rather than hierarchical," and warned that any formulations made for the time being should be seen as provisional.[17] Still, Sister Catherine Olsimo, CSC, drew upon the proceedings of a 1987 LCWR conference to argue that incarnational spirituality was "the center" holding things together for American Women Religious.[18] Its relevance to Sister Helen's work and how she regards it couldn't be more clear.

- Incarnational spirituality reminds us that the scriptures characterize Jesus the Christ as "the Word made flesh." Jesus thus represents God's willingness to set his own divinity aside and empty himself, "out of a desire to be with us." Flesh itself is thus lifted up and made sacred, as is, for that matter, the entire created world.

---

[17] Sandra M. Schneiders, *New Wineskins: Re-imagining Religious Life Today* (New York: Paulist Press, 1986), 5–6..

[18] Sister Catherine Olsimo, CSC, "Women's Center: Incarnational Spirituality," in *Claiming Our Truth: Reflections on Identity by United States Women Religious*, ed. Nadine Foley, OP (Washington, DC: LCWR, 1988), 9–34.

- The whole human environment is, therefore, a sacred place—
  not just altars, shrines, and the streets where Christ and his
  disciples walked, but all of it. *"Creation is good,"* and God
  is found *"in the midst of the web of life."* The secular world,
  moreover, was now "the place to encounter and to reveal the
  sacred." In fact, the idea of a secular as opposed to a religious
  world would make increasingly less sense to sisters engaged in
  social justice work.
- Fundamental to incarnational spirituality is an almost welcoming
  stance toward history itself. American sisters see this attitude as
  directly continuous with the spirit of Vatican II, for they see in
  that council a shift from a "classical" world view, which holds
  that truth is essentially changeless, to a more historical and
  evolutionary consciousness *"that expects change as the possibility for growth."* It followed for them that the Catholic Church
  itself would no longer be seen as monolithic and unchanging,
  but rather as unfolding in and through history. God's presence is
  especially manifest in activity that transforms and liberates. One
  must read the signs of the time, and "immersion in the world is
  key to authenticity."

Incarnational spirituality sees the church itself as standing in need of
conversion, and it envisions that difficult, painful process as a birth.
Women's experience and women's bodies are for this reason affirmed
and sacralized. Even the vulnerability that is associated with being a
woman and that is seen, typically, as a liability, becomes an asset for
women religious who seek to be "vulnerable to God's presence in all
of reality." With the choice to be vulnerable comes an acceptance of
risk: of risk taking and open-endedness, with a certain baseline trust
that they can work things out as they go along.

A reflective process, and by all means provisional, the sisters' exploration of incarnational spirituality has also been their quest for
religious identity, and they have taken considerable heat for engaging
in so open-ended a process.

When Father John R. Quinn was archbishop of San Francisco, he
touched on this conundrum in a 1983 convocation. In the course of his
remarks he described the deeply unfair criticisms American sisters had
been receiving from both Left and Right as they strove to carry out their
mandate for religious renewal, and he said that he believed they had
passed at last "through a profound experience of the paschal mystery."

They had attained, he believed, to a sense of identity that is "clear and profound," and that lies "with their configuration to Christ."[19]

To "configure with Christ" means to the sisters, above all else, walking with the poor. Jesus did not seek out crucifixion, they observe, but it was the consequence of his ministry, so they themselves anticipate "being drawn more deeply into a 'dynamism of dispossession'" as they identify more and more with those who are oppressed.

Incarnational theology proposes that if you truly love Christ, you won't be able to rest until that love is "enfleshed." Sister Helen has said of her move to the Saint Thomas Projects that her religious life up to that point had been ethereal and disconnected. That it had since become "a physical journey with Christ" makes special sense in the context of incarnational spirituality: Word had become flesh, and that is a very good thing indeed.

Since that first day in 1982, Sister Helen Prejean has visited Death Row at Angola—but in Mississippi, too, and Texas, and Virginia—at least once a month, more frequently when an execution was imminent. It's a seven-hour round trip from New Orleans, and she is asked sometimes, in the light of her arduous speaking and writing schedule, how she's managed to keep doing it.

The visiting and accompanying are not "an extra," she answers. She has to do "the other stuff" because she has to do something with "the anger, the fury, the fire, of having walked with human beings to their deaths." But visiting Death Row is "is the hub of the wheel of what I do. That, and visiting the victim's family members."[20]

"What I do," though, is not merely her work in the ordinary sense. Her Death Row visits have become the hub of her religious calling and her religious life as well. This kind of contact, she now believes, is "the only way the gospel happens." "You cannot be in the presence of another human being, and not know what redemption and the gospel of Jesus is about: *that every human being is worth more than the worst thing we do.*"[21]

It is only possible to "freeze-frame" someone in the act of doing that worst thing if we never go near them, and never experience the humanity we share with them. She has described "what I do" in utterly

---

[19] Archbishop John R. Quinn, "Extending the Dialogue about Religious Life," in Religious Life in the United States: The New Dialogue, ed. Robert J. Daly et al. (New York: Paulist Press, 1984), 27.

[20] John Dear, interviewer, "Getting Found by God: A Conversation with Sister Helen Prejean," March 14, 2001. Available on the fatherjohndear.org website.

[21] "Opening Address" Call to Action National Conference, Milwaukee, WI, November 3, 2000.

simple terms: "I become a human being with them, and I accompany them through whatever that entails." It is a treacherous business—one could so easily be engulfed. That she is not, and that she is able to keep summoning resources that allow her to lift her companion up out of his situation into something like acceptance and clarity, is, for her, grace pure and simple. Describing the night when Dobie Gillis Williams died, she says, "I know not to think ahead. I know that my strength is tied to his strength. I know that I am hanging by a thread of moral courage. If he comes apart emotionally, so will I. I know not to think of his being killed in just a few hours because I don't have God's grace for what lies ahead. But the grace is here now, and we are all abiding in this grace, which shores us up and links us closely to one another" (*DI*, 43).

Helen Prejean has accompanied six men to their executions, and the stories of four of those men are laid out in her two books, *Dead Man Walking*, published in 1993, and *The Death of Innocents*, which came out late in 2004. I would like to touch now on each of these four stories—again, not so much for what they tell us about the death penalty and what's wrong with it, but for the ways in which they illuminate the "paschal mystery" that Sister Helen and her colleagues have embraced.

Pulling into the parking lot of the Angola State Prison that first September afternoon she looked out across eighteen thousand acres of former plantation land named with unthinking cruelty after the African home of the slaves who had worked it. Angola was home now to forty-six hundred prisoners, most of them black, who worked these same fields today under the gaze of guards on horseback with rifles and attack dogs. Nothing, she points out, has really changed.

At the prison entrance she read a large sign that warned her she could be subjected to body searches, body-cavity probes, and a once-over by dogs trained to detect drugs. Her heart was thumping; her fingertips were cold. Through gate after gate she followed the guard, each gate clattering shut behind her, and at last she was locked, alone, in a room that was deep "in the belly of the beast." She waited, wondering how on earth they would spend two hours, and at last she heard leg irons and handcuffs rattle as Sonnier approached. She peered through the screen door, and saw *"the face of a human being."*

Only that. The monstrous, mythic "other," with his leg irons and handcuffs, looked remarkably like half the people she knew. This was one of her first and most telling realizations: the possibility that our society only allows the death penalty because we don't believe that those who live on Death Row are human like us.

Each of the journeys she has undertaken with a "dead man walking" would have its own character, but this first relationship would in certain ways set the pattern for those to come.

She still has two tremendous regrets where Patrick Sonnier is concerned. One is that she didn't engage herself earlier in the legal aspects of his case. He'd had deplorably inadequate legal counsel, and she believes that if she and others had intervened earlier, he might still be alive. The other is that she failed to reach out to the parents of his victims until after Sonnier's execution. She would not make these mistakes again.

Sister Helen probably didn't fully grasp at this point the significance of a choice Sonnier himself had made when he filled out the application that would allow her to visit him. Wavering between calling her "friend" or "spiritual adviser," he checked the second box, which meant that unlike even his family members, she would be allowed to be with him right up until the execution itself.

She felt her way into the role of spiritual adviser; she insists that there is no training for this kind of work. But she had been a formation director for her community, and she had taught junior high and high school boys, and both experiences were relevant.

She was neither sentimental nor naive about what she was there to do. She had come to relieve Sonnier's loneliness, but she had also come to help him prepare for death, and to do that she had to get him take responsibility for what he had done. A trustee who served meals on Death Row told her he'd never seen a man with more remorse than Patrick Sonnier, but she put limited stock in the observation. Regret for having thrown away one's life can look for all the world like remorse. As Sonnier's spiritual adviser, she couldn't settle for a close facsimile. Gently, relentlessly, she pushed him toward awareness. She would work through layer after layer of denial and acceptance with him, right down to the end.

But she would be working almost as hard with prison officials, working *them* down through layers of denial and pushing them just as relentlessly to take conscious responsibility both for what they had done and what they were about to do—to do it *not* as an act of passion, in a haze of drugs and alcohol, but because somebody further up the chain of command had told them to or, in the case of the guards, "You know, ma'am, it's a regular paycheck, and I've got a family to support."

In Sister Helen's descriptions of Death Row and the people who maintain it and carry out the executions, her perceptions clash repeatedly with official explanations and rationales. A stranger in a strange land, she notes down everything she sees, struggling to make sense of it, of all of these people, whose sole employment is to watch other people and see that they stay inside the prison. Everyone watching, watching, yet under orders not to become emotionally involved with anyone.

This is the woman, remember, who has just washed her hands of a religious life she'd found ethereal and disconnected. To refrain from feeling is, for her, to refrain from connection, and that is a form of death.

As Sonnier's execution date approached, Helen saw by how many means the people involved had been distanced from it: the electrical engineer who had been consulted to design the execution process had refused payment. The name of the executioner is kept secret, and he is paid four hundred dollars per execution by verbal agreement; nothing is on paper. The execution will take place just past midnight, well inside the prison gates, and behind Plexiglas, before a handful of carefully screened witnesses. She hears that one guard whispered to a man about to be electrocuted, "It's nothing personal." She vows that she will *make* it personal. She is following Gandhi's example in this regard.

What both Gandhi and Martin Luther King, Jr., had done, Helen writes, was to force government agencies to commit brutal acts *in public*, so that the conscience of the watching world was ignited.[22] The acts of violence would take place in any event; the job of the nonviolent resistor is to force them into the light. She couldn't literally do that, but she could be the eyes and ears of everyone who *should* be watching, which is to say every American citizen, in whose name the executions are being carried out.

By the time an execution is imminent, her senses are working overtime picking information. Like a veteran police detective at a crime scene, she notes everything she sees in case it turns out to be relevant. If she can "come down from the mountain" and tell us convincingly enough what she's seen, we might finally *get it*. Who knows which bit

---

[22] Helen Prejean, *Dead Man Walking: An Eyewitness Account of the Death Penalty in the United States* (New York: Random House, 1993), 196–97. Subsequent references to this book will be made in the form of parenthesized *DMW* plus page numbers.

of data might trigger a response in us: the high polish in the hallways of the warden's offices, the rows of marigolds outside, or the smell of fresh coffee percolating; or the look of a man whose head and even his eyebrows have been shaved so that they don't catch on fire in the electric chair—"like a bird without feathers"—or his humiliation at having to be diapered; the resolutely cheery bright green suit that a chaplain wears to the execution; or the detailed menu of the last meal of each of the men she has accompanied. Maybe just the random sound of someone putting coin in the drink machines and the clunk of the cans as they roll out.

The whole enterprise requires a suspension of feeling on the part of everyone concerned, and a tacit conspiracy to pretend that nothing is wrong . . . nothing wrong, for example, with the idea that on the evening of an execution the warden himself will host a white tablecloth dinner for the condemned man, his lawyers, the prison psychologist, any guards of whom he might be particularly fond, after which they hold hands and sing hymns together. After which they kill him.

The most extraordinary things, in other words, can be made to seem normal, and sometimes the single most important *religious* act one can perform is just to allow yourself to see what's before your eyes and hear what's coming in through your ears and then go on record with it.

I wonder whether Sister Helen wasn't better prepared for this work than she realized. Because I believe she'd had occasion to think hard about what it means to use your senses "in the service of God."

I've mentioned the Ignatian *Exercises* developed by Jesuit founder Ignatius of Loyola and their use by the Saint Joseph sisters. As a graduate student in English literature in the late 1960s who was also deeply familiar with the *Exercises,* Helen Prejean would undoubtedly have studied an enormously influential book published in 1954 by Renaissance scholar Louis Martz called *The Poetry of Meditation.* Calling the *Exercises* a "practice in the presence of God," Professor Martz proved that Renaissance poets like George Herbert and John Donne had adapted the first of them as a strategy for composing devotional and even secular poetry.

In "composition of place" the poet and/or meditator summons up through each of the senses in turn what it would have been like to be present at a biblical event: the annunciation, for example, or the crucifixion. It must have been particularly satisfying for Catholic students of literature to discover this connection and then incorporate it into their own work as writers and teachers of writing and literature. Reading *Dead Man Walking* and realizing that it was

written nearly ten years after the events it describes, one is struck
over and over by the vividness of sensory details. Sister Helen credits
her training as an English teacher for her habit of keeping a good
journal, but I strongly suspect that the thoroughness with which she
recorded telling details must have had to do with her commitment to
"composition of place."

What a great twist that the events she is conjuring up are not biblical events . . . except that in a certain sense, for her, I think they are.

She keeps careful track of "what my eyes have seen and my ears
have heard," and at the same time she knows that there is more to this
"knowing" business. "It's very important to assimilate what's happening in our lives. I find that I can't function if I don't have that sense
of being at the center of myself and in the soul of my soul, so that I
am truly operating from the inside out. And it's important to be very
self-directed, because it is so possible to be caught on other people's
eddies in the river."[23]

Her religious formation—eight years of it in a very traditional
mold—had certainly helped equip her for this work. But it's also my
strong sense that in carrying out her methodical "deconstruction" of
state-sanctioned killing, she has drawn heavily on a secular strategy
that she learned from Sister Marie Augusta Neal. It's a fundamental
rubric of sociology: *Always ask yourself who is defining the situation.* In any context where social justice seems to be at issue, that is,
whose interpretation of events—whose *framing* of events, and whose
language—is being accepted as real and true? Should we celebrate
Columbus Day as the day America was "discovered," for example, or
do we regard it as a day of mourning for the countless people who
were annihilated by European adventurers? On more than one occasion I have heard Sister Helen respond to questions about her position
on abortion by challenging the way the question is implicitly framed.

Deep sigh, wry grimace: "Who feels great about abortion? If you
really want to eliminate abortions, bring women out of poverty!"

In effect, she refuses to be boxed in to someone else's frame or
definition of the situation. She is suggesting that many of those who
would criminalize abortion assume or pretend that people who *don't*
want to criminalize it are pro-abortion, and that's just wrong. A
sincere desire to eliminate abortions, she observes, will recognize the
relationship between poverty and abortions and address that link
vigorously. The "if you *really*" part carries, of course, still another

---

[23] Jim Martin, *How Can I Find God?* (Liguori, MO: Liguori Publications),
1997, 43.

implication. And notice that she's gotten out of the exchange without letting herself be pinned down.

As Sister Helen encounters the various "Through the Looking Glass" unrealities of Death Row, Sister Marie Augusta's "mantra" goes on strengthening her. Because it has become second nature to ask herself at every turn whose definition is driving things, and who is benefiting, she has come to trust her own perceptions at least as much as anybody else's.

She is steadied, too, time and time again, by scriptural passages that slip into her mind unsummoned at the most charged moments, bathing everything that is happening in a timeless lucidity and even sacralizing it.

Sister Helen is keenly alert to the disasters consequent on the refusal to feel, whether she is observing it in a convicted killer, a Supreme Court justice, or a governor of Texas on his way to the White House. Ultimately, her weapon of choice against the cult of "not feeling" is her own openness. Like Jane Goodall, she leads with empathy and lets it instruct her. But, of course, being completely open means that she receives, as well.

To know that you are going to be killed on a particular night, to know the manner in which you will be killed, to watch as others are shaved and diapered and led off to the death you will face, and to watch the hands of the clock move toward the hour of your death, and *then* to learn of a last-minute rescheduling . . . to experience this over and over again: I don't think that many of us can begin to imagine how that would feel. Sonnier told Sister Helen soon after they met that he tried to get by on short naps around the clock, because deep sleep meant terror would erupt and take him over. He told her at first that he didn't want her to accompany him to his execution because "it would scar you for life."

He was right; it did mark her for life. As a child she had learned that some sacraments leave an indelible mark on the soul, and that baptism was one. She has experienced each execution, she says, as a new and *fiery* baptism. She would wonder after Patrick Sonnier's execution whether she was even the same person.

Over the course of Sonnier's last days, ordinary reality "bent" for Helen Prejean in certain regards, and she would experience this again at every subsequent execution. First, there was the disconcerting way *time* had of alternately rushing ahead and freezing. Given how unreliable the movement of time is at these junctures, she has reflected often on how curious it is that we fix on a precise moment of death: "He died at 12:32 p.m.," we say, as though he might not have died half a dozen times already that same day.

But she found, too, that she was able, toward the end, and without quite knowing how, to slip out of what was happening and move into a circle of light and strength. By exercising tremendous concentration, she could keep her "partner" in there with her. Just hours before his death, Sonnier was mulling over what he would say to those gathered outside the execution chamber. He'd been at peace a few days earlier, but now, he tells her, he is *angry:* angry at his brother (who appears to have done the actual shooting), angry at himself for "letting Eddie blow," angry at the two fathers for coming to watch him die, angry even at the teenagers themselves for being parked where they were in the first place. As she has over and over already, she tells him that yes, she can imagine feeling much the same way if she were in his shoes, but that there is another part of him "that wants to die a free and loving man." He should think about Loretta's and David's parents, and what they've suffered, and whether he wants to inflict even more pain on them.

She talks and talks; he thinks and smokes. The hours pass, and while she is away from the visitor stall he receives the third of a succession of phone calls, this one eliminating the last possibility that the execution might be stayed. She comes back as he's reentering his cell, and he looks at her and says, "Sister Helen, I'm going to die." At the same moment "his legs sag and he drops down on one knee next to the chair," and in her response we glimpse for a heartbeat the human truth of the stories about angels who fight the forces of darkness for someone's immortal soul. "My soul rushes toward him. I am standing with my hands against the mesh screen, as close as I can get to him. I pray and ask God to comfort him, cushion him, wrap him round, give him courage to face death, to step across the river, to die with love. The words are pouring from me" (*DMW,* 88).

All this while another figure moves in and out of the scene, managing to strike the wrong note at every possible opportunity. Sister Helen had met the elderly priest who was the prison's Catholic chaplain the first time she'd come to Angola. These men, the priest warned her, are the scum of the earth. They would try to con her. Her job as spiritual adviser was strictly to make sure these men got the sacrament before they died.

He'd urged her to wear a habit when she visited. His concern was that for a nun not to wear a habit represents a defiance of authority—not a good message to send the prisoners! He would fight her visitations later, arguing that she "stirred up emotions."

Sonnier had made his confession to the old priest several months earlier.

"You know, the heavy-duty stuff. "

He'd been stunned when the priest asked him afterward, "Have any impure thoughts? Say any obscene words?" Closer to the execution he had sauntered past Sonnier's cell one morning and asked him "Well, Sonnier, what are we gonna do with the body?"

The old man participated in a final prayer service that Sister Helen put together, building it around a recorded hymn sung by young Jesuits that echoed lines from Isaiah: *"Be not afraid. . . . Know that I am with you through it all."* The priest does his part, wearing the stole around his neck that symbolized his authority as a Catholic priest. He says the prayers in Latin, he places the communion wafer on Sonnier's tongue, and then he leaves.

He trusts the ritual, she realizes. He's sure it works, even in a foreign language and with no semblance of human intimacy. "For him, the human, personal interaction of trust and love is not part of the sacrament."

It's a moment of truth, and it alerts us, I think, to an extraordinary thing that is happening here in Patrick Sonnier's last hours. In effect, by sustaining that circle of light and strength and love, and keeping him in there with her, Sister Helen has called church itself into existence. The word *ecclesia* means "called out of the world," and she has done exactly that—she has called him out by name from a world that has condemned him to death and conjured up the reality of another, where there is no death.

This act is absolutely of a piece with her commitment to asking "who is defining the situation." She has systematically repudiated all of the conventional arguments for the death penalty, rejecting, in effect, the official version of what was taking place that night. She has just as systematically drawn Sonnier along, from overwhelming anger and confusion to real remorse and a certain semblance of peace. But in these last hours she takes things to still another level by defining the situation in a new light altogether. By being the face of love for Sonnier—by allowing Christ's unconditional love to flow through her to someone who has been exiled from the human community—she effectively lifts him away and sets him down in a new place.

That place, I believe she wants us to understand, is the church itself *as it was intended to be.* It's what we were told all along could always happen "when two or three are gathered together in my name." It only takes two, and there they are, the two of them—Body of Christ, Word made Flesh. By the sheer force of her presence and love she is holding onto him and telling him he won't die because he can't, because he is one with Christ.

The priest shows up to give the last rites, but Sonnier refuses to see him.

"No," he says. "I don't like that man. All of you, my friends who love me, you make me feel close to God. Sister Helen, when it's all over, *you receive communion for both of us*."

I mentioned two "bends" in ordinary reality, but I think there is a third that takes place at each execution she describes, and that is when the barrier between her and the man she is accompanying seems to dissolve. For Sonnier, that appears to have happened to the extent he needed it to. She has "renewed," or even reinvented, the last rites as a sacrament: You can't possibly die, she says, because you are part of the body of Christ that is all of us. And in a stroke of spiritual genius, she communicates her certainty to him by saying to him at the very end, "Pray for me, Patrick."

He answers, and answers *eagerly*, clearly believing her, "I will, Sister, I will!"

In the end, he did not speak out in anger. He asked forgiveness, though only of David's father. Loretta's had reviled him to reporters. Sister Helen believes that Sonnier wanted his last words to be loving, and in the case of Loretta's father, he couldn't make that happen.

One gets the sense that engaging with human beings *in extremis*, repeatedly and for long stretches of time, has altered irreversibly her sense of what constitutes a sacrament. I believe she has fully internalized the gospel teaching that Jesus the Christ is right there *in* the dear neighbor, however misleadingly he is disguised. Asked once how she prepares for visits to Death Row inmates—and families of victims for that matter—she said at once that she doesn't prepare—wouldn't dream of it. "We're never prepared for people. That's part of the real sacredness of people, a uniqueness that's irreplaceable."[24] You might think she was just being rhetorical, but after a while you have to realize that she is being quite literal when she says of the poor, "We must find our way to them in holy pilgrimage. That's what happened in me with death-row inmates."[25] Being with the poor and the powerless is for her the equivalent of visiting Assisi or

[24] Vicki Quade, "The Voice of Dead Men: Interview with Sister Helen Prejean," *Human Rights* 23, no. 3 (Summer, 1996): 8.
[25] *America* (July 31–August 7, 1999), 12.

Jerusalem. Her meaning becomes even clearer when she is asked to talk about God.

"Where do you find God?" an interviewer asked her (a Jesuit, as it happens, and good friend, Father John Dear). You don't *find* God, she replied. It's not like a school project. "You get taken over by God. . . . Dobie's grace and courage . . . the energy and commitment within myself, this passion that won't stop in me. . . . The energy just keeps unleashing itself inside of you. . . . To me God is a life force, a love force. It's strong and unrelenting and full of compassion."[26]

The language is extraordinary; she could be describing the coiled force Hindus call *shakti*, the resilience that is at the heart of the natural world and that is the essence of the Mother. Sister Prejean is often asked "how she keeps going," and she nearly always answers that it is continuous contact with the poor. Of the black women she has worked with in Survive, the victim assistance group she helped launch in 1988, she writes, "All the sorrow and loss is overwhelming, yet I don't feel devastated. There's something in the women themselves that strengthens me. I think of the rallying cry of black women in South Africa, "You have struck the women; you have struck the rock" (*DMW*, 241).

Her confidence in the authenticity of what she is doing—the sacramental character of the work—appears now to be rock solid. That first execution was formative in this regard. A couple of months after Patrick Sonnier's death, Sister Helen would learn that the Catholic chaplains at Angola wanted her to be barred from future visitations. One of them claimed that her naivete might have caused Sonnier to "lose his soul" by thinking he could refuse the last rites in his final hours.

Her response is quietly momentous: "I run the fingers of my conscience along the fabric of this accusation and feel for the hard knots and tears that guilt brings." But she finds none. "The fabric feels smooth and whole and sound" (*DMW*, 121).

She's come a long, long way from the screened confessional booth back in Baton Rouge.

Sister Helen's visitations with victims' family members began haltingly. She was right that most of them would not want to talk to someone who had befriended the man who had killed their child. But David LeBlanc's father, Lloyd, was an exception. The two of them became very close. LeBlanc is a devout Catholic; and when Sonnier asked his forgiveness just before his execution, he managed to nod yes.

---

[26] Dear, "Getting Found by God."

In fact, on the night when sheriff's deputies brought him to the cane field where his son lay dead, he had knelt down and prayed the Our Father and gotten though the line about forgiveness without halting or equivocating. "He said, 'Whoever did this, I forgive them.'" Yet he acknowledges, he has told Helen, that he struggles hard and almost daily to deal with his bitterness.

Sister Helen regards Lloyd LeBlanc as one of the "living saints" she has encountered in her work. (Bud Welch is another. His daughter Julie died in the Oklahoma City bombing, and he has traveled around the country since then speaking out against the death penalty.) LeBlanc called her one day, several years after Sonnier's execution, and invited her to come pray with him at the small "perpetual adoration" chapel where he prayed every Friday from 4:00 to 5:00 a.m.

In a chapel of perpetual adoration the host is exposed continuously. Worshipers take shifts so that someone is there praying around the clock. This one was located in an old wooden church deep in Acadian Louisiana surrounded by huge oak trees. Helen describes the long trip through darkness with her brother Louis, and she describes the young woman with long dark hair who lets them into the chapel, a blanket wrapped around her, and she tells us the chapel is "warm and close and filled with silence and the smell of beeswax." She *places* us there, right beside her on the wooden pew, and she explains, for those of us who don't know, what it is to pray the Rosary. That you touch and hold each small, smooth bead, and then you let it go. This is the great secret, she says. *"To hold on, let go. Nothing is solid. Everything moves. Except love—hold on to love. Do what love requires"* (DMW, 244).

This spellbinding scene is the very last in *Dead Man Walking*, and to the extent that the subtext of the book is a reconstruction of Christian belief and practice, it suggests, I think, the possibility that what really sustains "church" is the direct engagement of ordinary men and women, way, way "off the grid," in the perennial and often agonized struggle against darkness of spirit.

Helen had worked with other anti–death penalty activists trying to get legal recourse for Patrick Sonnier, and that relationship evolved after his execution into a commitment to work full-time talking to people about the death penalty.

She couldn't *not* do this because, as she puts it, "watching and seeing suffering has a way of getting inside of you, and you catch on fire. . . . I came out re-baptized. . . . I knew I was one of the few people in this country who had really seen this thing close up. A mantle of responsibility had fallen on me." After consulting with her community, she accepted the mantle, and *"The decision unfolded like a rose."* There is a saying Sister Helen loves to cite by Saint Basil: "Annunciations are many, incarnations are few." Those who share her tradition will recognize in her unfolding rose the yes by which the Virgin Mary turned annunciation into incarnation—Word into flesh. As a full-time activist working against the death penalty she would develop a sophisticated grasp of all the issues involved, and in both her writing and her talks she deploys that understanding in closely reasoned, powerful arguments. But closest to her heart, clearly, is the argument that springs out of her faith. When she is speaking with likeminded folk she lays it out plainly: "Paul called us the body of Christ. This means that we are all connected. We can never say to one another, 'I don't need you.'"[27]

Ordinarily the "we" understood to make up the body of Christ are understood to be the members of the church, but for Sister Helen society itself is also the body of Christ. Jesus' whole life, she argues, was about establishing a kingdom of God, and today that has to mean people of privilege crossing over into the inner cities and building community together, so that if someone in New Orleans' Ninth Ward is homeless, people in the Garden District will rush to help.

This body that we are, collectively, she maintains, bears wounds that are as deep as those of Christ crucified: "The death penalty epitomizes the deepest wounds in our society . . . militarism, poverty, and racism. . . . .We've got a social problem? Send in the marines. We target the enemy, dehumanize the enemy, then terminate the enemy. . . . .Poverty? . . . Only poor people are on Death Row. . . . Racism? Eight out of every ten people on Death Row are there because they killed white people."[28]

She would dedicate herself to abolition of the death penalty, but she had no intention of ever accompanying another person on Death Row. It had been too much. But when her friend, attorney Millard Farmer, asked her only five months after Sonnier's death to counsel two more Death Row inmates, she couldn't say no. He wasn't holding back, how could she?

Only one, though. She could only manage one at a time. And she would only do it at the direct invitation of the inmate himself. Which is how Robert Lee Willie came into her life.

---

[27] Helen Prejean, CSJ, "Walking Through Fire," *The Other Side* (September-December 1997), 3.

[28] Dear, "Getting Found by God."

Willie had been convicted with another man of the May 1980 kidnapping and murder of eighteen-year-old Faith Hathaway. Younger than Sonnier, but more seasoned in violence, he'd been involved in two prior murders, and he'd affiliated himself with the Aryan Brotherhood during an earlier imprisonment. Sister Helen visited him for the first time in October 1984, and he died in the electric chair just a couple of months later, on December 28, 1984. Like Sonnier, he had had abysmal legal counsel, and he compounded his own difficulties by making neo-Nazi proclamations to the press.

With each of the four executions that Sister Helen describes in her two books, she seems to drop down into the very same place in consciousness. At the same time, each story has its own twists and reflects in its own way on the sacramental nature of what has just taken place. With the story of Robert Lee Willie, Sister Helen looks at the high cost of *machismo*.

She had taken with a grain of salt a guard's depiction of Patrick Sonnier as the most remorseful man he'd ever seen on Death Row, but in Robert Lee Willie's case there was no evidence he felt any remorse at all for the rape and murder of eighteen-year-old Faith Hathaway. Remorse, she believes, "presupposes enough self-forgetfulness to feel the suffering of others" (*DMW*, 144), and she doubted whether this man, who seemed to live very much in his own world, had that capacity.

She would have only two months to get to know him and nudge him toward self-awareness. When she arrived at Angola two days before his execution, she'd barely made any headway. She would spend most of this day and the next with Robert at the "death house," where he'd been moved a few days earlier.

Fear has enveloped her along the way, and it feels like a hurricane: "swooping blasts, then eerie calm, and the sense of waters rising." Her prayers are stripped down and "essential" now: "*Jesus, help him, help me.*"

Which must have made all the more disconcerting Willie's own relaxed demeanor. Yes, thank you, he's slept fine. He listens closely while she takes him to task for telling the press that he admires Hitler and would like to come back as a terrorist. By way of explaining his position he tells her about the Aryan Brotherhood, and his time in the maximum security prison in Marion, Illinois. After a while lunch arrives—meat loaf, mustard greens, corn bread—and he eats heartily. His ease is so contagious she finds she's eaten most of what's on her tray, too. She is having to make an effort to keep the reality of his imminent death before her, because for long stretches of time, "through mysterious resources of his own," he is utterly at home in the moment, even enjoying himself.

He has a request: he wants to take a polygraph, because he's maintained all along that it wasn't he who had actually killed Faith Hathaway. It would mean a lot to his mother, he figures, if he could pass the test. Sister Helen is able to arrange for the test to be taken the next morning, though she is told, and tells him, that his overall stress load would probably be too high to allow for reliable results.

She spends the night with her family in Baton Rouge, and when she returns the next afternoon Robert's family has come, and his spirits seem still to be reasonably high. The sun is bright; his mother chain smokes but doesn't give way to grief. Robert joins the older two of his stepbrothers in teasing the youngest. The warden sends them away three hours earlier than he's supposed to, though, and by 4:15 p.m. Sister Helen is the only one left. She would be with Robert until his death just past midnight.

"And here it is, the coldness in my stomach, the aloneness, and this time *the exact knowledge* of what each hour of this night will bring" (*DMW*, 201).

She revises the thought within moments, realizing that what she doesn't know is how Robert Lee Willie will react at each stage. Will his self-control snap? Will he rage?

Eerily, the "spell of control" holds. At 6:00 p.m. a tray loaded with fried seafood, potatoes, and salad arrives, and once again he eats with gusto, "and eats and eats and talks and eats." One would never know it was his last meal.

Even as the stream of his life is ending, he seems to her to have found "some space, some grace," and she wonders whether somewhere along the line he hasn't figured out that "nothing is really solid, that everything is flow." But she catches herself and comes closer, surely, to the truth: "Or maybe his fierce 'macho' stance has inured him to appropriate feelings." He has said as much in earlier conversations, that he'd always had to take care of himself. There had never been anything to gain by revealing even to himself how he felt about much of anything.

One senses that Helen is of two minds concerning this parody of detachment. Time is slipping away quickly now, and she badly wants him to accept a greater degree of responsibility for what he's done. But there is so little time—and what if, in these few remaining hours he were *only* to awaken to the horror of guilt? What if he were to die in that state?

Something remarkable happens at that point, though almost sub-liminally. As she watches him, alarmed on his behalf, feeling the time career away from them, she seems to enter his plight so deeply that she starts to feel what he *should* be feeling but isn't equipped to. From real depths, and from longstanding habit, Psalm 51, the *Miserere,* has begun to unspool itself at the back of her mind. This was the prayer she and her sisters had been accustomed to reciting every day when the *horarium* was still in place, as they walked to the dining room after the midday examination of conscience. It was also the psalm they had recited when a sister was dying. "Have mercy on me, God, in your goodness; in the greatness of your compassion wipe out my offense. . . . Do not cast me from your presence, and your holy spirit take not from me."

A genuine examination of conscience is way beyond Robert Lee Willie's reach. And yet, in his own limited way, and through a back-door, Helen believes that he has made a gesture in that direction by asking for a polygraph test. Sister Helen watches him after his family leaves, "taking slow drags from his cigarette." It's getting dark, the ugly greenish yellow fluorescent lights have come on, and the words of the prayer return to her: "*Create a clean heart in me, O God, and a steadfast spirit renew within me.*" Robert, meanwhile, asks her about the results of his test.

Could he in his last hours lay claim to a heart that was even rela-tively clean?

She has to tell him that the test, as anticipated, had been deemed in-conclusive. He is chagrined. He'd been sure of himself, hadn't thought he was particularly stressed.

The remainder of the strange night passes, and she finds her way again into the circle of light and strength. She prays to God, asking him to help the mother and stepfather of the girl Robert had killed and who have come to watch the execution, but she prays to Patrick Sonnier, too, and asks him to help Robert. She prays, too, *as* Robert— as his surrogate: "*A clean heart create in me, O God, and a steadfast spirit renew within me. . . . for you are not pleased with sacrifices . . . a heart contrite and humbled, O God, you will not spurn.*"

At the moment of Patrick Sonnier's electrocution, she had shut her eyes. This time, though, she doesn't spare herself.

After Patrick Sonnier's death Sister Helen had begun meeting with the parents of one of his victims, and later she would also become friends with Vernon and Elizabeth Harvey, whose daughter Robert Lee Willie had killed. It took her a while. She assumed, correctly for the most part, that as someone opposing the death penalty her presence was not particularly welcome to victims' families, but it was more than that. She was afraid of their anger and rejection, and she felt utterly helpless in the face of their suffering. "In all my life I have never felt such feelings and counter-feelings, such ambivalence" (*DMW*, 229).

It was three years after Robert Lee Willie's death before she attended her first meeting with a support group for families of murder victims. She came at the invitation of the Harveys, who'd started the group. The group's motto was "Give sorrow words," she notes, and "Oh, God, they do." Shortly thereafter she proposed that Pilgrimage for Life, the Louisiana anti–death penalty group to which she belonged, inaugurate a program in New Orleans to support murder victim's families. In 1988, in the inner city, where the homicide rate is highest, the program Survive was launched, and from then on anyone who joined Pilgrimage was encouraged to support the activities of Survive as well. In 1991 she attended her first meeting, and as the litany of personal accounts unrolled, she recalls the plagues visited on Egypt described in the book of Exodus—in particular, the last and worst one, when the firstborn sons were slain by the Avenging Angel. She could barely take in the resilience of these mothers—all of them black: "Maybe it's because black people, especially black women, have suffered for such a long, long time. . . . *God makes a way out of no way:* For these women this is no empty, pious sentiment. It is the air they breathe, the bread they eat, the path they walk" (*DMW*, 241).

Over the next few years she would come to see her initial ambivalence—"cross-feelings," she calls them—in a new light. She may only have divulged this reading of things publicly in 2000, in an exuberant keynote address she gave to the members of the Catholic reform group Call to Action, where she knew she was in a solidly (and progressively) Catholic context. The film *Dead Man Walking* had been "a bloomin' miracle!" and even the book had been "a bloomin' act of God!" When her mother had met her at the door after that first execution, she was "my Catholic mama with her rosary still in her hands." And the night Susan Sarandon received the Oscar? Another act of God, and besides, "It was the Feast of the Ascension!"

But the most remarkable part of the address came toward the end.

> Our culture says you're either going to be on the side of the Death Row inmate or on the side of the victims' families, but you're sure not going to be on both. But spirituality and reconciliation says: Yeah, I'm going to be on both sides. But I didn't

know yet how to do that, so I stayed away from the victims' families. . . . We can't short-circuit it. We've got to go to both sides, to feel the pain of it. *The cross has two arms, and we must get on both of those arms:* the Death Row inmates and what we are doing to them and their human rights on one side, and the murder victims' families on the other (emphasis added).[29]

There it was. Those who choose to configure with Christ and identify with those who are oppressed have to figure that somewhere along the line they are going to experience something of what Christ did. There will be no *ease* on this path, in other words, no comfortable place to rest. The two-way pull will go on forever.

That two-way pull had, in fact, shaped every chapter of *Dead Man Walking.* Her editor, Jason Epstein, had instructed her to make sure that the reader could barely turn a page without being whiplashed back and forth between the terror of the individual facing execution, on the one hand, and the chilling facts of the crime itself, on the other. The book was published in the spring of 1993, and it enjoyed modest success. Its numbers were especially good in Seattle, and she remembers wondering whether people just read more there because it rains so much.

But a book, she opines, is like a child—it goes where it will, "and this one climbed into Susan Sarandon's lap." Miracle or not, the film would create a national and international forum on the death penalty that continues today, rekindled in 2002 when the story was presented as an opera and in 2003 when it was first performed as a play.

In 1991, Sister Helen began accompanying another Death Row inmate. She would visit Dobie Gillis Williams for eight years, and the signal difference this time was that it was simply impossible to believe that he had committed the murder for which he had been convicted. He was an *innocent* in a traditional usage of the word as well; Dobie's IQ tested 65 (a score of 70 or below defines mental retardation). In 2002 the Supreme Court would rule that it was unconstitutional to execute people who are mentally retarded, but that was three years too late for Dobie. He would be killed by lethal injection in January 1999 after fourteen years of imprisonment and no fewer than eleven execution dates. Two of those had been in the preceding June and November: both times he was within hours of being executed when last minute stays came through.

---

[29] "Opening Address," Call to Action National Conference.

The record of Dobie's trial reads like a truly bad movie. He was black; the murdered woman was white; and the circumstances under which he was supposed to have killed her were barely short of preposterous. Yet it took only a week for an all-white jury to decide his guilt on the basis of a confession that three sheriff's deputies claimed to have heard him make, though their recording machine had unaccountably failed to work.

Sister Helen's 2004 book *The Death of Innocents* begins with her description of Dobie's last days. By the time he died, he was the fifth man she had accompanied, and the depth of her experience is manifest. She knows what to do as the hour nears: dwell in the present, "because the strength comes that way." She will talk to him, thank him for the gift he is, and pray with him. She will keep calling him forth, ask how he's doing and what he's feeling, and that might seem odd to people who haven't been through this. Why encourage him to feel? Because "the enormity of the death that is about to happen is so great that it is easy to feel engulfed and muted and paralyzed. In words there is life, there is communion, there is shared courage" (*DI*, 10).

With Dobie's story we see compassionate witnessing in its purest, most direct form. There is no question of getting him to own up to anything; she's just here to love him and alleviate his fear. In what feels almost like a gentle parody of the struggles Sister Helen had undergone as spiritual adviser to two men who had in fact committed terrible crimes, she entertains Dobie's questions about the state of his soul. Was he *saved?* he asked her. Had he taken Jesus for his savior? Did he have faith in God? His uncle and his mother kept asking him, and he really didn't know. What did Sister Helen think?

In response, she acts as a loving mirror to the man: Look at how patiently he'd endured his time on Death Row and the rheumatoid arthritis that had gnarled his fingers and all but crippled him; look at how generous he'd been to other prisoners with treats and cigarettes; think how truthful he was, and how he'd been using his time in prison to pray and read his bible and attend days of spiritual reflection.

But over the next few hours she recognizes the more urgent drift of his question—his confusion about Jesus, and God, and death—and she hears herself responding to that in a way that surprises her: Yes, she tells him, death is a big mystery; she doesn't know where he'll be when he dies. "But I believe that you are going to be welcomed into the arms of God and that somehow you're going to be at the heart of all the loving energy that is at the heart of everything, and I'm going to call on you to help me in the struggle to end the death penalty. Will you help me, Dobie?" (*DI*, 46).

Dobie answers with the same trust that Patrick Sonnier had. Yes, he would help her. She reflects on how she had "stretched out like that in belief to a communion with Dobie beyond death," and she realizes that yet another conventional Catholic belief has fallen away. "I used to think heaven was a far-off other world for souls that had been separated from bodies. Now I believe that life is a continuum, that dying and living are like knitting and purling, all woven together, that somehow love binds us beyond death, and God is the life force that brings life out of death and loves us through all the dying" (*DI*, 46).

Something else is different about this death. Fifteen years have passed since the last two, and a far-flung network has formed of people who oppose the death penalty and who are, in fact, well aware of Dobie. The Trappist monks of Gethsemani monastery in Kentucky are praying, and so is the Community of Sant'Egidio in Rome; so are sisters in her own and other religious communities and people in Great Britain who've seen BBC documentaries about Dobie. Thousands of friends.

"It is like an underground stream, unseen but real, and I feel the strength of the communion" (*DI*, 48).

Joseph O'Dell died in July 1997, two years before Dobie, but Sister Helen had already been accompanying Dobie for six years when she met O'Dell just before his death. The focal point of his story in *Death of Innocents* is the colossally dysfunctional judicial process that brought him to Death Row in the first place. Sister Helen believes him to have been innocent, as, I suspect, will most readers of *The Death of Innocents*. Unlike her other three subjects, he was executed *in and by* the state of Virginia (it's an odd usage, another of those ways in which human responsibility is all but denied).

O'Dell had been on Death Row for ten years, and he'd already been scheduled to die December 22, 1996. Just two days before the appointed day, the US Supreme Court handed down a stay of execution and agreed to review his case. Within a few months, though, the Byzantine legal maneuverings were over, and his sentence had been upheld by the Supreme Court's familiar 5 to 4 vote. He would be executed July 23. His cell was directly opposite the shower stall where prisoners were readied for execution; he had already watched two close friends forced to shower and put on "execution clothes" just before they died by lethal injection. On execution days, he fasted.

Helen did not know Joseph O'Dell nearly as well as the other three men. Until the very end she exchanged letters with him, but most of her dealings with him were carried out through his chief supporter,

Lori Urs. Nonetheless, she was able to ease his passing in one vital regard.

Joseph O'Dell's execution was one long headache to the state of Virginia. O'Dell had been so sure his innocence would be self-evident to a jury that he chose to be his own attorney, a choice Sister Helen characterizes as "kind of like deciding to do your own brain surgery." He was convicted with breathtaking speed, largely on the testimony of another prisoner who swore under oath that O'Dell had confessed the crime to him and who admitted after O'Dell's death that he'd lied to get leniency in his own sentencing.

Like so many death penalty cases, O'Dell's was one long string of fiascos. Lawyers did eventually come into the picture to write appeals, but nothing came of their efforts. The *petition* for appeal they submitted was rejected because they had called it a *notice* of appeal.

"In my anger," Helen would recall, "I think of the words of Jesus to the spiritual ancestors of these justices: 'You strain out gnats and swallow camels.'"

The problem for the state of Virginia was that the Italian parliament got involved, as did the mayor of Palermo, thousands of Italian children, and Mother Teresa of Calcutta. It was a public-relations nightmare for state officials, and to make matters worse, Lori Urs, Joe's most ardent advocate, traveled to Italy in January 1997 to capitalize on it.

Lori took with her a letter from Sister Helen Prejean to Pope John Paul II (see *DI*, 124ff.). It's a masterful piece of writing. *Bearing witness,* Helen describes what Joseph O'Dell has been going through. He is still "in grievous trauma," she believes, from the near brush he had had with death just a month earlier, when a stay of execution had come through just five days before he was to have died. His tears are uncontrollable. "'They tried to kill me,' he keeps saying."

She has no doubt, she tells the pope, that the death penalty is torture. No matter how humane the means is supposed to be, "conscious human beings anticipate death and die a thousand times before they die" (*DI*, 124).

She invokes the familiar scriptural phrases, saying she has "seen with her eyes and touched with her hands" the very face of Jesus the Christ in the faces of these dying men, all of whom had said at the last, "I am so tired."

She notes the link between poverty and the death penalty. Of the thirty-one thousand men and women on Death Row in the United States, she says, 99 percent are poor. While most of the people she knows who are seeking justice for the poor oppose the death penalty, those who live at a distance from the poor support it ardently.

The letter continues, and addresses the reasons why the pope holds such a crucial position regarding the death penalty. In his 1995 encyclical *Evangelium vitae (Gospel of Life)* he had come very close to opposing the death penalty, urging that it should be "rare, if nonexistent," but he had left a loophole in stating that governments are justified in killing their citizens in cases of "absolute necessity." Death penalty advocates like New Orleans district attorney Harry Connick, Sr., had justified their positions with that very phrase. Given that penal institutions now allowed societies to incarcerate violent offenders for life, wasn't it time for the church to take an absolute stand against government executions?

She describes how "from the depths of my soul, from Christ burning within me, I found myself saying to them, 'Look at me. Look at my face. I will be the face of Christ for you.'" She pays him a deft and, I believe, entirely sincere compliment that arises directly out of her own experience: "What a large heart and what strong faith in Christ you must have not to be overwhelmed by the suffering of so many that you constantly encounter." Her closing words are magnificent—she knows that he is particularly devoted to the Holy Mother: "May Mary, who brought Jesus to the world, comfort and sustain you as you continue her holy birthing task, bringing Jesus to our hungry, suffering world."

Pope John Paul II received the letter on January 22 and read it immediately. One week later Cardinal Joseph Ratzinger, prefect of the Congregation of the Doctrine of the Faith, announced that the *Catechism* would be changed.

"At last," she writes, "the river bends. At the end of the twentieth century, the official Catholic teaching about the death penalty has become aligned with the core value of the 'inviolable dignity of the human person' that Pope John XXIII first illumined in *Pacem in terris* forty years ago" (*DI*, 131).

"'What's the name again," Joseph O'Dell asks her on the evening of his death, "of that Catholic book that I helped to change?'"

The answer? "Joe, you helped change a very big Catholic book, the *Catholic Catechism.*" When the pope heard of the suffering he'd already gone through, she tells him, it must have helped him see the death penalty as torture and therefore unjustifiable.

Woven into the story of Joseph O'Dell is another far more personal narrative. For all their apparent informality, Sister Helen's books are very carefully edited. In particular, as I've said, she says nothing of her personal life that doesn't have strong bearing on the story of her work and the people with whom she's carried it out. Her description of the last months of her "best friend in all the world," physician and Sister of St. Joseph Ann Barker, would seem at first glance to be an exception.

By January 1997 it was clear that Ann was dying of cancer. As a believing Catholic, she prayed for a cure, but as a doctor she was able to track the course of the disease from one day to the next. She read the laboratory reports herself, and she taught her friend how to clean and salve her radiation burns.

Sister Helen emphasizes the particular anguish of this passing. It was *different* from her mother's death, because her mother had been old, and sick, and could no longer do the things she'd done all of her life. Ann isn't even sixty, though, and she wants to live. How could the cells of such a woman be running amok? How could they resist "the power of her imagination and the force of her spiritual strength"? But then, she decides, this in itself must mean that her death is God's will. "And once I know that, I turn the energy of my prayer to align with God's love calling her home" (*DI*, 113).

Ann died in March, and Sister Helen would say afterward that she felt as if she had undergone an amputation. When she found a scarf that Ann had worn after her hair fell out, "I kissed it and pressed it to my face just to smell her one more time. Our relationship wasn't sexual, but we were so intimate that it's like being widowed."[30]

This grief was intensely personal, and yet she has given it a place in her public narrative. I suspect her choice of the verb *align* may tell us why. She will use it again when she refers to a week spent at a Trappist monastery in Kentucky a few months after Ann's death, "grieving and aligning my soul to her loss."

When she describes herself as "aligning my soul to loss," she is seeking the only kind of relief she believes exists for us when a loved one has been snatched away, no matter what, or who, has taken them, which is to say that "restitution" in the form of someone else's death couldn't be more irrelevant.

Sister Helen hadn't gone to Italy when Lori Urs invited her ("You'll have a chance to talk to the pope!") because it would have meant leaving Ann. But the immediate effect of Ann's death besides the grief—the "jagged empty space" in the center of what had been her life—was

---

[30] Raymond Schroth, SJ, "Sister Helen Prejean: On Death Row," *Commonweal* (October 6, 2000), 13.

"a lonely new freedom." And that meant that Sister Helen could give Lori Urs all the time she needed.

There had been a moment when she'd first met Robert Willie that in a very real sense prefigured this one. He asked her in one of their first conversations whether she didn't miss "having a man," and she acknowledged that sometimes on Sunday evenings, when the smell of smoke from family barbecues is floating through the neighborhood, she wondered whether she hadn't been crazy making the choices she had.

But then she said to him, "Let's face it. If I had a husband and family, chances are I'd be home with them this afternoon, instead of visiting with you."

Sister Helen's friendship with Susan Sarandon and Timothy Robbins runs deep and strong. The two of them grew up Catholic, so hanging out with a nun doesn't faze them, and their engagement with social justice issues is of a piece with hers. She likes to remember making him remove all the "nun-isms" from the *Dead Man Walking* screenplay—lines like "Oh, bless you, sir, you're a saint!"

My sense is that there is something Sarandon and Robbins know as actors that has come to be second nature for Sister Helen as well. Questioned about what it was like to play the part of someone who'd managed to relate on a human level to a convicted killer, Sarandon has replied that for her acting itself is often "enforced compassion." If you're playing someone who *isn't* a sympathetic character, you still have to find your way into the emotional realities of that character. You have to be able to look out at the world through the character's eyes.

Sister Helen has that one down. Actors understand the fluidity of identity, but so do opponents of the death penalty. One of Sister Helen's recurring themes is that we are better than the worst things we've done in our lives. We shouldn't be "freeze-framed" at our worst moments. Why not our best moment instead? There are eight or nine different kinds of nun, she has said, and she's been all of them. Asked why she thinks Sarandon wanted to play her, she replies: "She saw it as a strong role. Besides, she hadn't been a nun yet!"

I've asked myself what sort of connecting lines we can draw between Sister Helen Prejean and the women's movement. She has spent a phenomenal amount of time in environments inhabited and controlled and shaped by men, and she certainly has her issues. "We sisters are the hands of the church," she proclaimed to her friends at

Call to Action. "We don't need a lot of plumes and processions. We are the hands."

Yet, setting aside the tensions between her and members of the Catholic hierarchy, Sister Helen Prejean's relationships with men *as men* strike me as enviably uncomplicated. She has at every point in her work been able to count on the support of terrific men, from her allies in New Orleans when she first began fighting the death penalty to Random House editor Jason Epstein to her Jesuit buddies to, of course, Tim Robbins. She seems to be completely comfortable with men. One of my favorite photographs of her was taken in 1996 on Celebrity Bartender night at Molly's, a neighborhood tavern in New Orleans. She is holding court for a couple of enthralled young public defenders who cannot believe they've lucked into an evening with their heroine.

I've thought about how being a nun can bestow a certain kind of advantage. It pulls a woman out of the sexual dance and gives men a neutral place that I think many of them relax into gratefully. But more than that, it seems to me that her whole manner conveys the deep interior work she's done that has to a large extent finessed the problem altogether.

"Spirituality," she maintains, "is about the reconciliation of opposites—about diving deep inside yourself beyond the polarities to a place of unity where everything holds together."[31]

If I were to read those words in a theology or self-help book I might not even pause. But Helen Prejean gives every evidence of having actually been to that place of unity. When she meets someone for the first time, I don't think she is really thinking about their gender. I think she absolutely means it when she says that you can't "prepare" for another human being because "every man or woman is a universe."

It's July, and the world's foremost advocate for abolition of the death penalty is padding around the lobby of an auditorium on the campus of Holy Names University in Oakland, chatting up anybody she happens to bump into. She's set the tailored blazer and slacks aside for a loose, faded blue denim jumper, a white t-shirt, and sandals. Her complexion is olive-toned anyway (from her mama, she explains, who was French; "my daddy was short, that's where I get my stubbiness"), but a week in the Montana sunshine has warmed her skin to the rich golden brown of *crème brulee*. She has the look of a kid just one week into her school vacation with the whole summer stretching ahead of her.

---

[31] Wolff, *In Sweet Company*, 15.

Sister Helen describes herself as buoyant for the most part, but from the beginning of her Death Row work, she saw that she wouldn't be able to do it if she didn't take time to restore herself along the way. She has spent time at the Trappist Monastery near Gethsemani, Kentucky, and when she's home she plays saxophone and guitar. She has a Nordic Trak, she memorizes poetry, she reads and reads and reads, she paints watercolors, and sometimes she goes fishing. She cultivates friendship consciously and deliberately—"like a garden." But the wider she goes in the work, and the deeper it takes her—into grief, loss, and the general obduracy of things as they are—the wider and deeper she has had to go to replenish herself. She meditates, and she says that when she prays now it is not so much about petition as focus. It may be the measure of how all-consuming her work has become that she clears her speaking schedule for the whole summer now and heads north and west to Prayer Lodge on the Northern Cheyenne Reservation in Montana.

Her connection with Prayer Lodge began when she visited Genesis Farm in 1999 and met Sister Marya Grothwahl, the Franciscan nun who has developed the place. Helen had begun interviewing women for the book she'd begun to write on women and the Catholic Church, and she recognized Sister Marya right away as someone she would want to include. Sister Marya spotted her almost as quickly as someone who could badly use a home away from home. For the past ten years Sister Helen has spent every summer in Montana. She wrote most of *Death of Innocents* there, but her connection with the place goes way beyond writerly needs. She does sweat lodge, she spends time with the Northern Cheyenne, and she takes seriously the coming- and-going ritual of saying her name to each of the four directions when she arrives and then calling it back when she leaves.

Sister Marya is here at Holy Names too. They are participating in a weekend conference under the auspices of the Sophia Summer Institute. The focus of the conference is engaged cosmology, and when it is over, Marya and Helen will lead a two-day retreat titled "The Earth Is a Mystic, Full of God."

Helen Prejean has said all along that she wanted to *go wide*, and engaged cosmology is probably the culmination of that longing, insisting as it does that we concern ourselves urgently with the fate of even the smallest, simplest organisms. In fact, one could see this new involvement as one logical step further along the continuum that incarnational theology has been pursuing all along—and very much in the spirit of Saint Francis, for whom the vow of obedience only began with obedience to one's religious superior: "Holy Obedience

. . . makes men subject to all the men of this world, and not only to the men but also to all animals and wild beasts."[32]

She would speak that evening about how much fun she's having setting out on this completely new venture. She had read Margaret Wheatley's *Leadership and the New Science* several years earlier, and she'd heard Father Thomas Berry speak about the cosmos, and then she'd bought Brian Swimme's *Story of the Universe*. "I'd be reading it on the plane, saying 'Oh, my God, this is such great stuff!'"

"And you know, it's nice to be the new kid on the block, because not a lot is expected of you . . . and you get to learn and ask questions out loud and you get to have a beginner's mind."

Maybe that's the ultimate replenishment—to be "as a little child again," and to confirm her inveterate playfulness with the ideas of Margaret Wheatley, whose organizational theories had dovetailed so perfectly with her own views.

> "It's about chaos! You let it flow. You maximize the information and you maximize relationships, and when you do, you're going to have something *alive* on your hands."

> "Being in the web of life is about intimacy, and efforts of justice are a form of intimacy, and the work of democracy is intimacy, and love of self and learning to network in every way is another kind of intimacy. And the exciting and exacting work of aligning ourselves with the powers that course through us as universe is intimacy."

The retreat is under way. The words on intimacy and the web of life are Sister Marya's, but they could just as easily be Sister Helen's. The Sister Marya/Sister Helen act is pretty funny. Both women were schoolteachers, but Marya taught elementary school and Helen taught junior high and high school, and the difference keeps making itself felt. If Marya's ever heard of irony, she isn't letting on. Helen, on the other hand, can only sustain *gravitas* for a few minutes before she's mouthing off like the smartass thirteen-year-old at the back of the room.

("Oh, hey, Marya, did you hear that? I think we're changing levels. . . . We're getting *deep* now.")

Marya has orchestrated the day's conversations and activities, but she announces before dinner, with a telltale microsecond pause, that "Sister Helen will carry the ball this evening."

---

[32] Rafael Brown, *Our Lady and Saint Francis* (Chicago: Franciscan Herald Press, 1954), 24.

Sister Helen will, in fact, lead the group in a meditation, a meditation on the hand as it is celebrated in song, art, literature, daily life, scripture, and more. It's a familiar strategy for retreats of this kind. We take something ordinary, stare at it for a while, open it out, and recognize in the process that when we're *not* on retreat, an awful lot of meaning and richness speeds right past us. Straight faced, but only barely, Sister Helen promises, in keeping with the theme of the weekend, that as we consider *the hand,* we will move together into a special *field.*

She proceeds, then, in an informally Socratic manner, drawing forth the wisdom of the group. Is she serious? For minutes at a time she would seem to be. We ponder the hands of God and Adam on the Sistine chapel, we learn about the symbolism of the hand and fingers among Australian Aborigines. But suddenly she is leading the group in an *a cappella* rendering of the Elvis Presley classic, "Can't Help Falling in Love with You," with its chorus, "Take my hand, take my whole life too . . ." and she goes on, through verse after verse. How could she possibly know the lyrics to this entire song?

Or she is talking about her nephew who's traveled in Thailand and told her that in Asia you never touch food with your left hand, and exactly why that is.

Or she is mercilessly teasing Roger of the Colorful Shirt in the back of the room.

Regression sets in within moments. People are remembering hand games from nursery school like "The itsy-bitsy spider," and now someone chimes in with an enthusiastic, "This little piggy went to market."

"That's about your *toes!*" says our leader in mock alarm, but adds immediately in a soothing, therapeutic tone, "But it's *good* that you've come to us with this. It's clearly helpful for you to have come up with this. . . . It's a deep *archetype* in you!"

The room dissolves in laughter, and just when the whole business has begun to feel like a shaggy-dog story, Sister Helen falls serious.

"I want to tell you this."

And it's about Patrick Sonnier, and how she asked him once near the end what he missed the most, and that he'd told her, "Sister Helen, no one ever touches me."

Ever since then, she says, she's been negotiating with the warden of the prison to allow contact visits a couple of times a year.

And suddenly, loosened up by laughter, defenses down, we are looking, together, at a terrible truth. If you've read *Dead Man Walking,* it is impossible not to remember the last few minutes of Patrick Sonnier's life, when for the first and only time Sister Helen could, in fact, place her hand on his back, reaching way up because he was well over six feet tall, as he walked to his execution.

We pride ourselves in the West that we've never sunk so low as to have institutionalized untouchability. And yet, of course, we have. We do have our ways of conveying to another human being that he or she is no longer, in fact, human. And as that awareness sinks in, these ordinary hands that we've been teased into regarding as if for the first time—the veins on the back, the age spots, the ragged cuticles—have a very different look and tell a very different tale.

As to the larger story—the extraordinary tapestry of which Sister Helen Prejean's life and work are just one vibrant thread—it remains to be seen. I will say that the sisters I know best are among my most cherished heroes. They remind me very much of my favorite medieval women mystics, and it's hard for me to believe how nearly invisible they are to the world at large.

Because, finally, isn't this what renewal looks like? Invited fifty years ago to think seriously and in concert about their religious identity, to-day's sisters have peeled back layer after layer of unexamined thought and action and found their way to a radiant authenticity that reminds me of Clare of Assisi, Julian of Norwich, and Catherine of Genoa.

But perhaps they resemble the Beguines most of all—the "order that was not an order"—realizing that they didn't have to take permanent vows or place themselves under male religious authority to follow Christ. The Beguines were, on the one hand, the most irreverent where outward forms are concerned—the medieval equivalent of the guys in *Treasure of the Sierra Madre* who "don't have to show you any stinkin' badges"—and on the other hand, the most uninhibited in giving voice to their mystical experiences.

The relationship between today's more socially engaged sisters and the church hierarchy appears to be more tenuous by the year. Sisters describe the situation—no, they define the situation—in different ways, and often with a dry, dark sense of humor. I was familiar with the expression "defecting in place," coined years ago by Sister Miriam Therese Winter, who wrote a book by that title, but things seem to have taken a new turn. "Think of us," says another Sister Anonymous, "as loitering in place."

And she adds, obliquely, "You know, it took Moses forty years in the desert to convince his people they were not slaves. And it's taken forty years for the sisters to realize they are free."

Benedictine writer and speaker Joan Chittister says much the same thing, though in a considerably more somber key:

There is no doubt that women need to tell their stories. But at the same time, there comes a time when you are too tired of trying to be heard in a place like the church where no one wants to hear you. Then, you walk out of it, past it, beyond it. And often, invisibly. They think you're still there, because your body is, but your heart is long gone and your spirit free. I know.[33]

As to the question that hangs in the air, "Why do we—I—continue to align myself with an institution so closed, so heretical, so sinful? Because Jesus stayed in the synagogue until the synagogue threw him out, that's why."[34]

But let's close with Sister Helen's own formulation, because instead of looking back in grief or anger—at the synagogue, the cathedral, or the convent—it turns our attention gently toward the radiant mystery of what is yet to be. "God is everything in this, the power and the life that brings you into the big waters, then dissolves the boundaries quietly, gently, like the unfolding of the petals of a rose."[35]

---

[33] Joan Chittister, *Called to Question* (Lanham, MD: Sheed and Ward, 2004), 174.

[34] Ibid., 169.

[35] Wolff, *In Sweet Company,* 16.

Conclusion

As I became immersed in the research and setting down of these four stories, a conversation seemed to get under way that was quiet and tentative at first but grew gradually more intense until sometimes the room where I was working felt as crowded as a downtown coffee bar at a quarter to nine in the morning.

By the end I saw that a powerful consensus had formed around several issues, but in particular this: every one of these women had after considerable effort found a way to drop down to a place deep within herself where she got access to something I can only call a healing force. Each of them appears to have *aligned* herself, to use one of Sister Helen's favorite terms, and opened out in such a way that something much larger than her, and timeless, began to flow through her, and sustain her, and allow her to sustain others as well:

"My heart is a floodgate for a never-ending tide of misery,"

"As thy days so shall thy strength be."

"The dakinis were there."

"Grace never comes ahead of time. It unfurls under you as you need it."

In this regard it seemed to me that each of these stories is a living explication of a poem by Adrienne Rich that has lingered for years in the back of my mind as a kind of feminist *koan*. In "Integrity," Rich recognizes that a longstanding internal division seems to have healed itself when she wasn't looking. She had experienced anger and tenderness as her *selves,* for each had that strong a claim on her. But now the two selves are at peace.

> And now I can believe they breathe in me
> as angels, not polarities.
> Anger and tenderness: the spider's genius
> to spin and weave in the same action
> from her own body anywhere—
> even from a broken web.

All the women in this book have had to contend with firestorms of absolutely legitimate anger, and every one of them has made an angel of her anger—not a saccharine little feathery-winged wisp of a thing, but a fierce seraphim with a sword. An angel nonetheless, tender and unyielding at once, and magnificently effective.

But the *spider,* spinning and weaving at once, where does that come in? It took a hike in the hills behind my house early one October morning to make sense of that part of the poem and what it had to do with my four subjects.

There are certain mornings when the hills here are almost blanketed with large spider webs, beautifully constructed, some a good foot across. They look like satellite dishes, all facing in exactly the same direction and at the same angle. Thousands of years ago their builders had determined that the first breezes of the day move up the hill in that direction, carrying the first bugs: in a word, breakfast.

This particular morning I stopped, knelt down, and looked hard at one of these webs. It was so lovely, the delicate threads sagging under the weight of the tiniest dewdrops you could imagine, glittering in the sunlight.

And there *she* was, right at the center, the architect herself. She was huge. Her fuzzy legs were striped, and down her back ran three more bold yellow stripes. I wondered whether she wasn't full of eggs.

Before I knew what I was doing, I picked up the tight bud of a dandelion head and pushed it toward her. She ignored me at first, seeming to know it was a tease, but I persisted, and suddenly she threw several legs around the bud and tugged at it. I tugged back, and then we both realized there was a big gash right there at the center of the web.

Everything got very still, and seconds later something astonishing happened. A bright pink orifice opened up where I would swear I hadn't seen one before—an *umbilikos* of sorts—and a stream of white light issued out of it. It wasn't a thread, it was thicker than that, and white and lighter than air; I knew it was lighter than the air, because it just hung there for an instant, like smoke. She seized it then and began to whip it around until it did turn into a thread. She seemed almost to be pulling the silk out of herself and spinning it at the same time—*Yes!*—spinning and weaving in one motion, just as the poem said. Because she could, because she had so many legs!

I could barely breathe. Gossamer skeins were flying about now, and seconds later she had completely repaired the breach. It wasn't as pretty as it had been, but it was fully functional, and there she was, back at the center, the still point of her own owner-built world.

When the Mother is provoked beyond all patience, says the Indian tradition, by human greed and corruption and cruelty, she barrels up out of depths of the earth and straightens everything out—heals the wounds, feeds the hungers, repairs the broken web of life. Sometimes she appears as one radiant figure, and people argue over whether she is divine or human, but when times are truly hard, she embodies many times over, as women who look for all the world like perfectly ordinary human beings until you follow them around for a day and see the amazing things that happen around them. And if you ask one of these women how they do what they do, they're likely to tell you *they* aren't actually doing a thing. Something just keeps flowing in . . . grace? The life force? Shakti?

My friend Jean Bolen would draw a connection, I think, with the myth of the Holy Grail, and the Fisher King whose wound couldn't be healed, and I think she would be correct. Because the critical thing about the grail, and all of its mythic counterparts in other traditions—the crystal bowl, the intricately woven basket, the kettle, the womb—is that it is empty.

Relinquishment: A profound letting go that is directly proportionate to an immense welling up of grace and light and sustenance.

The greatest single difference between writing *Enduring Grace* and this, its companion volume, has been that the lives of three of my subjects are still unfolding. Shortly after I finished writing about Sister Helen Prejean, her home and offices in New Orleans were swallowed up in the floods that followed Hurricane Katrina. She has relocated for the time being in Baton Rouge and is trying to piece together her upcoming speaking engagements. She knows where and when she's speaking, but she's lost all of her contact information. On the other hand, she's elated at the fact that a great many court records have also been destroyed. If someone is sentenced to death, and has the right to appeal but can't because the records that would be the base of the appeal no longer exist, how can he be executed?

Jane Goodall's new book *Harvest for Hope* was published in 2006. It's a lively, multi-dimensional treatise on "mindful eating" put together very much in the spirit of Roots and Shoots. She looks at the dangers of genetically modified foods, the loss of seed diversity, a looming water crisis, the harm done to animals by factory farming, and much more. She points out some of the ways our own choices can address the problems—becoming a vegetarian, supporting local farmers who grow organic produce, and turning off the water while we brush our teeth. The book is not a tome or a treatise, and right in the middle of it we find out what Jane herself eats: the slice of whole wheat bread cut in half, the first half eaten with marmalade for breakfast alongside a cup of coffee, the second in the evening with a scrambled egg and a glass of red wine; the broccoli and small potato she eats for lunch followed by a few squares of chocolate; the odd apple or cookie between meals, and Oh, yes, at seven o'clock every evening, without fail because it's a family tradition, a shot of good whiskey.

In India, meanwhile, as we learn from the Dongyu Gatsal Ling website that Tenzin Palmo has been meeting with other Tibetan Buddhist nuns to address whatever resistance still remains to granting full ordination to women. She and Tenzin Dolmo met with a number of high lamas, who were supportive, "while kindly raising some points which would need to be addressed before the Full Ordination could be bestowed within their tradition." Subsequently, twenty nuns from eight nunneries met to discuss what action they would take. Committees were formed, letters written, and experts in monastic disciplines appointed to look into procedural matters. Bottom line: "Now that nuns are becoming educated and confident young women, living in well-run Nunneries, there is no reason why they should continue to be denied the benefits of the Higher Ordination as bestowed by the Lord Buddha Himself."

I find it fascinating that as each of these women moves along the trajectory of her own life, she becomes more incontrovertibly and idiosyncratically herself. If one could have set Jane Goodall and Diane Perry side by side when they were eighteen—two slender, blonde, boy-crazy English girls, bright as all get out and too strapped to go to college—we might have predicted closely parallel lines of development. But just look at them today.

The diversity of the spiritual descendants of Teresa, Julian, and Clare is one of the most heartening discoveries we make as we become acquainted with them. The world has gone awry in so many different ways that we *need* a diversity of gifts and passions to set it right. I wonder whether that isn't what Catherine of Siena was getting at when she passed on something that God is supposed to have told her: "Of my many gifts and graces . . . I have distributed all in such a way that no one has all of them."

God went on to explain that he could have supplied all of his children with everything they needed, both materially and spiritually, but he didn't because he wanted them to depend on one another. He wanted them to "exercise the virtue of charity" in all kinds of ways: "For there are many rooms in my house."

Many chambers in that interior castle made of a single crystal.

Postscript

In 2007, I took part in the (then) biennial Sacred Circles for Women held in the National Cathedral in Washington, DC. One of the keynote speakers was Pumla Gobodo-Madikizela a clinical psychologist who had served with Archbishop Desmond Tutu on the Human Rights Violations Committee of South Africa's Truth and Reconciliation Commission. It had fallen to Gobodo-Madikizela on behalf of the commission, to conduct a series of interviews with Eugene de Kock, the commanding officer of state-sanctioned death squads under apartheid. The interviews took place in Pretoria's maximum-security prison, where de Kock is serving a 212–year sentence for his crimes against humanity. Gobodo-Madikizela had described her meetings with de Kock in her 2003 book *A Human Being Died That Night,* and she recalled them again in her talk at Sacred Circles, broadening out into profoundly thoughtful reflections on post-trauma forgiveness as an alternative to vengeance and on what it means to forgive the unforgivable.

The talk was riveting. I found my way right afterward to the conference bookstore to buy a copy of *A Human Being Died That Night,* and then to a quiet corner in the back of the cathedral where I could read it without interruption.

Later that day, everyone who had presented at the event gathered for a farewell glass of wine, and I waited for a chance to tell Pumla in person how enthralled I was by her book and why. By the time I'd closed in on her, she was clearly trying to get out the door to catch her plane, but I got in her way and blurted out my piece anyway— said that I loved her book, and that I was struck over and over by its resonance with *Dead Man Walking.* Abruptly, she stopped, and her eyes lit up. "That book *gave me permission,*" she said, "to tell my own story in the way I did. It was very important for me."

I won't try to encapsulate what I think she meant. In fact, I am loathe to do so because I would so much rather readers explore both narratives themselves and discover firsthand all of the ways in which the two books almost converse with one another. Certainly though, the first sentence of the fifth chapter, "The Language of Trauma," laconic and understated, is indicative: "To experience empathy for someone who has committed terrible acts against other human beings, as I did with Eugene de Kock, puts one in a strangely compelling and confusing relationship with the perpetrator."[1]

I wish I could remember exactly when it was that I got a phone call, absolutely out of the blue, from Helen Prejean. I know that the hardcover edition of *Enduring Lives* had been out for a couple of years, so it was well into 2008. I'd sent her a copy when it first came out, but I hadn't lost a lot of sleep over her failure to get back to me. Who knows in how many ways I might have made her wince?

But in fact she apologized profusely for the delay, saying that she never read things written about her (why didn't that surprise me?) but that at a friend's insistence she'd finally sat down and read it, and now she wanted me to know how very much she liked it. She was particularly happy that her own story had been told in the context of the wider story of American women religious, but she was happier still that I had focused on the spiritual dimensions of her work. This was something she'd always wanted to do, but she hadn't had much encouragement from her editors, who insisted that she would be wiser to "stay with her passion," which they presumed was social justice, period. What she particularly wanted me to know was that by foregrounding the elements I had, I had in effect *given her permission* to get cracking again on her spiritual memoir.

At that point—after I'd told her what a thrill it was to hear this, and after I'd reminded her that all I'd actually done was compile a whole lot of things that she had said or written and let them speak for themselves—I had to tell her also about the permission *she* had unknowingly given to another woman who'd been struggling to tell a story that *she* knew, though for rather different reasons, would also encounter resistance.

This really is just a postscript. I only wanted to make note of a phenomenon that we see over and over in the lives of women like Helen Prejean and Pumla Goboda-Madikizela and every one of us who steps out of the cocoons and bubbles of conventional living. We'd so like to think of ourselves as free, but internal inhibitions run so strong. It's a fascinating exercise to sit down and think for a while about all the people in our lives who have "given us permis-

---

[1] Pumla Gobodo-Madikizela, *A Human Being Died That Night: A South African Story of Forgiveness* (New York: Houghton Mifflin Harcourt, 2003), 79.

sion" to be more truly ourselves and to tell our stories honestly and fearlessly. It is thrilling to realize that when we *do*, we pass that permission on—indefinitely—quietly, gently, like the unfolding of the petals of a rose.

Suggested Reading

Etty Hillesum

Hoffman, Eva, et al. *Etty Hillesum: An Interrupted Life and Letters from Westerbork*. New York: Henry Holt and Company, 1996. (Misleading in that it appears to contain the complete diaries and letters, which in fact were only published in English in 2002 in *Etty*; this book is nonetheless an excellent introduction to the subject.)

Smelik, Klaas A. D., ed., and Arnold J. Pomerans, trans. *Etty: The Letters and Diaries of Etty Hillesum, 1941-1943*. Grand Rapids, Ml: Eerdmans 2002.

Jane Goodall

Goodall, Jane. *Africa in My Blood: An Autobiography in Letters*. New York: Houghton Mifflin Company, 2000.

———. *Beyond Innocence: An Autobiography in Letters—The Later Years*. Edited by Dale Peterson. New York: Houghton Mifflin Company, 200I.

———. *Reason for Hope: A Spiritual Journey*. New York: Warner Books, 2000.

Montgomery, Sy. *Walking with the Great Apes: Jane Goodall, Dian Fossey, Birute Galdikas*. Boston: Houghton Mifflin Company, 1991. (Montgomery's book locates Goodall within the "trimate" sisterhood and features Goodall, interviewed, at her most candid.)

The Venerable Tenzin Palmo

Palmo, Ani Tenzin. *Reflections on a Mountain Lake: Teachings on Practical Buddhism*. Ithaca, NY: Snow Lion Publications, 2002.

Hart, Hilary. *The Unknown She: Eight Faces of an Emerging Consciousness*. Inverness, CA: The Golden Sufi Center, 2003.

Mackenzie, Vicki. *Cave in the Snow: Tenzin Palmo's Quest for Enlightenment*. New York: Bloomsbury Publishing, 1998.

Sister Helen Prejean

Prejean, Sister Helen. *Dead Man Walking*. New York: Random House, 1993.
——— *The Death of Innocents*. New York: Random House, 2004.
Wolff, Margaret. *In Sweet Company*. San Diego, CA: Margaret Wolff Unlimited, 2004. (I believe that Wolff's interview with Sister Prejean offers
the most in-depth look into Prejean's own spirituality.)

Index